MARY WESLEY AND ERIC SIEPMANN

Darling Pol

The Letters of Mary Wesley
and Eric Siepmann 1944–1967

EDITED BY
Patrick Marnham

VINTAGE

1 3 5 7 9 10 8 6 4 2

Vintage
20 Vauxhall Bridge Road,
London SW1V 2SA

Vintage is part of the Penguin Random House group of companies whose
addresses can be found at global.penguinrandomhouse.com.

Penguin
Random House
UK

Letters © Estates of Mary and Eric Siepmann
Editorial material © Patrick Marnham

Patrick Marnham has asserted his right to be identified as the author of this
Work in accordance with the Copyright, Designs and Patents Act 1988

First published in the UK by Harvill Secker in 2017
First published by Vintage in 2018

penguin.co.uk/vintage

A CIP catalogue record for this book is available from the British Library

ISBN 9781784704476

Printed and bound in Great Britain by Clays Ltd, Elcograf S.p.A.

Penguin Random House is committed to a sustainable future for our
business, our readers and our planet. This book is made from
Forest Stewardship Council® certified paper.

MIX
Paper from
responsible sources
FSC
www.fsc.org
FSC® C018179

For Chantal

CITY AND COUNTY OF SWANSEA LIBRARIES	
6000332336	
Askews & Holts	01-Nov-2018
823.914	£10.99
SWKL	

They were dancing a slow waltz now and they never saw me enter, two old people bound in the deep incurable egotism of passion ... I called out to her as she went by, 'Aunt Augusta', but she didn't answer to the name; there was no sign that she even heard me. They danced on in their tireless passion into the shadows.

From *Travels with my Aunt* by Graham Greene, a book that Mary kept on the shelf by her bed.

Contents

List of Illustrations

1. 1936: a portrait of Mary Farmar, aged twenty-four.
2. 1923: Eric Siepmann, aged twenty, an undergraduate of Corpus Christi College, Oxford.
3. 10 July 1945: a letter from Mary to Eric.
4. 21 September 1958: a letter from Eric to Mary.
5. 12 May 1937: Lord and Lady Swinfen, before the Coronation of George VI.
6. The children who spent the war at Boskenna: Toby, Ann Bailey, Nicky and Roger.
7. Colonel Camborne Paynter and Paul Hill at Boskenna.
8. July 1942: Flying Officer Henry Osbert Zetland, Heinz Ziegler.
9. Group Captain Charles Patrick Green. *Daily Telepraph*, 17 *May 1999.*
10. Father Paul Ziegler.
11. Eric Siepmann's former wife, Phyllis, arriving at the Divorce Court. *Evening Standard, 26 July 1951.*
12. July 1954: Eric with Billy and Pebble at Broughton.
13. 1952: Toby, Sonya and Mary at Knoll House.
14. Toby, Roger, Mary and Eric at Broughton House.
15. 1959: Mary and Roger kissing goodbye.
16. Mary in Cullaford Cottage. Photograph by Kate Ganz.
17. Cullaford Cottage, Dartmoor.
18. Mary, the bestselling writer. Photograph by Kate Ganz.
19. Mary and Sonya in the 1990s.

Unless otherwise stated, all the photographs are from private collections.

In 1983 an unsuccessful children's author called Mary Siepmann, by then seventy years old, published her first adult novel under the pen name 'Mary Wesley'. It was called *Jumping the Queue* and its heroine was a widow who lived alone in poverty on Dartmoor and was considering suicide. The story was inspired by the situation in which Mary had found herself following the death of her second husband, Eric Siepmann. Over the next twelve years Mary Wesley wrote nine more novels and enjoyed great popular and critical success. Her marriage to Eric had been the happiest relationship of her life, and is catalogued in the long correspondence which is published here for the first time. The letters are the account of a 'no holds barred' love story, passionate and uninhibited. But they are also a chronicle of despair on one side and of growing determination on the other, as the balance of responsibility shifts, and disaster nears.

Introduction

They met by chance in the Palm Court of the Ritz Hotel on the evening of 26 October 1944. Both Mary and Eric were married but the marriages, made or broken by war, were over.

That evening Eric Siepmann was noisy, intrusive and slightly drunk. Mary was with an old friend who was an officer in MI6. They were dining at separate tables, but Eric persuaded a waiter to bombard Mary with notes entreating her to join him in a night-club, which, after dinner, she did.

At the end of the evening Eric accompanied Mary back to her hotel where his efforts to join her in the lift were repulsed by the 'tiny Swiss night porter'. Next morning, as she checked out early to board a taxi for Paddington Station, he was on the pavement; and by the time she eventually caught the train to Penzance two days later they had fallen in love and Eric had declared that he was determined to marry her.

London in October 1944 was once more a dangerous place. In the last year of the war, the Blitz, which had petered out in the summer of 1941, had returned. This time it was a still more frightening bombardment, by V1 flying bombs and V2 rockets. The V2s struck without warning. The massive explosion, which could be heard miles away, was the first warning of their existence. A single V2 could destroy an entire street and the casualties were once again running into thousands. Over a million Londoners had left the city to avoid the danger, but Mary, true to her contrary nature, continued to come up to London from Cornwall to meet her friends and have a good time.

With victory in sight she knew that her pleasurable wartime was coming to an end. Born Mary Farmar, she had in 1937, at the age of twenty-four, married Carol, the 2nd Baron Swinfen, a wealthy young barrister whose father had been the president of the Court of Appeal. Mary liked Carol but she never loved him. She preferred the company of clever young radicals, one of whom had proposed to her before volunteering to fight in the Spanish Civil War. He was killed in 1938 in the Battle of the Ebro.

Carol was lazy, and quite rich enough to neglect his profession. He was also generous, kind and affectionate. His main disadvantage from Mary's point of view was his exaggerated sense of decorum. This required him to defer to the wishes of Mary's parents in such matters as where they should live, who should be their son's godfather and whether Mary should be allowed to model hats for *Vogue* (permission refused). Since Mary had married to get away from her mother, Carol's polite but feeble acquiescence infuriated her. In 1938 she had presented her husband with an heir when their son Roger was born, an event which she later described as 'a near-miracle' since she and Carol had seldom slept together. The war that came in the following year gave her an opportunity to escape from her husband as well as her mother; at long last she could lead an independent life.

Early in 1940 Mary was recruited into MI5 and put to work tracking Soviet and German radio call signs in an office near St James's Park. Her hectic social arrangements started in London while she was working for MI5. She said later that she was ashamed of the fact but in truth the war, for young women like her, had been an intensely exciting time. There was the exhilaration of danger and a degree of sexual freedom that would have been unthinkable in time of peace. One of the earliest of her wartime lovers was Heinz Ziegler, an exiled political scientist from Bohemia who was the son of a German–Jewish banker established in Prague. Heinz was very worried about his parents who were trapped by the Nazi occupation of Czechoslovakia. He spoke a lot about his mother and one night, while they were dining in Soho, Mary decided that she would like to bear his child. By the time the Dunkirk evacuation was at its height in June 1940 she was pregnant, which meant that under wartime regulations, with invasion apparently imminent, she was obliged to leave London. She headed for Boskenna, an old stone manor house in Cornwall, on the cliffs near Land's End, where her second son, Toby, was born in February 1941.

Boskenna was a lost world with its own rituals and customs. She described it as 'the house that was to become my home and steal my heart', and with her children settled in the nursery and her husband at work in London Mary decided to lead a more interesting life. It was during the war years in Cornwall that she earned her nickname of 'Wild Mary'. Boskenna stood conveniently close to an RAF fighter base, and as she said later, 'War is very erotic ... We thought why the hell shouldn't we do what we want? ... They were all going to be killed ... It got to the state where one reached across the pillow in the morning and thought, "Let's see. Who is it this time?"'

Mary was the youngest child of Colonel Mynors Farmar and Violet Dalby. The Farmars were risk-takers and warriors, a military family with connections at court. In the eighteenth and nineteenth centuries, by waging war with a view to profit, they had acquired land in Ireland, Pennsylvania and Virginia. One Farmar governed Singapore; another – Captain George Farmar RN – promoted Midshipman Horatio Nelson, recaptured the Falkland Islands and went down with his guns blazing in the English Channel after engaging a squadron of French warships. Over the years, the Farmars made and lost several fortunes; they ended up in the late nineteenth century with little money and no land but excellent connections. Mary's grandfather, Major General William Farmar, served in the Sikh Wars, the Indian Mutiny and the Crimea. Then, in old age, he entrusted his remaining fortune to the family solicitor – who absconded with the lot. This meant that the general did not have enough money to send his youngest son, Mynors, to Eton. But he could still introduce the boy to Queen Victoria. After meeting the Queen, Mynors Farmar was awarded a Queen's scholarship to Sandhurst. He passed out in time to join the Lancashire Fusiliers, and fight with Kitchener on the Nile.

Mary was born in 1912. She had clear memories of the Great War and recalled her father returning from the trenches towards the end of the conflict looking thinner and more exhausted on each occasion. He fought at Gallipoli, where his battalion suffered a 50 per cent casualty rate on the first day and he was wounded and decorated with the DSO, having been recommended for a VC. Two years later, at Passchendaele, he was wounded again and gassed. He never fully recovered from these wounds and remained a gentle but withdrawn presence throughout Mary's childhood.

That childhood was dominated by her brother, Hugh, and – particularly – by her sister, Susan, who was bossy and interfering. As the youngest, and a girl, Mary's education was entrusted to a series of sixteen more or less incompetent foreign governesses, all of whom found her extremely difficult to manage. But they did teach her fluent French and some Italian.

Mary admired her mother, who was snobbish, forthright and brave but who frightened her. As a small child, she trusted only her nanny and her grandmother, who had been born Hyacinthe Wellesley and who was the wife of Sir William Dalby, a famous surgeon. Mary said that her grandmother became her adored one, and that despite her calm exterior 'she bubbled inside, like I do, like a kettle'. Much of Mary's childhood was spent in her grandmother's house in London surrounded by pet dogs, guinea pigs, a goldfish and a caged canary.

After the First World War her father remained in the army and was posted to India. Her mother and sister accompanied him and she was left behind at a boarding school where her education continued to be largely neglected. She also spent the holidays at the school and did not see her family again for two years.

Mary first discovered Boskenna though her friendship with Betty Paynter, a young woman of her own age who had invited her to stay before the war. Many years later Mary described her friend as 'funny, a pathological liar, extremely dishonest about money, a very loyal friend, the first person I would choose to have with me in a tight corner'.

Boskenna had been in the Paynter family for 250 years and Betty lived there with her eccentric father. When Mary first visited, Colonel Camborne Paynter employed twenty-three servants and owned two thousand acres and ten farms; his property took in Lamorna Cove, the adopted home of a colony of artists including Alfred Munnings and Laura Knight. The colonel kept open house for Betty's friends, and for his own amusement would invite 'dancing girls' down from the London music halls to spend the weekend. He was a law unto himself and once reported Betty for dangerous driving after she had crashed her car into his on a narrow bend in West Cornwall. Since he was the chairman of the bench and heard the case in person he was able to impose a lengthy driving ban. The colonel was a merry widower and a generous host. He sometimes rented out his cottages on original terms; bridge players were preferred, Roman Catholics were not. During the war he ran the local black market in petrol and food, and smuggled daffodils up to London.

In 1937 Betty married a Danish aristocrat. Mary was her brides-maid and after that she became a great favourite of the colonel. When Mary arrived in the autumn of 1940, pregnant and with two-year-old Roger in tow, he was delighted. The Blitz was under way and refugee children had started to crowd into the house.

By chance, Betty was also pregnant. She had met an attractive young Russian in Paris, her Danish husband having disappeared into the fog of war. The two babies – Toby, and Sonya – were born within months of each other. Quite soon the nursery at Boskenna, run by Alice Grenfell, the colonel's housemaid, was joined by a fourth child, Nicky, the infant daughter of Diana Blackwood, another fun-loving mother.

The young mothers came and went, sometimes to London, sometimes to Penzance or the nearby RAF fighter base. Years later Nicky Blackwood recalled Mary and her own mother making rare appearances at Boskenna, 'looking mysteriously glamorous ... swathed in mink and in a hurry'. For the children of the nursery, running wild on the cliffs and farms and beaches of West Cornwall, Boskenna was a paradise.

Looking back in old age, one of Mary's RAF pilots wrote: 'Boskenna needs a book ... the path through the hydrangeas to the sea, the haunted wood ... and drinking in The First and Last at Land's End at Christmas ...' ...'. In Mary's words, 'War freed us. We felt if we didn't do it now, we might never get another chance.' Another Battle of Britain veteran, Wing Commander Pat Hancock DFC, remembered Mary at Boskenna during the war: 'She was a very, very pretty girl with raven black hair and a deep laugh. She and Betty used to hunt in pairs. They were deadly.' For the fighter pilots a few days and nights at Boskenna were a precious resource. They sometimes confessed to being 'scared witless, before going back into battle. One woke up at night screaming and punching the air, and Mary would have to bail out of the bed to avoid getting a black eye.

Then in October 1943 things started going wrong. The national press printed a 'black market scandal' story beneath the headline 'LADY SWINFEN BUYING CLOTHING COUPONS FROM HER MAID'. This was entirely Betty's fault. She was the one who had been buying the clothing coupons, and Mary was eventually acquitted of any offence. But the misleading publicity ensured that the damage to her reputation had been done. As far as her conventional family were concerned, Mary was out of control.

Next, in May 1944, Mary heard that Heinz Ziegler was dead. Heinz had left a safe job working as an interpreter with a Czech RAF squadron to join Bomber Command. The professor of economics had retrained as a rear gunner; his Wellington was shot down over Budapest. He and Mary had made plans to move to Prague after the war with Roger and Toby. She had been asking Carol for a divorce since the autumn of 1942 and he had finally agreed. Carol had always accepted Toby as his son but Mary was nonetheless dreading the family scandal that was bound to erupt when her divorce was made public, and now, with Heinz's death, she was faced with a solitary future without any means of support. She thought of applying for a peacetime job with MI5, but then another setback occurred.

In September 1944, Mary was invited to lunch in London with a former lover, Raymond Lee, who was in the French section of SOE (Special Operations Executive). Also at the lunch was 'a tall Czech' who asked her if she would help him to get locked up in 'a nice English prison'. The Czech explained that he was a fugitive from the post-occupation purge of collaborators in Paris and was anxious to avoid French justice. Lunch turned into drinks and then dinner; Raymond Lee admitted that he had rescued the Czech in Paris, escorted him back to England and then tried to get him onto a boat to South America rather than turning him in. Eventually Mary called a friend in MI6 who arranged for the fugitive to be arrested that night. The Czech (who was actually Austrian) was later tried for war crimes in Germany and received a life sentence, and Raymond Lee – who had an outstanding war record – was cashiered and deported.

It was because Mary was worried that this incident would blacken her name with the security services that she was dining with her MI6 contact at the Ritz. She was in search of a job and a stable life to provide a home for her children.

The noisy party dining at Eric's table was composed of Betty Paynter, a couple called Sylvester and Pauline Gates, and Pauline's brother, the actor Robert Newton. Pauline and Robert had known Betty all their lives. They had been raised in Cornwall at Lamorna Cove, where their artist father was one of the colonel's tenants, and by 1944 Robert Newton had become one of the most famous actors on the English screen and stage. He had just filmed *Henry V* with Laurence Olivier and David Lean was about to cast him as Bill Sikes in *Oliver Twist*. He was amusing, alcoholic and cruel when drunk, and in many ways a typical member of the set Mary spent her time with when she came to London. Although Eric appeared to be equally well suited to these rackety friends, he was in fact, like Mary, in a state of anxious indecision.

Eric was the third son of Otto Siepmann who, having been born in the Rhineland, left Germany as a young man to settle in England, disillusioned by Bismarck's aggressive nationalism. Otto Siepmann became a brilliant language teacher, employed for many years at Clifton College, in Bristol, where Eric grew up. Otto's wife was English and Eric's two older brothers, Harry and Charles, had joined the British Army and fought throughout the Great War. The fact that Otto had two sons in the trenches did not protect him from the anti-German abuse of several of his colleagues in the Clifton masters' common room. Eric afterwards said that the years of the Great War brought 'the bad days for an Anglo-German family'.

Eric, born in 1903 and regarded as highly intelligent, won scholarships to Winchester and Oxford. At Winchester, he made an important friend, Anthony 'Puffin' Asquith, son of the man who had been prime minister two years earlier. Margot Asquith, Puffin's mother, treated Eric as a member of the family and he often spent the holidays with the Asquiths at Sutton Courtenay. There as a schoolboy, he met the great men and women of England, and Europe, Lord Birkenhead, John Maynard Keynes, Lady Diana Cooper, the King's private secretary Lord Stamfordham, Igor Stravinsky, 'Papa' Joffre, Marshal of France, – and of course H. H. Asquith, the last prime minister of England to win a double first. Asquith, a classicist, never read a newspaper; his fall from power amounted in Eric's view to 'the fall of the intellect' in British public life. Remembering those years, Eric later wrote: 'For the time, I lived in magic ...' But a fatal conflict had been set up in his mind – which he was never able to resolve – between the glamour and worldly values of Sutton Courtenay and Otto

Siepmann's emphatic teaching that virtue would never be found in the pursuit of worldly prizes.

At Oxford, Eric was a contemporary of Evelyn Waugh, Peter Rodd, Basil Murray* and Graham Greene. He left without taking a degree having decided that his friends, who also included Maurice Bowra,† were much cleverer than he was. He then enrolled at RADA where John Gielgud was a fellow student. Eric showed no talent as an actor, but he did once understudy Gielgud when the latter was playing the male lead in *Romeo and Juliet* in Drury Lane.

When Eric left RADA he decided to earn his living by writing plays and novels. At the age of twenty he had become engaged to a fellow student, Benita Hume, who was sixteen. They married, but Benita left him after six years to pursue her career. She later married Ronald Colman.‡ The failure of this marriage caused Eric to have a nervous breakdown, the first of several.

He started to write film scripts for Alexander Korda and collaborated with Winston Churchill, attempting to turn the latter's 'eighteenth-century prose' into popular dialogue. Churchill's draft script included the phrase 'virtuous withal' and the project turned into a fiasco. When it was cancelled, Churchill was inclined to blame Eric who, he said, had 'behaved lamentably'. Korda next set Eric to work writing dialogue for Laurence Olivier, a more successful project which led to 'Eric Siepmann' getting an enormous screen credit for *Moscow Nights*.

Faced with this success, Eric promptly abandoned the film industry to write a novel, which was a satire on the film industry. He completed this in four weeks and it was published by Chatto & Windus. Then he wrote a play in three weeks and it was produced in New York, but these triumphs did nothing to reassure him. So

* Evelyn Waugh made Peter Rodd and Basil Murray the models for the character of Basil Seal in *Black Mischief*.

† Maurice Bowra was later warden of Wadham College, Oxford.

‡ Ronald Colman, athletic British heart-throb and Oscar-winning movie star of the 1930s and 40s.

he turned to journalism, working for *The Times* and the *Manchester Guardian* as a foreign and diplomatic correspondent. He was sent to cover the Spanish Civil War and his reporting of anarchist anti-clerical atrocities was admired. But in due course he walked out of both jobs in fits of depression. During this period he also wrote and threw away several books.

When war broke out Eric, who had been feeling increasingly aimless, joined the Royal Marines and was assigned to 8 Commando which embarked for the Middle East in 1941. A few days before sailing he met a very determined young woman called Phyllis Morris who pointed out to him that since he was almost certain to be killed and since he did not have a wife there would be a widow's pension going begging. They were married in January, four days before Eric sailed for Cairo.

But Eric was not killed, so Phyllis's plans were thwarted. When she eventually joined him in Cairo they had a spectacular falling-out. Eric became violent and they separated.

He spent most of the war in North Africa, working as a front-line information officer with the Eighth Army. On returning to London in the summer of 1944, he was encouraged to apply for a job with the French Intelligence Section of the PWD (Psychological Warfare Division). He was highly qualified for this position which would have meant him accompanying a combat unit into France after D-Day. But the officer in charge of the posting was R. H. S. Crossman.* Twenty-five years earlier Crossman had been Eric's fag at Winchester, where Eric, in a fit of high spirits, had caned him for no reason. The job went to someone else.

Eric, who was still a captain in the Royal Marines, did finally manage to get an appointment as commander of a small psychological warfare unit operating in south-west France. It was the only prospect before him and he was due to travel out at the end of October 1944.

---

* Richard Crossman, a millionaire farmer and socialist, later a prominent minister in the 1960s Labour government.

The novelist Antonia White, with whom Eric had a brief and unhappy affair in the 1930s, once wrote: 'He is terribly split and divided against himself ... His mind strikes here and there like a sharp searchlight, but whole tracts are unilluminated ... He has built up this swaggering, cynical Byronic self as a defence. But his cruelty, his impulse to destroy his own happiness and that of the people nearest him is very deep indeed ...' Eric Siepmann, she said, was 'the wickedest man I ever met'.

This was the man with whom Mary, in search of security, fell in love, in a hotel bedroom overlooking Kensington Gardens in the autumn of 1944, while the streets around were being flattened by rockets and flying bombs. 'I read him the *Georgics* in bed, and the *Four Quartets* ... and we lay above the sound of the traffic looking out onto the Broad Walk ... So casually do you find your rubies,' Mary recalled. Later she wrote a poem that included the following lines:

> *I no longer need to drift alone*
> *In the mist of searching*
> *For the door into our garden ...*
> *I will watch for the wind*
> *And guard our solitude*
> *Let no one invade it*
> *Before your return.*

———

The letters of Eric and Mary Siepmann stretch over twenty-four years and start four days after their first meeting. It is a two-way correspondence, a conversation that was only interrupted when they were together and was promptly resumed whenever they were separated.

Mary was thirty-two when she met Eric, and she survived his death by another thirty-two years. Their love affair was by far the most important relationship she experienced, but there are practically no traces of Eric, or of their time together, in the ten novels that brought her wealth and fame in her widowhood. For her fiction, she generally drew on other periods in her life, particularly the earlier wartime years. The twenty-six years with Eric remained private; she kept her original promise, and 'let no one invade' their solitude, the sealed world they shared.

But eventually she changed her mind. I first met Mary in 2002, nine months before she died, when we spent several days talking in her house in Totnes. These visits were repeated throughout the year. She had asked me to be her biographer after reading *The Death of Jean Moulin*, my account of the life of the French Resistance leader. As I was leaving after that first visit, she handed me a large carrier bag containing two shoeboxes and a bulky ring file, and on returning home I discovered that they contained these letters. In her opinion they provided the key to any understanding of her life. I drew on them for *Wild Mary: A Life of Mary Wesley* but very little of the correspondence has been published before.

It was quite appropriate that Mary and Eric should have been introduced in the louche surroundings of the wartime Ritz Hotel. During the war the great London hotels, particularly the Dorchester and the Ritz, became the sanctuary of London society. The Dorchester attracted the more prudent since it was constructed of steel and concrete; risk-takers preferred the more chic atmosphere of the Ritz. The Duke of Bedford's great-granddaughter gave birth to a boy in a suite at the Ritz in January 1940, at the height of the Blitz.

Mary was an habitué of the Ritz. Her wartime diaries were punctuated by 'Nips [drinks] Ritz' followed by lists of restaurants, bars and nightclubs such as Ciro's, the 400, the Ambassadors, Rules and the Café Royal. And it was in the Ritz that she was arrested in October 1943 by government enforcement officers who had followed her from Boskenna and then searched the pockets of her fur coat for those clothing coupons while she was lunching in the restaurant. Mary escaped a probable prison sentence after explaining to a lenient court that she had been handed a sealed envelope by an unnamed acquaintance.

The friends who introduced Mary and Eric in the Ritz were also part of that raffish and slightly desperate wartime world, a world that was volatile, erotic and bent on distraction. The 'very, very pretty girl with raven black hair and a deep laugh' fitted in perfectly – though a very different person was waiting to emerge. She remained a risk-taker of course. Eric once told her that one reason he loved her so much was that she took such incredible risks, and Mary added, 'He was one of the risks.'

Throughout the long years of Eric's struggle Mary remained admirably loyal, never doubting his talent or abandoning her belief in his eventual triumph, until the day in 1968 when she realised that he was dying.

Their correspondence does not just paint a vivid picture of life in post-war England, it tracks the story of a marriage. In 1945 Eric is the dominant partner, a published author and playwright, a scholar of Winchester and Corpus Christi College, Oxford, a man whose time has come. Mary is his pupil, headstrong, high-spirited and very funny – but without any confidence in her own ability, uneducated (she never sat an exam), shunned by her family and incapable of earning a living. By the end the pendulum has swung and it is Mary who is keeping the show on the road, paying the bills, raising the children and, in the process, teaching herself to be a writer.

PART ONE

Hope: 1944–46

The correspondence starts on 30 October 1944, with Mary, who has taken the train back to Boskenna in Cornwall, writing to Eric on the day following her arrival, although she is due to return to London later that week. Boskenna, the seat of Colonel Camborne Paynter, has once more become a refuge for children evacuated from London to escape the V1 and V2 bombings. The resident children are Mary's sons, Roger and Toby, Betty Paynter's daughter, Sonya, and Nicky, the daughter of Betty's friend, Diana Blackwood. Mary and Eric have just spent three days together, most of the time in bed, and are determined to get divorced and remarried to each other as soon as possible. Because Eric was still serving in the Royal Marines, the correspondence was subject to wartime censorship.

———

Boskenna, St Buryan, Cornwall
Telephone: St Buryan 202
30.10.44

My dear love,

I hope your journey was not too disagreeable. Mine was but only because I was travelling away from 'you'. I collected four stray Americans – <u>girls</u> – and contracted to find them rooms in Penzance and take them in my taxi. The taxi instantly broke down and their polite voices reiterating how kind the English are to

3

travellers in distress gradually lost conviction as we sat stranded in darkness, discomfort and rain, while the driver – never sweet-tempered at the best of times, roostled [sic] about underneath the car. It ended alright.

This morning the nasty evacuee child has a fine display of measles spots and all four other children look very suspicious to me. I am waiting for the doctor. I do hope if they must get it that all get it at once. If they do, I must stay here even if you don't go to France at once as there is no one else to cope.

... I had a charming letter waiting for me from my lawyers to tell me my divorce is in the January list so I suppose it will be ground out during the next year.* Viva!

I shall ring up Pauline† this evening to thank her for making such a lovely thing possible. And when she says what did Eric do I shall resist saying 'oh well he carried the coals and emptied the slops'. Or any of the other things I could say.

I hope you are dropping every fourth drink and getting some sleep ... [censor's blue pencil] I miss you dreadfully already and can see every sign of it getting worse and worse but it is a pleasure to miss you, for otherwise I wouldn't love you and cherish loving you so much.

Fundamentally you have made me happier than I ever remember so the waves of missing and loneliness don't so much matter though they feel very real.

With you I can become the person I really am – and bearing the grave in mind be buried as such. Dear love consider yourself kissed,

Mary

* Mary and her husband Carol, Lord Swinfen, had spent the war apart. In 1941 Mary gave birth to Toby, her son by Heinz Ziegler. Carol acknowledged the boy as his own and saw no reason why he and Mary should divorce. But Mary wanted a new life and in 1943 asked Carol to divorce her for desertion, which he reluctantly agreed to do.

† Pauline Gates, sister of the actor Robert Newton, had introduced Eric and Mary four days earlier, in the Palm Court of the Ritz Hotel. Her husband, Sylvester Gates, a fellow scholar with Eric at Winchester, was now a barrister. He would later become chairman of the British Film Institute.

Boskenna — 4.11.44

Darling,

It was nice to talk to you this morning. The first nice thing since I got back here last night, creeping into a sleeping house with only the parrot to greet me and he was rudeness itself. (Apart from the children who set on me like a pack of terriers at six this morning. They were heaven.)

Otherwise it's been the traditional homecoming, with all the horrors hoarded for one's happy return dished up with my breakfast tray and ranging from 'The cook's left' to 'The fox has eaten your chickens' and passing lightly over the fact that the children are in quarantine for measles. Ending with 'I thought I'd wait till you got back to deal with it milady'...

So — I feel nothing will be nicer than to come straight back to London, see you and snaffle the job if it's possible.[*]

I'm sorry the wind of malice is blowing round your head. It was bound to. When attacked I shall keep mum, when cornered, which is unlikely as I can always put the receiver down, I think I shall flaunt you as a red herring across the trail of the millionaire Betty's yapping after at the moment.[†] ... I don't think I'll go to Ann Newton's house.[‡]. I don't want us to be chewed up by gossip.

I don't quite grasp which of us is supposed to be co-respondent in the other's divorce? I don't want one... and nor do I see any necessity to be yours ...[**]

[*] Eric was due to take up the post in France, working with a Psychological Warfare Unit under the control of the wartime Ministry of Information. France was still a war zone, under military control and partly under German occupation. Eric had suggested that Mary should join him as his secretary.

[†] Betty Paynter, daughter of Colonel Camborne Paynter, Mary's wartime host at Boskenna.

[‡] Ann Newton was the former Annie Maclean, second wife of Robert Newton.

[**] In 1941, just before being posted to North Africa with the Royal Marines, Eric had contracted a wartime marriage with a woman he hardly knew called Phyllis Morris. After meeting Mary he decided to divorce Phyllis, who was still posted abroad on war duties.

Anyway if you tell me your plans when you know them I will come. I want to very much.

Alec is here.* The horrible suspicion that I am his next intended is growing, only for goodness' sake keep that dark or Betty will veer in that direction and I couldn't stand it. That I caught the milk train last Friday night on leaving Pauline and have been having gastric flu ever since has a sediment of truth. I find no difficulty in remembering you, darling, and will refresh my memory for myself – soon. This is a fine burst of pomposity against the gossips and doesn't in the least express how much I want to see you – but you said you were imaginative, my love.

M.

Boskenna [undated, between
4 and 23 November]

Darling,

Your Aragon back, I've made a copy for myself.† I calmed my ruffled feelings trying to translate it – an obvious case of Fools rushing in – after our sober–tipsy talk yesterday afternoon. I'm afraid Pauline was too drunk to hear me tell her I'd thrown *all* the curtains into the creek. I am soberly throwing every fourth cigarette away. Setting fire to the house Colonel P. says, and watching the measles spots burgeoning. My children haven't any yet but Betty's Pekingese has bitten her child's nose so badly that she looks as though she might have something far far worse ...

* Nevil Alexander Beechman MC MP, wounded nine times at Passchendaele serving with the King's Royal Rifle Corps, a friend of Colonel Paynter and National Liberal MP for St Ives, the local constituency.

† Louis Aragon, the French philosopher poet, a leading intellectual of the day, had become an icon of the post-liberation Resistance. Mary had made a translation of 'Elsa Before Her Mirror', which the poet had dedicated to his communist muse and wife, Elsa Triolet.

I thought teatime was the moment to telephone Pauline and say thank you as she usually fetches Oliver home from school sober. I wasn't right. This is a nasty letter but I feel a long way away.

I love you.

M.

Boskenna – 23.11.44

My dear love,

I was glad to hear those coins clinking into the slot and then to hear your voice this morning. I'm still wondering whether you got off, as if the weather here is any indication it must have been quite chancy.

I am glad that you spent the evening with the enemy and routed them. Claud* rang Betty up, soon after you and after saying in a slightly surprised voice that he had a headache, gave a spirited description of the party. Apparently at one moment he knocked Joy clean out and she was supine for two hours. I ran into a slight barrage of curiosity here but was so damping that it died away with an apologetic fizzle. So I am fundamentally in very good heart missing you horribly (and naturally '*je m'ennuie terriblement*'), but so full of loving you that I am as happy as it's possible to be without you in sight, or at least with a date to meet you in an hour or two's time.

Do not doubt my darling that I like this state of mind and shall remain in it until you come back. Let that be soon. My measly child is very much better and having high jinks in bed. Toby looks as if he is brewing but not just yet. He scrubbed my back in my bath this morning and made no tactless references to 'mangles' [love bites or bruises]. Family rumour has it that my brother is going to get married on Saturday but there is no proof that he is not still in Brussels so I can't worry about that yet. Alec B. is here, and Betty but no one else.

* Claud Morris, a farmworker who had become a dashing young man in the district. He was later a successful, radical publisher. No relation to Phyllis.

When I got into the train yesterday feeling very sick at leaving you, I sank into a coma and was dead asleep when we got to Plymouth, with my legs up on the seat opposite so that the only other occupant of the carriage had to shake me and yell in my ear 'This is Plymouth'. He was old and explained not sufficiently nimble to leap over my legs or crawl underneath when he wanted to get out. I woke up again at Truro in time to get a tremendous kick of nostalgia and wish I'd had the sense to steal Dennis's snow boots for you to wear in France.*

Be very careful won't you, my darling, not only of wet feet but of bearing me in mind. Oh dear! I do want you back. Great waves of it are coming over me as I write. I hope I shall arrive at the joys of anticipating your return fairly soon. That's going to be wonderful. It really is lovely to love you, all of it comes with this. I hope it reaches you quickly, and yet I feel to tell you I love you is a deplorable understatement of fact and things to come.

Mary

Boskenna – 24.11.44

My darling,

After the anti-climax of yesterday ... I've suffered great uncertainty as to where to project my loving thoughts – London – mid-air – or Paris.

Did you I wonder enjoy the Bridie play?† Or was it that I was in an enjoyable mood the night I saw it, and met you afterwards.

An amusing tweak to our lives is that Betty is terrified that Paul is going to clapper [sic] Claud, Mr Morris. If not Paul, Joy.‡

---

* Dennis Bradley was one of Mary's admirers. On returning from the war in the summer of 1944, and while staying at Boskenna, he had proposed to her – although she was at that time still the undivorced wife of Lord Swinfen.

† *It Depends What You Mean* by James Bridie, the play Mary had been to see on 26 October, the evening they first met.

‡ Betty Paynter was having an affair with Claud Morris, as well as with a local solicitor Paul Hill. Morris was also involved with a young lady named Joy.

I look like taking the train again very soon as my brother has arrived and threatens a wedding any day now. No settled date but autocratic telegrams at hourly intervals. It's nice to be wanted but I do dread the train. Otherwise no news. My voice is hoarse from reading to Roger with measles. I've been pecked by the bull turkey and it never stops raining ...

It's early to tell but my love shows up in an unfaltering manner. Sweet, don't falter either. Missing you as I do there simply isn't room to do anything but love which when I come to think of it is the only sensible thing (as well as enjoyable) that I can do, or want to. I'm longing for news of you and don't forget to send me your next address as it makes me feel nearer to you. My love this is short and hurried but I'm off to bed where I can indulge my imagination and memory as much as I please. The subject has a great sameness but how I like it!

All my love all of it,
Mary

Boskenna – 26.11.44

My Darling,

It's so cold here, I hope you are not perished in Paris and pray you are getting hot baths. I spent all yesterday marketing in Penzance and ended up looking and feeling like a strawberry ice (wearing the loathsome Pink). The horrors of the morning were slightly mitigated by the genuine pleasure shown by the policeman who caught the Lord Lieutenant's daughter, Lord Puff-Puff* and me – 'how she loves her title' all parking our cars wrongfully outside the fish shop. And by finding *Fowler's Modern English Usage* in the book shop. What good reading, I laughed so much reading it in bed this morning that I spilt my coffee and upset my dog.

* Frederick, 2nd Baron Carnock – brother of the author Harold Nicolson.

Betty's child had her birthday and Diana Blackwood's child, who is dumped on us here for the duration, succumbed with [sic] the measles. Roger is almost over it and Toby holding out ...

I shall go [to London] measles permitting, on Wednesday night for my brother's wedding ... [I look forward to] the sight of my family and all the relations who creep out of the country houses and South Kensington Hotels on these occasions, to pass remarks and make comparisons ...

Darling, I do miss you so only you left, it seems to me, some part of yourself behind so that I feel happy all the time, no need of company and completely yours ... I must speed this into the post so that perhaps it will catch up with you before you leave Paris. I love you in every conceivable way.

Mary

===

Eric's first letter to Mary is written almost a month after their first meeting. He has arrived in Paris to take up his post with the Psychological Warfare Unit.

===

Major E. O. Siepmann,
Information Services,
British Embassy, Paris
c/o F.O. with 2 halfpenny stamp.
By Bag. Put your name and address
on outside of envelope.
27.11.44

Darling –
    <u>Address as above</u>: *F.O.* [Foreign Office] *has been notified. The only thing you have to avoid is sending messages to other people*

(not entitled to Bag) which I don't suppose you'd do anyway!
No letter – I'm told they take 2 weeks, alas ...*

*Paris is odd. Went to a party at which my host told me there
would be some Americans who know nothing about anything,
some French who know too much about everything, some of the
haute noblesse who have forgotten nothing, and some of the
haute noblesse who have learned something.*

I thought it was dull.

*Most comfortably installed at Hôtel Louvois – minus heat and
hot water, but otherwise good – where I live chiefly because my
colleagues live in the Castiglione. I am also entitled to eat there,
but eat at the Crillon, for the same reason. This gives me time
and quiet to think about my work and you – the only two things
that matter to me – without interruption.*

The tour looks better than I expected. Guests of FFI [*Force
française de l'intérieure*, title of the Resistance forces incorporated
into the French Army] *at the good hotel in Toulouse which they
have requisitioned; and sallies to Carcassonne, Albi etc. as occasion arises. This will give me time to found my own office, and I
foresee sending for staff to hold the fort in early January, and
rushing back myself in mid-January to return with P.A. and car.
My chief impression at the moment is that it is staggeringly difficult
to learn anything – owing to the segregation of various interests
(which are far from merged, as one had hoped) and which is also
partly due to the sheer transport trouble – I walked ten miles the
first day, but have now found use of a car when needed!*

*I took an exhausted Pauline to see the Bridie play on my last
night – and on to the Ritz! This obviously sentimental pilgrimage
smashed her last efforts at malice, and she decided that I am a
brother to her ('a better brother than Bobby'!†) and made sincere
efforts to be nice – which she can be – spoiled only by the wish
of all one's well-wishers ... to see one ruined by a 'bad' woman*

---

* All military correspondence with England was sent by Diplomatic Bag.
† Her real brother, Robert Newton.

rather than happy with a good one. The fact is, they can't bear to see two people happy; it <u>is</u> an unbearable sight, which is why one should shut up about it! I will, in future.

I thought the play the best in English I'd ever seen (rather like a very good Jules Romain's) and I couldn't get over my astonishment at its ever being produced commercially. A great encouragement for the play which I'll try and have ready to write by the time I see you (the 'Olivier-Bobby' soldiers' return one) and which I shall make – as Hemingway used to say – just as intelligent, Reader, as I can make it. Incidentally, Paul – and several others – were thrilled at the 'Negro' play idea, but I think she wanted it for Bobby (she at once suggested an English film produced by Puffin Asquith) – such is the Newton mind, and possibly not a bad idea at that, Puffin being a great friend of mine and all of us being friends etc.! But I prefer Jack Houseman* and [Paul] Robeson.

If you'll stick to me, I'll concentrate on all these things. This is a re-hash of a very long letter full of 'bits' and jokes which I've had to cut out, for obvious reasons. But don't stint yourself – I mean me – I need some 'bits' to live on, and the censor is curious only as regards official secrets or personal messages.

I am playing with the idea of 'faith' as defined by you (possibly in your sleep?) and the great journey across the Alps from the bed opposite the Broad Walk to the marriage one, let alone the grave, appeals to me.

It is a bore to have to write in short-hand, and I shall have some very big 'bits' to deliver verbally when I see you again. Your photographs console and torment me, but Cornwall is very clear and everything else and especially the Georgics and your eyes at 2-inch range when they smile, and when they don't.

<u>*Write often!*</u>
E.

We left my books at the De Vere! Please give them to Dennis.

---

* Jack Houseman, British-American actor, attended Clifton College with Eric in 1915.

Boskenna – 2.12.44

My Darling,

It was very lovely to get home this morning from London and find your first letter. <u>Much</u> appreciated.

May I throw back the cry of WRITE OFTEN? The only suggestions or criticism I have to make are that, as you once said to me, you should learn to spell my name, and that one sentence might have been omitted 'If you stick to me'. It conjures up visions of glue – an unattractive substance usually connected with things broken – I prefer Aragon's '*Nous serons tous deux comme l'or d'un anneau ...*'

I too have been playing with the idea of Faith. One aspect, a simple one, seems to be that having found one person in whom I have faith I am in a fair way to growing smugly impervious to the winds of malice. It's a startling and enjoyable feeling, rather like meeting God at a party.

Darling, I will telephone to Dennis to rescue your books. I wish I'd known yesterday ... as I passed 'Rubber is Scarce' – a placard for which I have a strong sentimental attachment and could have fetched them myself.

I had news of the enemy in London – none of it would make Sylvester writhe quieter at night ... *

My brother's wedding was a splendid and agreeable performance. In the grossly overcrowded church there were two themes of conversation carried on in carrying whispers. Mary's divorce, the first to disgrace the family for a hundred years, and the curious fact that Hugh and Constantia look exactly alike.†

There was lots of champagne at the party afterwards, in the house of one of the late King Edward's mistresses, a racy old

---

* Sylvester Gates had begun to suspect that his wife was having an affair.

† Hugh Farmar married Constantia Rumbold, daughter of Sir Horace, 9th Baronet and anti-Nazi ambassador in Berlin. The ceremony took place in the Grosvenor Chapel. Mary's sense of isolation was sharpened by her brother's decision to ask Carol Swinfen to be his best man.

lady who got bored and bore me off to see the secret stair down which as she put it 'one can nip down secretely [sic] if surprised'. There was a fine collection of Ambassadors, and their widows, gamekeepers, ex-loves of Hugh's, mobs of relations, old nannies and friends. My husband was there ... He tells me they kick off with the case in January. So many people went out of their way to be pleasant to me that I realised just how greatly in family disgrace I am. At the time it made me rather giggly ...

I dined with Alec and Betty, Phyllis Allen and that man Nack [unidentified], both of whom I took a violent dislike to, and unable to stand the company took refuge in the Paddington Hotel where I waited for my train and read *The Idiot*.

Getting into my sleeper absolutely whacked I was assailed by night horrors about my family's disapproval, wept stormily and gave myself a sore throat and the feeling that I really had been through the mangle this time and wished violently for you ... I just wish they'd shut up ... My sister* without ever referring to the subject managed to convey an infinity of loyal support and went bounding up in my estimation ...

While I was away Toby started measles, and is in full swing. Not in the least ill, eating like a horse and tormenting the two little girls who are still rather ill with it. The night nursery has a row of cots filled with scarlet-faced children eating oranges and wearing hideous paper hats I brought them from Harrods.

I am glad to be back so that I can stay put geographically until mid-January, clear up the measles epidemic and get on with the typing lessons I have imposed on myself. I'm being taught by an old maiden with a fluffy white beard who says I am not <u>quite</u> as stupid as some.

I envy you Carcassonne and think it a pity that there hasn't been a little bit of fighting round it, it might have undone the harm Viol[l]et Le Duc did when he prinked it up so much ...

* Mary's sister, Susan, was a war widow.

Boskenna – 3.12.44

My Darling,

I am exceedingly interested in your play and don't see why after it's been done by Houseman and Robeson it shouldn't be filmed only I distrust the English Films. In my meagre experience of English film production, they seem to have learnt to do nothing well except miss the bus with unfailing regularity. I would love you to buck up with the writing of it – as I wanted to tell you one day when we were in the Café Royal, and you shut me up at half-cock (now at a safe distance I <u>shall</u> say it!), as I think it should be produced during 1945.

I have recovered from the exhaustion of the family wedding and feel most healthy. Our new cook makes life most comfortable. She is an imposing personality – thinks us all half-witted and on her days off wears sensible shoes, a Harris Tweed overcoat and a porkpie hat. She looks as if she bred Great Danes. I shall probably be very fat when next you see me as she brings me little snacks all the time.

I must have changed as Alec looked at me the other day and said, 'I don't know what's happened to you Darling but I'm very glad.' Looking at the nursery rocking horse which I painted not so long ago I wondered whether it isn't true that all forms of bad art are self imative [sic]. I see I have given it eyelashes like ostrich feathers, spots like American bruises [wartime slang for love bites] on its haunches, and as for its mane and tail – Well!

... Possibly impatience of the time between now and mid-January will counteract the cook's snacks. And there is what I trust will be a very long journey to the grave to look forward to ... Lots more letters please. I love the one I've got and love you.

M.

Major E. O. Siepmann,
Information Services, British Embassy, Paris
Café, Bd. des Italiens – 5.12.44

Darling –

As I never seem to write a 'proper' letter, and yet you are always in my thoughts, I now carry about notepapers and I shall send you scraps. This is nicer for me than for you, because I enjoy brooding about you whereas the 'scraps' are apt to give only moderate pleasure.

I am in the 'old café', underneath my office – of 1930: waiting to go and see Le Quai des Brumes, in the same cinema where I saw it before. These nostalgic exercises do not prevent me from looking towards the future: a habit which I had lost, and thanks to you have found again. The T. S. Eliot poems on Time which I read with you at my feet strike me as very good in retrospect. They and the Georgics would make an excellent Christmas and birthday present: I shall try and spend the latter with you, January 21st.

I have ordered a French woman to find you an umbrella, and please name your scent as otherwise you will get (a) Bourgeois 'Soir de Paris', which Malcolm Muggeridge's* beautiful secretary says you ought to have, or (b) Je Reviens, which is my favourite but which I do not connect with you.

No word from you since wedding.

Malcolm, carrying an ultra-secret bag to London tomorrow, has refused in violent terms to carry any umbrella in it (I didn't tell him for whom). Churlishly he said that if I sent one round he'd give it to the secretary whom I've described as beautiful and whom he described as 'wizard'.

I shall be in Paris at least until Monday or Tuesday (11th or 12th). So please continue to send by Bag, and even after I've gone they will forward to Toulouse as best they can – probably fortnightly.

---

* Malcolm Muggeridge, later a celebrated journalist and editor of *Punch*, was a wartime MI6 officer who had been posted to Paris to investigate whether or not P. G. Wodehouse should be charged with treason. As a result of his report Wodehouse was cleared.

I had 50 minutes' talk with the Ambassador* who was interested in any report I can make on my region. I have been concerned to have the idea of my office (now backed by the F.O.) accepted by the Embassy here – MOI having done nothing to gain their sympathy as usual, so that if I hadn't acted I might well have found myself detested as an interloper. Meanwhile I've also had the necessity of a P.A. accepted by my MOI boss and I shall probably send for my secretary in early January to hold the fort while I fetch the said P.A., and a car, from London.

Luncheon today with Adrian Helman, the Minister known unfortunately as 'l'impuissant' since he married Tyrell's daughter with éclat in Notre-Dame, only to have it annulled shortly afterwards by the Pope. He has a new, serious wife (rather good for Résistance purposes) whereas he is Catholic and jolly and gave us lots to drink. They live in the flat of ex-Herr Mumm, the champagne merchant, with a lovely view. One French woman and one French F.O. official were capable of talking me down (without frowning at, even, interruptions) so that it was quite a good party. Anyhow, it was quite obvious who were the intelligent members of it.

Everything is interesting. I've seen old friends. Two hours with Georges Boris† who more or less started the Résistance and BBC in London. Very depressed, very depressing. They mostly hate themselves at the moment, are nervous, exasperated. The city is sad, wet, dark at night, no buses and taxis, amazingly beautiful, cold. I went to see the most beautiful woman I've ever seen in my life – only I was nine when I thought so, and that was 32 years ago and I hadn't seen her since! She was still beautiful, had been hiding youths from Lorraine (her country) in her house, fussed with her brooch which she kept on taking off (her breasts were, indeed, white) and began to take my life in hand, reduce my daily expenses-sheet and tell me that I should

---

* Duff Cooper, wartime minister of information and confidant of Churchill's, had taken up a new appointment as British Ambassador in Paris.

† French socialist and journalist who liaised between General de Gaulle and the BBC during the war.

meet 'All Paris' in her flat. In fact, she instantly produced a lively one-eyed youth who was described as a major in the Résistance and the future Minister of the Interior. I left, alarmed but imperceptible, in the middle of a sentence and I suspect that she is talking still. I forgot to say that her two sons are prisoners [POWs], and her daughter's flyer-husband killed, that's what it's like here. Other friends – after 10 minutes' uneasy conversation I asked: 'Et Pierrot?' A brilliant boy of 18. He had disappeared a year ago, having – I believe – become a communist. His parents are white reactionaries.

I find you brave and amusing, understanding and beautiful, simple and sophisticated, and I love you. More than that, I mean to get you. Off to the film.

E.

Hotel – 7.12.44

My darling – what joy to find your two letters: as if I'd never expected to get one again …

I was entranced by the account of the wedding, I could not help being pleased by Alec's remark, and derive delight from the narcissistic decoration of the rocking-horse.

With a loving eye, I observe that you are the only woman I have ever known who would have said she was returning from a wedding on the following night – and done so. And with a meticulous eye, I observe that the only thing of which there is no account are the goings-on _after_ the wedding on the Thursday night …

In spite of your audacity in offering me advice on vocabulary and the art of letter-writing, I must admit that you have some magnificent phrases. I, too, 'writhe quietly' at night – more quietly than poor Sylvester, perhaps; but no believer (like you) in separation, and truncated without you. I met a young woman with almond-green eyes the other night, and over innumerable brandies I extracted from her everything that she knew about *sexual or emotional relationships. She protested against 'being the spokesman of her sex' – which indeed she couldn't be; but what she told me did not make me happy about separations. We ended up in a boite, where we decided that we had exchanged such intimacies (my question and her answers) that we couldn't possibly meet again, so I handed her over to a charming (if slightly bewildered) American officer, while I wrote a long letter to you, and we separated without knowing each other['s] names and with a fervent and mutual vow never to find them out.*

As to the plays, there are two; The Negro and The Return (of soldiers, to London). But as you heard about one in a state of exhaustion at the Ambassadors, and about the other in a state of exhaustion at the Café Royal, it is hardly surprising that you confuse the two. Your encouragement – as they say – is noted, and more than noted, appreciated; and 1945 it shall be, glue or no glue. And I too prefer gold. More complete love than I have ever felt goes to you with this 'scrap'.

Eric

Boskenna – 11.12.44

Darling,

If you knew the pleasure your scraps give! ...

I am amused that I already know you well enough to have guessed that you would have noticed my omission in my description of the wedding. The Thursday night was spent innocently with the girl I was staying with in her flat, an over-garlicked dinner cooked by me, gossip and ensuing indigestion.

I look forward to the umbrella, as the only one I have has original habits which do not include protection from the rain, and *Bourgeois Soir de Paris* is the scent I use and if you like it will go on using ...

We have had a solid week of hail. Most unpleasant, especially the day spent meeting a very lovely horse Betty has bought off the train. Widely advertised as 'dead quiet, a child could ride him' he came off the train like a V2 leaving base ...

I love your story of the annulment. Diana Blackwood whose child we have here is going in for it too. So is her sister, and the man Diana wishes to marry now, and <u>he</u> has two children. All hope for the Pope to wink at the little children, pocket the money and annul. I understand that there are 57 varieties of annulment, like Heinz Sauce ...

Later

I was interrupted by a macabre search for a missing coastguard. (Due back from his beat at mid-day they began organizing search parties at dusk!) Considerable hue and cry over the telephone and storm lanterns and torches bobbing along the cliffs, starlight and bitter cold, beautiful and frightening. The children knew all about it before anyone else. He was found dead in a blue mackintosh, by his brother, having fallen over Lamorna cliff. Personally I think one of the elementals gave him a push. The search parties ended up here keening in the kitchen and drinking beer. The parrot joined in with some pithy remarks and made me giggle. He has about as much tact as my Aunt Violet.*

I had a typing lesson today and was interested to find that the most indelicate words are the most difficult, which explains perhaps why good typists are so seldom prim ...

Alec has taken a house ten miles away, from which to fight the election. He is afraid too much Boskenna damages his reputation. He should have been frightened sooner ...

It's late, I'm going to sleep, although thinking of you is no soporific. *Je m'imagine dans tes bras.*

M.

---

* The story of the dead coastguard eventually inspired a significant incident in Mary's second novel, *The Camomile Lawn*, published in 1984. The parrot lived again in *A Dubious Legacy* (1992).

Boskenna – 13.12.44

My Darling,

... Such a heavenly day yesterday. Betty and I rode miles across country. It [Dartmoor] was looking incredibly beautiful. B's new horse is a dream. I climbed up – it's a long way – and rode side saddle for the first time in twenty years feeling madly insecure and cursing Catherine de Medici for inventing such a thing. The horse goes like a train but we managed not to part company although I laughed so much I'd no grip at all. Betty looks just as funny riding astride.

Roger has mutilated the Blackwood child by ... cutting her hair off all on one side. She now looks as if the moth had been at her. I was enchanted at getting a Christmas Aerograph from Paddy* to whom I've not written for months with 'Boo!' written on it and nothing else. I bought a Christmas Card depicting a very <u>frosty</u> scene and wrote 'Boo! to you' and that I think is the fizzle finale ...

I have an extraordinary feeling nowadays ... [that I have] settled into quite a new mode of thought and nerves all due to loving you. I have never loved before without knowing I could somehow manage without it. Nobody can really hurt me except you now ...
M.

Boskenna – 17.12.44

My Darling,

... For three days the house has been bedlam with scenes between our Nanny† and the cook – both forceful personalities. Tears into the frying pan and tears in the sink – both threatening

---

* Wing Commander C. P. 'Paddy' Green DSO DFC. Paddy Green was one of Mary's most persistent wartime lovers. He was a veteran of the Battle of Britain who became a celebrated night fighter pilot. He had been posted to North Africa and Italy. On his return he was wondering whether Mary was still interested.

† Alice Grenfell. Alice had been working for Colonel Paynter as a housemaid since she was a child. She became a lifelong friend and support for Mary and her children.

to leave instantly. I took a hand with Nanny, but got madly bored with cook and kept away and read Chekhov. Betty ... lost all sense of proportion and I angered her by reading aloud. 'The husband killed his wife,' shrieked the parrot. Like all storms it blew over and they are still here being <u>too</u> sweet to each other ...

My precious [sic] Miss True* is on heat and has already slipped up with some low suitor. I was illogically disappointed the other day to find I hadn't. '*Tant pis*' as the Douanier said, '*On recommencera*' ['Never mind ... We will start again'] ...

There's a very good novel called *The Cup of Astonishment* by a woman called Mirsky [Vera T. Mirsky] who hasn't written before. Not yet reviewed ... about the women's concentration camps in '39 and under Vichy ...

Philip Toynbee's article on the literary situation in France in last month's *Horizon* left me gasping with the amount he has read. Peter [Quennell] contributed a quite unreadable article on the psychology of refugees ...

Boskenna − 21.12.44

My Darling,

No letter from France for ten days ... [Here] Christmas fever is at its height, fearful mortality on the farm. Old friends of the children in the pig line laid out and chopped up and the children helping with total lack of sensitivity. Yesterday was a hell of goose and turkey plucking, feathers and down everywhere, tempers exceedingly short and Colonel P. losing every key on the place. In the middle of seeming chaos the man who comes every year to arrange the Farm accounts to show a loss (and thus diddle the income tax) arrived to stay ...

* True was a stray mongrel, a cross terrier-hound bitch, that followed Mary home to Boskenna early on in the war. True had previously belonged to the butcher in St Just, who had trained the dog to steal chickens from farmyards while he was delivering meat to the front door. Over the years, as Mary's dogs died and were replaced, she called the new dogs by the old names.

[I have been] swaying on step ladders and garlanding the house with hydrangeas and violets, anemones and narcissus ... It looks very fantastic and gay, far more like a spring festival than Christmas. I need a large white Italian Ox to complete the effect.

The wine merchant is so overcome by a letter from a confrere in France telling him that he has preserved all his old stocks from the Germans that he has been most generous. How I wish you were here ...

C. [Carol] is acting so nobly about not coming down and being so generous ...

M.

Boskenna – 22.12.44

My Darling,

... I feel no goodwill to all men (only to you) and am wildly depressed by the war news, Greek news and Polish news, and should like news from you ...

My youngest child has decreased in popularity since he painted Betty's child all over with white paint and rubbed in mud and feathers from a goose. The effect was startling ...

Grand Hotel Toulouse – 27.1244

My Dear Love,

... I left Paris suddenly at two hours' notice without time to write to you again. Then, five days and nights (often) on the road owing to a defective Ford V8 – and no jack! ...

Then icy cold here, no fires, heating or hot water; and a rush of work opening my show of photographs ... Conditions are tough – too tough for you, possibly, until April ... Foul food in a dining room which is half-morgue and half-Frigidaire. No comforts ...

Lunch today with Julien Benda. * *Christmas Eve 'réveillon'with 'les beaux milieu intellectuels' until 4am – and then I spent Christmas Day in bed!... The show went well. I was photographed shaking hands with the Commissaire de la Région [Pierre Bertaux], replied stutteringly to two speeches, bad champagne. Then thank God that was over and I just meet people – accumulating en route quite enough material already for a Penguin size 'In Search of a New France'. (I've kept full notes – your influence. To get you I must finish my books in future. My past has been a succession of first chapters. I want you to be an epic.)*

Your letters reached me splendidly, only a week from Cornwall. Only there was a gap ... and after the 13th – silence. Ominous after what you implied about correspondence with Paddy drying up, and that being the end of it. Pride because I didn't write? I love you ...

Too much to tell you about Toulouse and the rest of it. This is Resistance country, quite different from Paris. The mood is self-conscious, touchy, aggressive ... (They literally believe the Anglo-Americans are slowing up the war 'for political reasons'). Plenty of Spanish repercussions. A France–USSR demonstration at the theatre; last night at which 'les sportifs de Toulouse' were followed closely on the stage by 'les intellectuels de Toulouse' ... Tremendous even dangerous freedom of thought; a new world fluttering, as it did in Spain in '36, the brave new world which is never born, I think.

Boskenna – 30.12.44

My Darling,

No letter from you for so long that I am saddened ...

Christmas has been exhausting and only really enjoyed by the children. I was unwise enough to put trumpets in their stockings

---

* A prominent critic and moralist who was both left-wing and anti-Marxist; he coined the phrase 'la trahison des clercs'.

so that we were all roused at 5 by a discordant cacophony. I took them to church hoping to quell them but they refused to be parted from toy tanks and ... trained the guns on the parson during the prayers and ejaculated Bang and Pop to my acute embarrassment and I had to send them out to the pub where they are infinitely more at home ...

The cook spoke so sharply to the daily housemaid that she went off her head ... Finally the cook showed up in her true wolf colours and walked out of the house never we hope to return ... I am temporarily replacing her which I can manage fairly well but I am rather at a loss dealing with the insane housemaid ... I am terrified of mad people but fascinated at the transformation in this poor woman.* She was a very plain, ugly, neat, respectable middle-aged frump in spectacles and false teeth. Now wearing only a nightdress (she barely wears that) and having thrown the spectacles and teeth at her bewildered husband, she has turned into a Blake drawing with wild red hair standing out from her head, blazing blue eyes and the appearance of youth. Even her hands have changed ...

Toulouse – 2.1.45

Oh darling,

Everything has gone wrong. What a fine beginning to a critical year! First, Mac – my American – left our car outside a night club on New Year's eve; a car which I had borrowed, by personal contact and with the prestige of renting premises, from the authorities. I wasn't there, but I reproach myself with being too lax and using it myself to go to restaurants and so on, whereas I should have given clear orders that it should be used only for work.

Disaster! – the transport situation here is serious. It was stolen – immobilised, without petrol and 'en panne', which is

---

* Mary's fiction would contain a number of references to socialised insanity, notably in *A Dubious Legacy*.

why he left it. Yet there are regular car bandits, and they must have towed it away between 3am and nine the next morning. I was luckily (not that it helps) in bed; but I've had to take the blame and how I loathe this Anglo-American integration anyway. I can't really give him orders: for instance, he wants to go skiing in the next car I've been able to obtain. He is among the best of them. New England, relatively conscientious and good-mannered, and he works hard. But the outlook is hopeless; no sensation of the tragedy around him, and his comments on France are just 'that she is evidently still unworthy to take her place' among the 'big' powers. And this is called 'propaganda'. I long to have my own team, and hate to take the onus of their shortcomings, of which they are ridiculously unaware, as well as of my own, of which I am fully conscious but which I carry around like a tin on my tail.

Then, as my journey to Bordeaux was thus stopped, instead of taking the ice-train (6am and the only one) I risked waiting for a lift with a Scottish HLI [Highland Light Infantry] colonel today; and now I've waited all day for their bloody car to be repaired. But I shall get off in an hour or so. And worse, worst of all your silence; no word since the 17th and god knows what the implications are meant to be. Either that you concluded logically that there were no communications; – or P on leave? ['Paddy' Green] – or else a slap in the face, implying that you assume I've walked off to my French girl or other thoughts; or merely a lesson in manners, which I don't need. When I don't write, please write. The cold is bad enough, and you have given me an inward glow with which I find I can't dispense!

This shall continue in Bordeaux. Mary, I delight in you. It's quite simple, you must belong to me. I'll do most things – (but much leeway to make up, before we are secure and prosperous) but you mustn't jib away like a wicked horse at the first silence or difficulty. Don't be heartless; you are not – I first loved when I discovered in the night that you didn't like hurting people. So write, you wretch, write.

And I shall see you almost as soon as this letter reaches you. Do, please, try to borrow a flat as I've got no money. I've asked Dennis to get me a room in his filthy lodgings ... I shall stay a fortnight ...

PS *Bordeaux – 3/1/45*

Mary – I find there is no reliable mail to Paris, so I send this by hand. I am leaving Bordeaux by air today week i.e. Jan. 10th and I shall telephone to you – possibly before you get this? All my love,
    E.

Boskenna – 3.1.45

My darling,

I spent the last day of the old year getting our lunatic off to the bin which was a complicated business as she lives miles from a road and we had to walk her up from the valley very drugged and raving – all this by moonlight – she shied like anything at shadows poor thing. We got her into our car with me and I had to drive her to the house where we had another car to take her to Bodmin. She nearly ditched me at one moment by giving a loud whoop and nearly snatched me out of the driving seat. I was torn between terror of the insane and giggles ...

Love such as I always hoped to feel comes to you with this –
M.

Boskenna – 14.1.45

My darling,

It's cold here ... No telephones working and no signs that they will ever work again and the postmistress has different ideas to mine of the importance of telegrams and only delivers them spasmodically. Everything drips in a beastly thaw from the eaves to the Colonel's nose. News percolating through from London is of Betty ensconced in a nursing home, Claud with an ankle broken catching a bus in the iced streets, and Paul and Mark having 'a very big thing' which may or may not be true but there certainly is no idleness during Sylvester's absence. Bob [Robert Newton] and Ann are keeping warm fighting. I see them at the close of the century lashing out at each other from their respective bath chairs with rubber tipped sticks. [In fact the Newtons were divorced later in the year.]

Not much company here. Alec flashed by on his way to London from Scilly – just like the White Rabbit. He drank all my gin and disserted at length on the discovery of a communist cell on one of the islands ...

One expedition to St Ives to spend the day with Romie Brinkman [sic]* who waits six months for her husband's letters to percolate through from Moscow. I felt a certain sympathy ...

15.1.45 – Post girl as nasty as ever this morning, but delivered an intimation from Gordon Dadds† that my case is no. 1389 on the list ...

All my love to you ...
M.

Boskenna – 16.1.45 [typed]

My opinion of Separation would make a long tale and a sad tale like that of the mouse in *Alice in Wonderland*. Only it would be even more dull.

---

* Born Rosemary Hope-Vere, in 1943 she married her third husband, Colonel Roderick Brinckman DSO MC, chief of staff, British Military Mission to Moscow.
† Solicitors acting for Mary in her divorce.

I suspect that I have already bored on about it enough, and to continue would place this separation in the category of FINAL instead of temporary, which I trust it to be. Between bouts of cooking I am reading a lot, but have had to abandon the Russians as the gloom is too much for me at the moment ...

Betty has got herself into a bad mess, and I may have to go to London and extricate her ...

The wish to contribute a mite to the reconstruction of Europe is like a fever in my bones. Here I am out of it and futile ... My God the majority of people in England, especially in country districts, are uninterested and incurious about Europe ...

There is something very unfeeling about a typewriter. All this hitting and the sly little bell, which rings away your thoughts. Giving them a mass produced leer. This reminds me of Betty's Danish husband who always sent her the carbon copy and sent the top layer to the lawyers ... Betty used to cry and get carbon all over her face which was funny too ...

17.1.45 [manuscript] – I <u>love</u> the post girl. I <u>love</u> you and I am wildly happy as after a blank of over five weeks I have your letter and you may be home at any minute ...

———

On 23 January Eric returned to England for fourteen days' leave. Mary spent the entire period with him either in London or in a pub in Devon.

Eric returned to France on 5 February, taking the Newhaven to Dieppe ferry. In Paris he prepared to set up his office in Toulouse, where the murderous post-liberation insurrection was just petering out. Before leaving Paris, Eric visited Louis Aragon.

———

Paris – 6.2.45

My sweet and enjoyable Mary,

My loving thoughts followed you from the Café Royal to Betty's and down to Cornwall ...

Journey was good, only 90 minutes to Newhaven ...

Dieppe, a shattered shell around the harbour at dusk, was moving ... I got a car immediately and reached a most comfortable hotel – the Bedford, in the rue des Arcades, behind the Madeleine (all-British, thank God); and to my delight hot baths, although no heating ...

Finances not so catastrophic as I thought. I'll repay you the further £80 on April 1st, calling it £100 altogether unless you find that you spent more. After that I should have about £100 a month, and I ought to be able to live on fifty and save the other fifty – allotting all or part of it to you. (And the divorce _might_ pay for itself, if the solicitors agree to my stopping allowance now?)*

... Good luncheon at the Bristol ... among the 'diplomatic corps' for which it is reserved ... I somehow never felt that I should become an 'official'. Nevertheless, one must admit that it carries great advantages. British war-time organisation, in particular, is remarkable ...

Your photographs are on the wall, and I love you deeply.
Eric

Paris – 11.2.45

I spent an hour with Aragon. He lives in a demi-proletarian flat in a fashionable quarter.† He spoke on the telephone in a rather high voice, and he is the normal 'type intellectual' in tweed coat and grey trousers. He is handsome and a trifle washed out. Who isn't in France? Answer – a lot of cads.

* The purchasing power of £100 in 1945 would be £3,854 today.
† 14th arrondissement, off the Boulevard Montparnasse.

I lay on Elsa's bed ... She had beads in her hair and much rouge but a strong face. * *The flat is like a Trade Union secretary's with posters on the wall, but they drove me off in quite a smart car. He talked all politics and no literature ... He said nasty things about the BBC broadcasts in summer 1943, driving people to death, which I propose to check.*† *They 'hated us' when the landings were delayed. I haven't heard a literary man in France say a good word about another. Nor have I heard one word of enthusiasm ... poor France!*

Today I fly to Bordeaux (where I shall write again). And probably to Toulouse tomorrow.

I love you,
Eric

PS I've slightly improved the poem, but it is still Beta minus ...

Based in Toulouse, Eric's official task, this time labelled as a press officer, was to guide public opinion away from Marshall Pétain's collaboration and towards a pro-Allied support for the provisional Free French government in Paris, led by General de Gaulle. His unofficial task was to weaken support for the USSR and diminish French Communist influence in the South-Western region. In his letters to Mary he painted a vivid picture of the complications of life in post-liberation France.

---

* Elsa Triolet, the wife of Aragon. During the occupation, Aragon and Triolet, though identified as Communist writers, continued to publish and sell their work. They were also discreetly associated with the Communist Resistance, which became active in June 1941, following the termination of the Nazi–Soviet pact. In September 1944, after the liberation of Lyons, they moved to the city, then under Communist control, and were feted as the symbols of France's intellectual Resistance.

† These broadcasts were part of a British deception operation intended to dissuade the German High Command from transferring more units to the Eastern Front.

Toulouse – 19.2.45

I flew back on Tuesday ... There was a blue sky, and it was a fine flight in an old Anson. Toulouse was hot! ... Work is accumulating and I look forward to my car and a stenographer.

I shall enjoy my first job, which is the reportage on Toulouse which I had commissioned by Picture Post ...

Bideford – 20.2.45

In search of solitude I escaped this afternoon into Bideford, an enchanting little town. The bookshop my first call ... then the junk shop. A dream of a junk shop. I had seen it in the morning and been headed off by my mother. But true to myself I got back to it. We now have some new possessions. Firstly a pair of absurd Bristol glass bugles of enchanting useless-ness and fantasy* (they really blow) and considerable rarity. Secondly a candlestick, also glass ... either Flemish or Italian late seventeenth century I think. This is for you. Thirdly a very beautiful <u>white</u> Bristol glass box which I could not resist. The glass is milk coloured with green-blue lights at the base, and last a very proud beautiful *capodimonte* bird in white porcelain. For you too. In fact they are all for you if you like them but sometimes I shall blow the bugles ... I did enjoy myself. The owner of the shop knew a lot about china and jewed me over the bird but nothing about glass. I stayed two hours ... and we parted with mutual expressions of esteem. I look forward greatly to the agonies of jealousy Betty will suffer (also a junk shop fiend) which I believe to be one of the chief pleasures of antique discoveries ...

Goodnight my dear love,
M.

* *The Glass Bugle* became the title of Mary's first (unpublished) novel.

London – 24.2.45

My Darling,

I have had a sober and practical three days here and shall go back to Cornwall tomorrow. First, what I have done about the British Council ...

Alec who I met in the Ritz for a drink very nearly got himself murdered by being unbearably pompous and in his worst *Monsieur le député* mode, saying he knew Sir M.R.* *very* well and would of course have to tell him about my divorce. I was so angered that I later rang him up and told him to go to hell ...

I have shopped for the children and my mother trying to replace Rocket [V2] losses and dealt as far as I am able with her flat which is a shambles of filth and broken glass, sodden and half-burnt furniture. So hard on the old ...

I have sent you the Polyphotos ... Looking at them I decided there was nothing for it I must obviously wear a yashmak ...

Simon Harcourt-Smith† made a speech in the Ritz in his best Author-F.O. manner about the distressing spectacle of my hair, he hadn't finished when I left but over my shoulder I saw Donegall‡ take him soothingly by the arm and lead him to the bar.

L'anneau d'or tiens ferme,
Mary

Toulouse – 26.2.45

My very dear love,
The porter, who has a delightfully old-fashioned bow, told me on my return from Bordeaux that he thought I should find 'full satisfaction' on my desk. So I did, indeed – three letters

---

* Sir Malcolm Robertson, ex-diplomat, MP, chairman of the British Council.

† Diplomat, novelist and briefly in 1944 the last of Mary's casual wartime lovers.

‡ Arthur Chichester, 6th Marquis, aviator, war correspondent, jazz fiend, disc jockey and gossip columnist.

covering the whole period from my departure to yours for London ... Who is the 'gangster friend'? I look forward to the hourly diary. (Tell Mrs Grant* to keep up her admonitions.)

Where is Paddy? This must be scribbled and sent as I am rushing off to Carcassonne ...

E.

Boskenna – 28.2.45

... Your first letter from Toulouse this morning gave me much joy but I am sad you had a bout of depression. You must not. I will try not to, since I love you increasingly in spite of loathesome separation. Your letters help immeasurably and bridge the geographical gap. Detestable as is this separation I see a certain danger in hating it overmuch as this. . . breads fear [which is] absurd since we are travelling down a path which neither of us have ever travelled before.

... Every year I am surprised afresh by the spring here, impossible to get used to the flowers. Narcissus and daffodils being packed off by the ton to market. And everywhere flowers, mimosa, violets, primroses, anemones and many more. Toby picks all day long and between us we have filled the house. Every available man and girl is picking, bundling, carting and packing ... today the sun was hot and the sea and sky violently blue and the children tumbled into a cart full of daffodils, looked absurd and vital ... Nor did it matter that Colonel P. pitched head first over a stile and nearly broke his neck but not quite, and the pump engine broke and the water failed and the boiler nearly burst. As I write I am being interrupted all the time by Colonel P. shooting questions at me so forgive me if I write inanities. Soon I shall forget he is eighty and say shut up ... (Thank God he's dozed off.)

---

* Mrs Grant, a Penzance widow by then aged 79. She had lost her husband in the Boer War c.1901. She was a neighbour and confidante of Mary's and once said that her jolliest times had been in her fifties – 'By far the best lovers, my dear'.

Boskenna − 3.3.45

Darling,

... These two days have been particularly beautiful − blue and gold. Frost in the morning followed by hot sun. I worked in the flower fields most of yesterday as we were short of labour and picked and carted flowers all day. The horse is called Albert and gets very bored. Even the children worked, at least mine did, the others were rather frivolous.

For an hour Toby and I struck and sat under a flaming gorse bush which looked exactly like scrambled egg on toast in the brown bracken, but smelt hot and delicious. I read him the *Georgics* which he affected to like ... On days like this everyone sings as they work and there is a strong similarity to a pagan festival and I feel very near the earth.

Today Geoffrey Bennison, one of my dancing pansy friends, came over from Mousehole where he is staying with Betty John. I am lured over there tomorrow to see Gwen John's pictures except for those in the Tate. They have never been exhibited. (She was Augustus's sister.) They are lovely I believe. She left them all to Edwin John* when she died and he keeps them hidden. Betty, his wife, is away so I'm going to sneak in and see them. (Geoffrey B. is or expects to be a painter.) ...

My dog has a favourite fox and combines the roles of her parents ... streaking across the cliff in full cry, down the earth, only to emerge hours later stinking of fox. It's awful for me at night. I can do nothing about it, any more than I can stop Roger falling into the water trough with all his clothes on which he has done two days running ...

Alec rang up. Most affable and knowing he had angered me had made great efforts on my behalf with Sir Malcolm Robertson.

---

* Edwin John was the fourth son of Augustus and Ida John. When his aunt Gwen John died in 1939 he inherited the contents of her studio. In 1945 he and his wife Betty were living in the Fish Store in Mousehole, a disused pilchard store. He was a trained artist who died in Wales in 1978.

He [Alec] is a good little man but tries to hide his timorousness in pomposity ... I love you,

    M.

Paris – 4.3.45: 9am

Mary darling – I came up by train on Friday night to fetch my car and driving it back early this morning. I feel tantalisingly near, and I seize the chance of a scribble which will reach you quickly. Your letter of last Wednesday [i.e. dated 28.2.45] *reached me here, and is actually before me.*

It is full of sense and reassurance. Indeed, we must not make of separation a strain and we must try to be natural – that is to say, not afraid of fear. I shall not cease to need you; and I trust you to let me know any changes of fancy! Meanwhile, the best thing is to work and prepare our future.

Darcie Gillie of the Manchester Guardian *came to dinner, and was full of de Gaulle's speech in the Assembly (which alarmed his friends by his lack of contact with the popular outcry; i.e. for some gestures of urgency). Then I went alone to a play –* Une Grande Fille Tout Simple *by a new young author* [André Roussin] *and company. Not very good, but eminently theatrical. I find myself absorbed in technique which (I hope) bodes well for the coming play.*

Paris in the sun yesterday was beautiful, but still odious with troops ...

The what *from Bideford? It looked like 'funk ...*

Darling, dear love, the polyphotos are awful. Please send two more enlargements of the beautiful shut-eyed one underlying urgently, *as I've succeeded in spoiling both, trying to mount and frame them.*

Eric

Boskenna − 5.3.45

The rooks keep flying past the window carrying long surrealist twigs for the nest building which their wives instantly discard. They have no manners and nasty natures I observe.

Darling, your leave on the 15th. I am already in a passion of anticipation. It might be possible to have Sylvester's cottage again … I would like you to meet R. and T. [Roger and Toby] but staying here has marked drawbacks …Perhaps it would be more sense to stay put in London …

I must answer your questions. The 'gangster' friend* has only nuisance value and never, thank God, materialised. I will tell you his story when I see you. He is a low friend of Boris Melikoff's [sic] who got into trouble with security and was an infernal bore.†
2. Paddy. I don't know where he is. In fact I can't work up a glimmer of interest there. 3. My gland ailment … is better …
I am conscientious in swallowing a nauseous mixture … which I firmly believe to be chiefly strychnine …

I bussed to Mousehole yesterday and spent the afternoon in Edwin John's lumber room seeing all Gwen John's pictures and drawings. They are in a shameful state and nothing is being done about them until after the war. Edwin and his wife keep them hidden and not a soul has seen them yet. We roostled them out and they are very beautiful. Some extremely like Toulouse Lautrec, and she has a remarkable sensitivity. Some of her portraits of nuns made me wish to steal, it would have been easy.

I am bored at the prospect of Geordie and Claire Sutherland‡ invading next week. They insist on coming, she to stay here and

---

* Raymond Lee, see Introduction.

† Boris Melikof, Armenian expatriate and Communist, friend and suitor of Mary from pre-war Boskenna days. They had an affair during the war. Mary once had to lock him into her bedroom wardrobe to make way for a more importunate suitor.

‡ George 'Geordie' Sutherland, 5th Duke of Sutherland, married to Clare O'Brien. He was the first chairman of the British Film Institute, Conservative politician and landowner. Barbara Cartland suggested that he was probably the father of her daughter Raine, Countess Spencer.

he nearby in Penzance. I don't mind him really, he is stupid and quite nice, but she drives me scatty, Miss [Mrs] Emanuel's sister. Having them about is as unrestful as a badly furnished room.

It's unbelievable, a rook has flown by with a spray of camellias. I hope it will be received in a proper spirit.

Boskenna – 7.3.45

My Darling,

... This life by letter is to me rather like conversations under an anaesthetic – such gaps in thought and time ...

I received physical support from America yesterday in the guise of two most elegant bust bodices, in answer to a *cri de coeur* to a friend in New York. Enchanted, I rang up Mrs Grant to tell her, and she said, unkindly I thought, 'What are you going to put in them Darling?'

It seems the Germans have the *toupé* ['nerve' – correctly spelt '*toupet*'] to use buzz–bombs again, there is considerable indignation felt in London. I had hoped for fewer shocks to favourite buildings ...*

I miss you more daily and have little patience. I might occupy myself usefully in learning to spell, but you told me I am in good company since your brother Harry cannot either ... JUNK, darling, not FUNK. And please admit I showed courage in sending the Polyhorrors ...

The post brought a letter from the B.C. to say try as he would Mr Simpson doesn't think he can place me. Nor did I think he would be able to as my academic qualifications are nil and that's what they like irrespective of anything else. But it was worth trying ...

Romie Brinkman brought her mother-in-law for the afternoon. A splendid specimen of the dying aristocracy. Very like Queen Mary

* Between June 1944 and March 1945 London and southern England were bombarded by 3500 V1 flying bombs and 1100 V2 rockets.

even to the toque and the Daimler.* A great gardener, she toured
the garden rolling out the Latin names of all the shrubs so glibly
that I began to suspect she knew she was safe, that Romie and I
knew none of them. I only caught her out on one. She is recovering
from a heart attack brought on by being heavily fined for getting
too much or too little meal for her hens. This happens to all of us
however hard we try to be honest. I adore old ladies. This one collects
swans (china and glass ones). She tells me she had eight hundred –
but that the Blitz had taken its toll. Romie kept hissing in my ear
'Don't make her walk too fast or she'll die before she's changed her
will'.† She is vastly rich and Romie the new daughter-in-law ...

Geordie Sutherland gave me a good laugh last night. He never
has recovered from being a Duke. He rang up in a petulant tone in
answer to a telegram I'd sent him to say it is impossible to get him
suites of rooms in local hotels at short notice. 'But did you use my
name?' I bellowed 'Of course I did and it had no more effect than
mine'. He rang off. I wish him stuffed for the nation ...

I have to go and shout at the horseman who is deaf. He is
shaping up to go mad like his wife or so he says, and I am inclined
to believe him. Insanity is becoming quite the mode in this place.
But who is to look after the horses? So I must trot off and soothe.
Practically impossible to be soothing at the top of one's voice but
I am willing to try ...

Toulouse – 8.3.45

Darling –

*To my delight, your London letter on arrival here. Thank you,
too, for Spanish Verse: which reminds one that I have forgotten
my Spanish, and I shall read Lorca with Spanish friends ...*

* Born Mary Frances Linton in 1870, she became the second wife of Sir Theodore
Brinckman, 2nd Baronet in 1895. They were divorced in 1912. She and her
husband had called their second son 'Napoleon'.
† Lady Brinckman died in 1948.

Coffee has begun to arrive. The first packet came last week, and I had stored up the rest as – for some peculiar reason – they served coffee here for a few weeks. Now 'café national' reigns again, and I am triumphant. Cigarettes have not begun to arrive. I'm told that they are sent, whoever your dealer is, via Imperial or American Tobacco Co. and that there is always a delay of 8 weeks, after which they trickle in regularly. Speriamo. No – alas – cigars! Possibly stolen, so you'd better check ...

Polyphotos hopeless (white jersey was a mistake, photographically; lovely in life). Do send more snapshots.

<u>Later</u>

Hero's Hemlock* *struck me as too melodramatic; but for a <u>sour-comic</u> play, it might not be bad. And that is how it is developing. I got a stimulus, last night, by referring to my notes written last October – (before the 26th). I found savage remarks like 'blast the English – attack them!' and angry records of people who told me that 'We've been under strain – people in London are tired – the war is over.' I find I was impressed by the clean, friendly cats (after Naples' spitting skeletons) and fat horses; by people's callousness, at movies or about casualties ('no feeling'); and by Sir Anthony Lindsay-Hogg,† the first acquaintance to whom I talked after 4 years' abroad, who spoke to me about the limitations of bombed London (i.e. the night-clubs were all dull).*

This, and the memory of Nancy Mitford's‡ voice – always a big stimulus to me at any time; I use it like benzedrine (I haven't seen her for 6 years) – gave my first Act quite a fillip. I am still

---

* Eric's play, which was never completed. Throughout their relationship, Eric was engaged on an endless stream of plays, novels, works of criticism, popular theology and current affairs, each of which was abandoned and destroyed in turn as it was overtaken by some brilliant new idea.

† Sir Anthony Lindsay-Hogg, 2nd Baronet, theatregoer and socialite, briefly married to the Canadian actress Frances Doble.

‡ Eric had become friends with Nancy Mitford in 1933 when she married his disreputable friend, Peter Rodd. Mitford's first successful novel *The Pursuit of Love* would be published in 1945.

at scenario stage, but I aim to bring a complete scenario and one Act, – which I may show to Curtis-Brown [sic], * – in April; with a view to production in autumn.

I feel more and more constant, alas (a most alienating attribute) and you have affected my daily life. Tell me the truth, and remember that I love you deeply.

    Eric

Toulouse – 11.3.45

... PROGRAM

May 1, 1945:	*Return to England with play*
September 1:	*Leave MOI; production of play*
May 1, 1946:	*Marry Mary*
February 1, 1947:	*Have a child.*

Boskenna – 11.3.45

... Yesterday I took Mrs G. to the advance show of all the pictures of local artists going up to the Academy. Mostly trash but two or three excellent. We maliciously barracked Alec who was there doing his Member of P. act. He purpled with annoyance, poor little man ...

How is ... the play? ... Wouldn't Gielgud be better than Olivier? He's got more body to him ... I love you,

    M.

Boskenna – 12.3.45

Darling,

My head is buzzing ... Betty has come back from London with the discovery of what sounds the perfect little house for us. It

---

* Spencer Curtis Brown, a leading literary agent and founder of the agency to which Mary eventually sent all her unpublished work.

belongs to a friend of hers who is rich and told to leave London because he has a bad heart ...

The rent is £185 a year* including rates. It is a modern non-basement cottage in Don Place SW7† not far from Harrods. The cooking, fires and hot water system are all electric so there is no shovelling or stoking. It's on two floors. It has on the ground floor a large sitting-room, dining-room, kitchen and larder and lavatory. On the next floor two bedrooms, bathroom and dressing room and a little roof garden for sunbathing. Apparently every room is full of fitted cupboards and book shelves and it sounds the most easy comfortable thing and the cheapest I've ever heard of ... There is no likelihood of the landlord turning us out or increasing the rent. It's the sort of house which I could very easily run myself with Biddy (or there is a maid who goes with it) daily. He turns out in June.

Darling, I thought it might be wonderful idea to take it and furnish it with my furniture and your books and either live in it if you come home soon to write plays, or if you are still in France I would have it with a lodger, some trusty girl friend who would pay her share and chaperone as well ... It is quite incredibly cheap for nowadays and I'd love to snap it up if it's as nice as it sounds ... One could let it for ten pounds a week until we wanted it for ourselves quite easily ... It would save you the £100 a week in hotels when you're on leave ... It does seem rather putting the cart before the horse but houses and rents are going to be impossible – worse than they are now after the war ... Do let's go and see it when you are back ... The present owner has sworn to offer it to no one else.

Her next piece of useful information is that there is what sounds a lovely pub in Devonshire for leave. Ponies to ride, lovely country and perfect peace. Let me know exact dates if you can ... Carol wants to come for a week in April and it would be nice for me to fit him in while you are home ...

The Duke arrives today. The Duchess to follow later. How tedious ...

* £7,200 today.
† Actually Donne Place SW3.

Boskenna – 14.3.45

My love,

... I have my first crop of freckles for your return since I escaped into the sun yesterday and lay hidden basking behind a rock.

I have reached a high peak of irritation and intollerance [sic] with the late Mrs Dunkerley whose yardstick only measures by money and who is so tough she pleasures in hurting people who love her for her own good. No news and none from you since there is a gap caused by my getting your last letter so quickly from Paris.

My children have put on order, what they call 'a real screecher' [a V1]. They say they would like one very much and are disappointed that I cannot guarantee the date of delivery. They have talked about it so much that various members of the household were for some days under the misapprehension that it was already en route.

At the moment I am despondent and feel time apart from you is time wasted and I'm in a state of violent impatience and feel unreasonable.

I do not think I am much good at separations after the first two or three months, it is only tolerable if I am very busy which I am not at the moment or when I have just had one of your letters ... I love you,

M.

Toulouse – 18.3.45

Darling –

Of course, take the house quickly. It is high time we cut our cloth to suit our coat (or, as you say, put horse before cart). We must be together; or have the means; or at any rate the certainty of being together – and this will be a great help.

Not that I shall let you loll, or ever trot around London for long (without me). This makes it more urgent than ever that I should return by September, at latest. (I am writing to R. Marines about my status; I don't believe they'd object to my doing civilian work e.g. journalism, that could be interpreted as helpful to the war effort.)

All these details need to be settled when I come to London; so let's settle <u>that</u> detail first. I'll definitely apply for leave in the first week in May, and suggest that I also do a week's work at MOI as there is much to be settled. That would mean, reach London on April 30th. But now <u>you</u> must come up on Friday, and we'll <u>see the house</u> – and go together to Devonshire on the Saturday!

What excitement.

Incidentally, these dates are cobwebs; as I don't want to <u>apply</u> for leave yet: but I'll let you know as soon as I've done so, and have confirmation. All we can do is to plan firmly according to these dates, and trust to carrying it off – which we will.

I am immensely stirred and excited about the house.

Finances are, temporarily, catastrophic. I got no reply about tax and other mysterious reductions. If I get a rebate, I can pay you the £100 I owe you. If not, I'll allot you £20 monthly from May to September ...

Apart from that, I can allot a further £20 as from May, as originally planned, for our mutual future i.e. for house and saving, if any. I've no furniture.

I am inclined, my darling, to throw in my hand and supply evidence for my wife; thus committing myself to a fine of 30% of income, for the rest of my life, for the folly I committed.* In relation to the folly, it seems moderate ... Personally, I am much attracted by the idea of setting up house together (<u>the</u> house, of course) and not giving a damn; especially as you'd presumably keep your children in Cornwall, and go to and fro until we'd worked out our future. So that nobody but our friends would clearly know what we were up to. But I don't know how far you're affected by your commitments – (a) conventional – i.e. family (b) matrimonial – i.e. how it would affect children, etc.?

---

* A reference to his divorce negotiations with Phyllis. If Eric supplies evidence of his adultery he will be the guilty party and will have to support her for the rest of his life.

Darling, the fact is, that we planned a journey across Alps which it takes 18 month to cross; but that we are gravely tempted, and possibly wise, to settle on the lower slopes. I don't want to lose you, in the Alps, or anywhere else.

Your letters are miraculous. Three big whoppers, all in one week; <u>and</u> Bystander [now The Tatler] (which I like) and <u>adorable</u> snapshot of you (looking angelic) …

Tell Mrs Grant there is plenty to put in those bodices; at least, that I'm satisfied.

I love you.

PS

My STOMACH – everybody at Grand Hotel ill, so that they sent for a doctor, suspecting sabotage and sacked the cook. We used to eat badly. We now eat badly.

Coffee comes in couples: very welcome. No cigarettes.

BOOKS – I'd like Bowra's,* Apollinaire and the latest Aldous Huxley.

Darling, can I send you anything? Do you see French weeklies?

Local authoress – is introducing into her novel – an English major, who is tall, <u>THIN</u> – blue-eyed, and CHINCHILLA HAIR!! (What is chinchilla?)

Boskenna – 19.3.45

My love,

… As far as I know your cheque passed quite alright. I've had no remark from my bank. I've had a surfeit of what Colonel P. calls the Ducal Invasion for the last week but mercifully Geordie has arrived and taken Elaine to stay at St Ives where they are at

---

* Maurice Bowra, notable classical scholar and wit, later Warden of Wadham College, Oxford, was an Oxford contemporary of Eric's and a friend of Mary's.

a moderately safe distance. He is rather nice and far less stupid than is supposed ...*

I think it a good thing that your play becomes funnier and funnier. Laughter is after all the strongest weapon. I trust you are disguising Colonel P. to some extent, since I have lived under his roof for four years and love him dearly. Also he has much goodness.

I am touched by your consideration in telling me that your blonde is dyed and happily married. Delighted to hear it!

After weeks of heavenly sun – the last two days of which were so warm I sunbathed naked – it is howling and blowing and what the Cornish call 'a nice drop of rain' is falling. It would not disgrace a monsoon ...

Mary

Toulouse – 19.3.45

Darling,

Please don't be silly.

I gather from your gloomiest letter (written so soon after the house excitement) that (a) you are lonely and (b) la ex-Dunkerley told you not to marry me, because I hadn't got any money.

I am not much astonished (though upset by) the discouragement, as I had seen the clouds gathering ...

Well, if you find anybody richer, whom you really want, let me know. Meanwhile, we know that it will take me a year to make the thing practicable; and that's a hell of a time (incidentally, a good many other people are facing that problem) ...

This has the makings of more than an affair ... Please know ... that you can transform my life ...

Second; what are the implications of your doubts? If you can't stand it what happens? Do you cease to write, fall into the arms

* 'Elaine' is probably a slip. George Sutherland's first wife, Eileen, died in 1943. He married Clare O'Brien in 1944. Mary clearly had a soft spot for 'Geordie' who was twenty-four years older than her and a notorious womaniser.

*of the 'premier venu', or just lose faith? It's all rot. What you've
got to do is help me to make it bearable for you, as quickly as
possible; but it won't be quick, and it won't be easy, and it isn't
even certain ...*

*I love you. Remember that. As I never loved even Benita (and
I loved her) because we were still cynical, as only the young or
the born-old (like Dunkerley) are. You have stirred me in some
way that no one else ever has ...*

*As to money and the world, of course we're in the hell of a
mess. It's taken me 42 years to make the mess. That if you
remember was one of the things that appealed to us ...*

Boskenna – 22.3.45

... Lovely sun again but we are getting too much of the Ducal
party who are shattering in their relentless pursuit of pleasure
which is only an attempted escape from boredom. How terrifying
non-working uncreative people are. I've reached the point when
I would gladly call for the tumbrill [sic] ...

I have a very good feeling about us, and don't worry we'll get
disentangled perhaps sooner than later ...

All my love,

M.

Boskenna – 24.3.45

... I am so glad, so excited that you think the house is a good
thing for us ...

For your leave I am writing to Devonshire, and if I fail to get
rooms there (from the 5th to the 14th) you can I think come here,
it will be heaven by then and Betty will most likely be away ...

Incidentally about finances, you owe me £60 not £100 and I
have quite enough for a few days in London.

If you throw in your hand and supply the evidence, I am all in favour of it. I don't think we shall ever get anywhere otherwise. You know what I want to do about the evidence and I know how to do it without publicity.* If you let me do it, it would make the fact of our setting up house just one sharp blow to my family and leaving the children here for the present. I know I can manage C. It seems much easier to be honest about it, I have a horror of being furtive. And if you are with me I won't mind the alarms. If your case has begun by the time you come home and mine is nearly over, which it will be, it will make things a great deal simpler ...

Chinchilla is a variety of rabbit. Its fur is slightly like your hair in colour but very soft and silky which yours is not thank God! ...

Carol is coming here from the 3rd to the 9th and I am going to stay with Romie B. at St Ives. I twitted him over the telephone this morning with having Victor Russell [sic] as his council [sic] which I can't help thinking is very bad taste since I've known Victor since I wore pigtails and his daughter is one of my dearest friends and Toby's godmother. I should have thought there were other KC's.

Mrs Emanuel† and a boyfriend have arrived to swell the Ducal party. We are in for visitors for weeks ...

Boskenna – 25.3.45

Vera Emanuele [sic] Guy Trundle,‡ an ex- or comeback flirt of hers, arrived to stay yesterday, and Alec, Billy Bolitho** and the Sutherlands came to dinner as well as various neighbours. We had quite a party and I was amused when Vera loosened by gin

* Mary is offering to be named as Eric's co-respondent.
† Vera Emanuel was the sister of the Duchess of Sutherland, née O'Brien. Mary later described the sisters, for some reason, as 'two Hungarian tarts'.
‡ Man about town, Ford car salesman, identified by the Metropolitan Police as the secret lover of Mrs Wallis Simpson in the months leading up to Edward VIII's abdication.
**Cousin of John Bolitho, Toby's godfather, who had first employed Mary in MI5 in 1940.

started to tell me how nice you were and fishing wildly for information, which she didn't get, tripped herself up and started
abusing Pauline for being such a gossip. The very fact that I am
completely indifferent to her affairs acts as a violent stimulous
[sic] to her anxiety about mine. But she goes hungry ...

Reading *The Jungle Book* to my children I reduced myself to
tears and a lump in my throat at the tragic passage when Mowgli is
turned out of the wolf pack, only closing the book to see Toby sound
asleep in his cot and Roger very nearly so and utterly unmoved! ...

Toulouse – 25.3.45

Mary darling,

*... The Pyrenees have just appeared, patched with snow. I am
in a new room with a view over the rooftops. Also in new offices.
Tomorrow to Montpellier for my last photographic show. Back
here to meet Anne-Marie – my parachutist assistant – who is due
to arrive, and to get the office going. Then in 10 days, I shall feel
fit to report that the wheels are turning and to apply for leave ...*

*After 4 days of an odd wind called 'd'autan' (nobody seems
to know the origin of this word) there was a purge of rain and
blackness. Suddenly the sun has appeared with the mountains.
The wind plays havoc ... Even the waiters have been putting the
wrong dishes on the wrong tables, in a kind of gloomy daze . .*

*The Pyrenees are now white and slate, and the sky very blue.
Damn that wind, it's still blowing this paper about, but I refuse
to shut the window.*

I can love you very much.

E.

———

*This letter from Eric was followed by one month's silence, which
alarmed Mary.*

———

Boskenna − 28.3.45

God knows, since I've forgotten, what I wrote to you my Darling that has put you on such a tack [reply to Eric's letter of 19.3]. Reading between the lines you have grasped the wrong end of the stick. But what matters is that you are upset. So am I. Very ... I am angry with you too for the violent insult you deal me in implying that I could be influenced by them [the Dunkerley crowd] or their standards ... The only enjoyment I have derived from them is in snubbing them when they have tried to talk about you. None tried more than once ...

Dunhill's write that they sent your cigars the day I ordered them and suggest that they are delayed not lost. Your cigarettes have been delayed by a V. bomb which fell on their warehouse but should reach you soon ...

Claire and her unfortunate duke have left and Vera and her flirt are leaving on Friday ... Roger sighted Vera and Claire together, shook his head and remarked all too clearly 'They have the same face.' There he is almost wrong as Vera has some heart whereas Claire has none. There have been some tragic effects of war in the neighbourhood [mutilated soldiers or civilians] which combined with the approach of my case have given me silly nightmares. Otherwise I am very well and have completely changed colour from lying in the sun ...

Boskenna − 28.3.45

My Love,

This is to send you a little midnight love. I wrote this morning when I got your letter about doubts. No good in saying much more about it ... I am very sleepy and I love you. Goodnight.

Boskenna – 29.3.45

My Love,

We are speeding the departing guests to-day. Very nice too …
I have made use of poor Vera by whipping off with some of her
clothes which I liked … She and her sister have angered me past
endurance by telling Toby to his face that he is beautiful. In an
upset mood already yesterday I threatened her so venomously
with physical violence that she was quite frightened …

Vera today at lunch said, 'Now Mary Darling tell us how you
fell in love with Eric.' So I said, 'I wouldn't dream of telling you
anything Vera Darling, it might spoil your version.' Her boyfriend
[Guy Trundle] most traitorously laughed and said, 'Yes, it surely
would.' …

Boskenna – 31.3.45

Darling,

In a month very close to you there will be no danger of my
writing to you something slipshod and misconstructable. I
want your next letter since your last still stings, absurdly since
you told me clearly you love me. And I love you, and am so
absorbed in our mutual life. Really loving makes me more
capable of solitude when I can't be with you. Your letter hurt
me because you chid me for wavering when I was far from any
such lunacy.

Exhausted by last minute Easter shopping in Penzance with
Betty this morning in the car which only starts with the cooper-
ation of passers-by to push – heavily laden with children bottles
of drink and food. A gale blowing and the little town crammed
with people.

Claud has arrived for Easter and Phyllis Allen is still here. Carol
coming on Tuesday and I am leaving. He has infected me with
nerves over the case. So stupid. I wish it were over.

Claud says Sylvester battered his way into the Markham Street house after Pauline and Mark [Pauline's lover] and beat Mark up in a big way. His nose was still bleeding days later.*

Alec's agent has told him it is now 'alright' for him to stay at Boskenna again. He was foolish enough to tell this to Mrs Grant. I suggested he should come next week and put a notice in *The Cornishman* that 'Lord S. [Swinfen] and Mr B. [Beecham] are staying together at Boskenna'.

I have the new Huxley [probably *The Perennial Philosophy*] for you but want to read it quickly before I send it to you if you don't mind. *Texts and Pretexts* is also coming as between us Mr Wilson and I made a muddle ...

A rocket has transformed the orators' stand [Speakers' Corner] in Hyde Park into a pit. Biddy sent a tremendous account of it. No casualties.† It will be nice if they are over as is likely when and if we take the house ...

Such wonderful news from Germany. I am most profoundly thankful that you are not there ... I love you more than the day you left Victoria and I miss you just as much.

My Love,

M.

Boskenna – 2.4.45

My Love,

I am so glad to get your next letter and relieved your gloom was mostly the wind. Mine was as you now realise Betty's visitors ...

Easter day was exhausting. Morning church with everyone cross ... then a long drive to Alec through a gale with the roof leaking and the car behaving temperamentally. Too much to eat

---

* Sylvester Gates, having identified the suspect he had had in his sights since December, beat him up.

† The explosion of this V2 by Marble Arch blew the windows out of the Hyde Park Hotel on the opposite side of the park.

at Alec's and when we wished to leave Colonel Paynter had vanished, it took two hours to find him ...

(Last night) I dreamt of Pauline crawling up drainpipes ...

C. is only here until Sunday as he has divorce nerves and wishes to be back in London in 'good time' for it. He is making very heavy weather over it and it is fortunate we are not meeting and that all he has had so far are quips over the telephone ...

Later, 4th

I have reached St Ives ... My leaving was funny as we all overslept and C. and I overlapped by an hour, which he particularly wished to avoid, feeling most unwanted and de trop and convulsed by Toby's violent remarks on the situation. I went to lunch with Mrs Grant who restored me to good humour and we laughed a lot. On to St Ives in the afternoon where Romie is being very sweet to me. We also have laughed a great deal. Chiefly on the subject of bringing up little boys, which we both take very seriously and shouldn't be a funny topic at all ...

I'm sending you a snip about Harry. It's very tremendous, isn't it?*

I love you with all my heart, all the more so since it isn't simple or ordinary for us. I want you badly and I believe in you.

M.

Boskenna – 13.4.45

Friday the 13th indeed. It is a terrible blow President Roosevelt popping off. What is the feeling in France? Here, first reactions

---

* News had just reached Mary of Harry Siepmann's appointment as an executive director of the Bank of England. Eric as a child had revered Harry, who was thirteen years older than him, and whom he described as 'my brother the god'. It was Harry who had arranged for Eric to go to Winchester. While at Oxford H. A. Siepmann was said to have gained the most brilliant first in Greats since Archbishop William Temple. He was a personal assistant to J. M. Keynes at the Versailles Peace Conference in 1919 and later became the right-hand man of Montagu Norman when Norman was governor of the Bank. Following his appointment as an executive director of the Bank, Harry was widely expected to succeed as governor.

seem to be blank dismay. I am praying hard that the next chap will be pro-French ...

Publicity over my case has been polite. Non-committal in *The Times* and *Telegraph* and 'Wife fell out of love in Cornwall' in the *Western Morning News*. Everyone has seen it except me but I'm told by Mrs G. that I came out of it unsullied and she remarked that so unspotted was my reputation that she would have to revise her opinion of me.

No other repercussions as yet. Tomorrow's post will bring them no doubt. On being told last night that a silly old woman who has a kindergarten Roger used to go to, is saying that she had to ask me to take him away as he consistently used foul language calling her a Bugger I flew into a tremendous rage and with Betty's help typed off an exceedingly pompous stinker in my name and Carol's. (Actually I took him away from her to send him to the village school as he learnt nothing and being a silly old snob she was furious.)

It was such a pleasure to do it the very day of the divorce and I knew you would have laughed at the mother-tiger demonstration. In point of fact it's going to make an enjoyable village row as the whole of Boskenna is up in arms as all the men adore him all the more since they taught him any 'foul language' he knows. He's a quick learner too.

The theory that nothing ever happens in the country has always struck me as ludicrous. There is a far greater proportion of husbands chasing wives with hatchets (and vice versa), madness, poison pens, scandals and intrigue ... and so forth than in towns.

Colonel Paynter is setting off to London next week to take Jean Batten out dancing. I do love his utter lack of self-consciousness at eighty-one ...

Boskenna – 14.4.45

... This morning very sweet letter from my father and mother. Greatly concerned about my financial future. They are very heavenly people but I'm determined not to be a drag on them. My love for them has always been a reversal of roles – more parental than filial. Also an explosion of denials over the telephone from Roger's ex-school mistress which nearly damaged my eardrums ...

Boskenna – 19.4.45

Darling,

Two days of heat wave and how I wanted you here. July heat, yellow gorse pouring in torrents down the cliffs into very blue sea and all the bluebells coming out as well. We have lain frying on the rocks, so hot that we've had to pop into the sea every twenty minutes. The water is icy so the bathing consists of an inelegant duck and no more. But it was lovely and I am biscuit already ...

Bathing is rather spoilt since the rocks are covered with oil from sunk ships, a disaster which took place some time ago – but the oil sticks.

I have complicated my life by co-opting a young rook which fell out of its nest. It has a voracious appetite and wakes me at dawn with raucous demands. It also snores and sleeps in a basket at the foot of my bed. True hates it.

You were right when you said unless I got a full report of my case I would never know what had really happened. It arrived on Sunday and the shock of finding who witnessed against me was a bigger blow than I've had for a long time.* It made me very unhappy and spoilt something I believed in and loved. I won't write anymore about it but I will tell you when I see you.

---

* Mary had discovered that her cherished brother, Hugh, was a principal witness for Carol and against her in her divorce case. Carol obtained a decree nisi in April 1945 on the grounds of Mary's desertion. He was given custody of the boys. He continued to pay Mary an allowance and met all the educational expenses. Mary and Carol remained on good terms, however, and they shared the care of the children in the school holidays.

It has its funny side as when I read the thing I was sitting in the garden with Betty. I was sobbing with rage and misery when there arrived two small boys who had come to tea with Roger. They were aghast! Emotion being infectious the tea party turned into a free for all in the garden and they all got into brittle moods and teased Roger, who goaded beyond endurance attacked his persecutors, and hurling a heavy fir cone at the largest boy who is twelve drew blood in terrifying quantities and gave him a lump on his head the size of a pigeon's egg.

His expression of detached satisfaction as he watched me bathing and plastering his weeping victim gave me great pleasure. The only smear on an otherwise perfect situation was that the wound was at the <u>back</u> of the head ...

There was a meeting last night to form a committee for the Welcome Home of the men from the parish who have been at the war. I missed it but Betty's account is good. Feeling ran riot as many of the committee have kept their sons at home.

No news from you for weeks. I miss your letters and the gap seems immense.

I have been thinking much about fidelity and come to the conclusion that all I need to concern myself about is my own. I feel confident of attending to it satisfactorily. To be unfaithful would spite my face. And faith.

Love greater than I have ever felt comes to you with this.

M.

Boskenna – 21.4.45

My darling,

Three weeks' silence on your part and I am depressed for lack of news ... Do not be angered – I have been made miserable this week by the backwash of my divorce but that is over now leaving only mental fatigue.

I lunched yesterday with Romie at St Ives and found her also in a state of deep unreasonable gloom, <u>her</u> husband has been away a year, Betty also is gloomy. We all fully realise it to be sex, my dear, let's face it, <u>and</u> the spring as Germaine Halot once said to me ...

The apple blossom in the orchard by the sea is breath-taking. I fled there by moonlight two nights ago after reading the concentration camp atrocities in the press. For the first time in my life I am thankful for the American gift for publicity. The world and England especially should take count, and if we do not we deserve another war ...

Mrs Grant, Alec and a woman who has been running welfare in Belgium are lunching here tomorrow and Ronnie Emanuel* is coming to stay for a few days on Monday. Colonel P. set off to London this morning ...

In two in the morning glooms I have given you fish poisoning in Marseilles, fatal accidents in your prison van, changes of heart, death from a strayed English bomb aimed at the Germans near Bordeaux and various other imaginary fatalities. The logical outcome of the spin of sadness I've had over my personal back-wash from my case ...

Now I must go and dig for worms as (my rook) is reproaching me ...

Hotel Castiglione, Paris – 23.4.45

Mary darling,

I am indeed ashamed of my silence. All sorts of things have been going wrong ... The position now is – no leave is possible till, anyway, June ...

---

* Wealthy visitor to Boskenna, whose noisy sister-in-law Clare, wife of the Duke of Sutherland, had established herself in the Boskenna stables, much to Mary's irritation. Ronnie's wife, Vera, had departed on 29 March, accompanied by her boyfriend Guy Trundle.

The complications have been incredible. Firstly, money; for some obscure reason they stopped paying me altogether last February. I certainly can't afford to move until it has all been put right ...

But there have also been incredible complications in my office ... Alas I seem right back where I began; having had to get rid of my French assistant to make way for Anne-Marie – who proved impossible (unbelievable mess-up, including politics ...) and whom I'm hurrying back to sack, which will leave me with no one even to wrap up parcels ...

I'll tell you all about it one day. One detail – my American lieutenant left, leaving one local girl (pregnant) on my hands ...

Outside my window, at the corner of the rue d'Anjou is displayed in large blue letters ... M.A.R.Y. (dressmaker?).

Two letters intercepted here give me joy and stability.

Jimmy Beaumont, dashing through Toulouse, observed that you'd been at first a plain fat girl, and then that you'd become a beauty. He wondered what had happened next. I didn't tell him ...

Maurice Bowra has just turned up in this hotel and I am trying to lure him to Toulouse ...

E.

Boskenna – 28.4.45

My Darling,

Great feelings of bitter disappointment that your return is put off made me feel sick all yesterday. Delayed action, since my first reaction on getting your letter was immense joy on hearing from you at all! Also I am peevish with Ronnie Emanuel who now seems reluctant to part with his house. However there must be other houses and I am sending out my spies. As soon as you know definite dates for your leave will you tell me? Then I will get to London a few days before you and snoop around houses, and find us somewhere to stay in London and if you would like to go to Sylvester's cottage again I could perhaps lay that on too. We could come straight here for one night, from London, you could see the full horror of Roger and Toby and I could collect immense quantities of provisions to take to the cottage.

Like you I desperately want a house. I am sick of living in other peoples [sic] however nice. But until we are together and can discuss ways and means and probable dates I can't really do much more than dream. Supposing you do get back finally in September I would like to have the house a month or so before so that I can move in furniture and muster the army of 'little men around the corner' to hang curtains and mend the furniture broken in the move …

Colonel P. returned very sprightly from London last night and meeting him I also met Hugh and Constantia passing through to Scilly on leave. A mixed pleasure for Hugh since it was he who was witness in my case. He eyed me rather like a horse passing a tractor. They are coming here for the night on their way back.

Having bowled the old boy [Hugh] off his feet in a totally unexpected attack I feel revoltingly magnanimous.

My darling I am most worried about all your office troubles, wishing I could help, and only able to write constant reiterations of growing love.

M.

Toulouse – 29.4.45

Mary darling,

Now that I am back in Toulouse, it is more difficult to write clearly than ever!

… All this is puzzling to you, and you must read between the lines … Favourable developments are A. Money … Establishments in Paris thought I was bound to get back my £80 tax after all, agreed that MOI owed me arrears of salary … and announced a rise of pay (of £50!) … It looks as if I shall recover about £300

by May 1st – which is sorely needed. (I am sorry that you, too,
have suffered on the wayside.)

B. Finally I put out some grumbles about leave and was
instantly greeted with: 'Certainly, you are entitled to it'! So I can
come as soon as I can get my office going. But when will that
be? I am now single-handed ...

Anyway, something will happen soon. It's quite possible that
I shall return jobless – only keep that private ...

As for Spring – the White Russian maid on this floor said this
morning that she expected me to commit suicide any day now.
Apparently, my 'cafards' are obvious ...

═══

In Toulouse French political complications and British office
politics began to defeat Eric.

═══

Toulouse – 1.5.45

... I came with a plan to avoid the obvious dishing out of brochures
and propaganda German-wise. I cultivated the Résistance and set
about a reportage on them. Alas, I found that that the New France
is not the Résistance, and that the Résistance itself – whatever its
past – goes around with what is called a chip on its shoulder and
positively refuses to be understood! There are schisms of the past
involving us, about which you learn painfully. (I have just been
told pat: 'the English did nothing for the Résistance'.)
The result is that, having gained little ground there, I find myself
assailed by the bien-pensant and soi-disant anglophile element
for having neglected them for – this is the latest, from an official
source – the communists! I've fallen between two stools. Worse,
I've become disgusted, hating Toulouse, rather weary and disillusioned about France ...

Boskenna – 3.5.45

My Darling,

Your first letter back in Toulouse came quickly. I love you, and am deeply sorry you have struck a boggy patch. Please don't worry too much or get too depressed and exhausted as it won't last ...

Betty and I have been gardening, a useful outlet for spring energy. It is an enjoyable one too, but usually complicated by the assistance of three or four children, two dogs, one pony and two rooks. Each has a different conception of horticulture and most of the time is spent in stopping unnecessary pruning and digging ... The pony treads on everybody's feet but it provides manure, and the rooks tweak precious buds off the rarest shrubs and keep up what is obviously an uncomplimentary commentary ...

It's a miracle to me how any work ever gets done in this place. The Cornish are natural child lovers which I am <u>not</u>. Each workman has a child attendant. The carpenter spends half his day looking for stolen tools, the mechanics in teaching the inside workings of the tractor, and the ploughman never seems to be without some odious child shrieking and swaying on the horse pulling the plough. Betty and I on the other hand are constantly seen racing for cover at the sound of infant voices.

There is a good deal of nursery satisfaction on the demise of the dictators.*

Yesterday evening we had to do a long round to collect money for the returning soldiers of the parish and combined it with a sightseeing tour for Gluck and Edith Shackleton.† It was an exquisite evening and most agreeable. We went to Penberth which was looking very pure and friendly, then to the Cades open-air theatre at Porthcurnow. Have you seen it? It's wonderful. A little amphitheatre on the cliff and the backdrop is the sea and rocks and the whole

---

* Mussolini and his mistress Clara Petacci were shot by Italian partisans on 27 April, their bodies photographed in Milan on 28 April. Hitler committed suicide on 30 April.

† Gluck, niece of founder of J. Lyons & Co. and celebrated painter of floral subjects, lover of Constance Spry, lived with bisexual journalist Edith Shackleton Heald – last mistress of W. B. Yeats – at Chantry House, Steyning, Sussex.

thing a mass of flowers. Then to a farm near Nanchisel [Nanjizel] where Betty went in to extort money while I took Gluck and Edith for a walk. The cliffs were bewitched and we got lost. Gluck and Edith were poor performers over the banks and had some inelegant falls. It was very wild and beautiful and exhausted swallows were arriving from Africa, in the distance the Scilly's [sic] lay sharp and black in a steely sea. Next to Porthgwarra where an old lady of eighty was persuaded to show her china collection and finally to the pub at Sennen where we ate and drank and laughed a lot and none of the fishermen stopped playing darts to listen to the news.

Colonel P. says the only difference the Victory is going to make is that we will gradually stop feeling guilty when we enjoy ourselves. I feel a great sadness and emptiness.

I suppose that is the effect of a war. There are so many shocks and disappointing surprises in the first years that one becomes battered into insensitivity and unable to rejoice. I remember how my mother cried when the milkman told her the last war was over. I suppose she felt as I do, that she'd spent it cramming food down the children's necks so that they'd be ready for the next, and relief that my father wasn't killed.

Hitler has had a full page obituary in *The Times*, which surely creates a precedent? And how beautiful Mussolini's mistress looked lying dead in the piazza at Milan. Nothing seems quite real, or is it that I have the wrong yardstick for reality? ...

Edith tells me that Yeats always said the infallible preventative for having one's letters read, or steamed open by the postmistress, was to begin most formally and end the same, and then you could be as free as you pleased in the middle. I think it's a splendid idea ...

Toulouse 6.5.45

Darling,

Cats are jumping out of bags. Last night the new Vice-Consul said that he felt bound to warn me that the Consul and

Vice-Consul at Bordeaux are gunning for me with a vengeance, and that reports are going to FO; so he strongly advised me to get my own reports in to MOI ... He says that he was even warned against me in London, and that after getting to know me and seeing my work he had already reported favourably on me to Bordeaux – which had done him no good! He says that he attributes it to jealousy of 'MOI's power in the south-west'.

... I have cultivated the Resistance, and this doesn't suit the Consuls at Bordeaux who are wildly pro-Franco and consider left French, as well as Spaniards, as red revolutionaries. There has been another spy in the region who has dug up that the Rector of the University accused me of 'cultivating communists' and that the Regional Directeur d'Information disapproves of me – he is a strict Catholic (and ex-Pétainist) (plus 'anti-alcoholic'!) ...

It's quite obvious that I can't last. I don't know to what extent I can fight back, but it's an FO versus MOI war and I'm on the weaker side and I don't even expect much backing.

In fact I fully expect to be back in London and out of the MOI within a month. I expect that the Marines will release me, as there isn't a huge demand in the Pacific for 42-year-olds who've been abroad 4 years ...

We will build a life. From now on, I shall not do second rate jobs. I must do what I consider worth-while ... we must mobilise help in London, as I shall be running against a wash of préjudice. I have some friends around Harry ... and Curtis Brown, the agent whom you met at lunch ...

I am angry with Pauline, though I resented Sylvester's cold rudeness. All she wants is to leave him, and trail back in a few months, I think. I agree he should beat her ...

I think if Harry were convinced that the grave is in view he might help with rent etc. and getting started, on a limited scale. I don't want to ask him, but it may be a solution. I must say I'd rather that grave than a wet one in the Pacific ...

Boskenna – 5.5.45

My Darling,

Truly appalling weather, very cold and drenching wet (a 'nice shower of rain' to the Cornish) ...

The idiotic false alarms of Victory day seem to be dying down a little. Who ever started them? There seemed an extreme absurdity in celebrating or talking of it before all fighting has stopped in Europe and all the countries are liberated. Betty in Penzance two days ago caught it badly – a rumour widely spread of 'a four hour stand down and special announcement at 11.20'. She sent me a message, so I flew to the wireless at 11.20 and listened to a very interesting Geography lesson for schools on The Andes. She bustled back for lunch having lost her head and bought champagne. Sad anti-climax ...

The gardenias I stole from Geordie Sutherland with his gardener's connivance are flowering and scenting the whole house.

It may interest you that the whole of Gordon Dadds bills for my (divorce) case came to under £200. Very little isn't it? ... I found a house near here yesterday which may do for Ronnie and wrote him a stern letter either he move out of 17 Don Place by Sept. 1st or find me a house even nicer and cheaper than his. Of course if we saw it we might loathe it but I think not.

=====

Germany's unconditional surrender came into effect on 8 May.

=====

Toulouse – 8.5.45

I heard the news yesterday at 8pm ...

Last night the collaborationist mistress of the English captain in the next room, the non-combatant US forces and the youth of the town made a certain amount of 'tapage'. I celebrated the occasion by staying on the waggon (which I had ascended since my troubles began), going to bed at 10 and getting up at 7 ...

There is a public holiday for two days. My balcony is decked with flags and the students are marching past in single file in the street, hands on each other's shoulders, cheering. Ages 17 to 12. (What will they cheer in their lifetime?) ... Are your children on your bed? What do they say about V-Day? ...

I'm amused that the Glucks spoke of brother Charles. He and I have not been on writing terms since the war, but family love exists ... We were brought up as rivals, rather a bad thing. Especially for me, as I was the brilliant one who would achieve anything, and he the plodder. The result was that for 10 years I thought myself so clever that it was quite unnecessary to do anything; and by that time it was a bit late ...*

The feeling [here] about Pétain is 'au Poteau' ['to the stake'] ...

Arrive, slightly to my surprise, my driver (Spanish, hatless, dirty and red-eyed) and my temporary assistant, cool, neat and dressed in blue.

Boskenna – 9.5.45

Just a little hangover from yesterday. Even the children lapped champagne. Diana arrived and then left, and Bill Armstrong[†] from Germany, and Hugh and Constantia from Scilly and all the neighbours flocked in and the children went quite mad putting out more flags. At first I felt very flat. Nothing seemed real. They have all gone now except Bill who leaves tonight and Hugh Sellon[‡] who

---

[*] Charles Siepmann, the middle brother, won the Military Cross at the age of nineteen while serving with the Royal Field Artillery on the Western Front. After leaving Oxford he became a housemaster at Borstal. He was later Director of Talks at the BBC, a key position from which he resigned after a violent argument with the Director General, Lord Reith. He then emigrated to the United States.

[†] RAF friend of Mary's who remained devoted to her for the rest of his life.

[‡] Possibly Conservative political writer, author of *Democracy and Dictatorship*.

is just coming for the day. London on the wireless sounds bedlam and Betty reports that it's in an uproar and no one has yet gone to bed. I would have loved to be there if you had been at home. As it was last night I was alone with Toby, everyone else having gone to the village to get drunk ...

Boskenna — 10.5.45

I was interrupted by celebrations gaining momentum. I now feel absolutely defeated by The Victory. Bill and I spent yesterday morning in Lamorna pub with Gluck, Edith and Vicky Williams, getting back very gay to meet a completely sober Hugh Sellon. He caught up rapidly. Betty telephoned from London that when she arrived at Paddington tipsy Americans were letting off rifles so she's under fire at last. Yesterday was boiling and the sea rough. I half sprained my ankle and by the time I had got Hugh S. and Bill off to London and done the last lap of celebrating with Colonel P. in St Buryan I'd had enough. Diana is coming again tonight but she's in a filthy mood so I don't relish the prospect. Tomorrow I'm taking Mrs Grant to hear Michal Hambourg* who is playing in Penzance. I look forward to it.

Nice announcement on the wireless yesterday that the law against spreading alarm and despondency has stopped. So that we can now be as alarming and despondent as we please. I feel both about Pétain.

Hugh and Constantia's visit passed off admirably. No awkward subjects raised. I seem to have been an unconscionable time writing this letter. You must forgive me ... The house has been so full and as we've hardly any servants there's been little time ...

* Member of a Russian-British family of virtuoso musicians — Michal, Max, Jan, Boris, etc. Their father had been accused of being German during WWI and had successfully sued for libel after showing that he was of Russian descent and had been a naturalised British subject for twenty years — see the similar story of Max Erstweiler in *The Camomile Lawn*.

I love you most dearly and I hope I shall see you very soon. Three months is a long time to go without necessities ...

M.

Boskenna – 12.5.45

I am so glad to get your letter written on the 1st. I rather like disaster and its subsequent battles so don't let that worry you ... You sound as if you were having to swim for it through glue, but it may bring you back sooner ...

Yesterday ... I took Mrs Grant to a concert – the Penzance Orchestral Society, Michal Hambourg was the attraction. How she plays ... I think she is very beautiful as well as a considerable artist. The Orchestral Society arrived with a mass of musical instruments and began the programme by battering through *The Bartered Bride* and the Serenade for Strings, glaring at one another [as] they fiddled and trumpeted faster and faster. Feathers flew and Mrs Grant in a clear voice commented that the conductor seemed to be making a soufflé. Then Mozart and Michal Hambourg at the piano. My heart warmed to her when I saw her go pink and begin to shake with giggles as the orchestra bolted. Knowing her to be a friend of Lydia Phillipson's in Brussels I went to see her in the interval. She is enchanting and we made friends in the Mayor's parlour while the orchestra massacred Beethoven's Second Symphony. Never have I heard it sound so like 'The Ride of the Valkyries'. Laughter and a victory hangover from which she was suffering should have put her off when she came to play again but it didn't, and the way she played Chopin was sheer bliss ...

Visited Gluck and Edith on my way home and we drank gin among the bluebells. It's hot again and lovely and this afternoon I propose to fry in the sun ...

Sylvester has turned tough, armed himself and threatened to murder both Paul and Mark and they are terrified. Everyone is reported to be happy except Paul but it's nice for her too. Mrs Newton* used to say to Mrs Grant 'Poor little Pauline, her face gets <u>wizened</u> with scheming'.

Complete faithfulness here and no American bruises but a lot of scratches from Ernest [her pet rook] who is learning to fly and uses me as a landing ground, which is agony ...

I love you. It will take me years to show you how much.
M.

Boskenna – 13.5.45

Victory Sunday so I carted all the children to church except Nicky who is a papist. Rather a moving church parade of British Legion, Girl Guides, A.R.P. etc. Moving because it was so simple. The farmers in bowler hats and Colonel P. – *ancien militaire* – giving crisp orders (which no one paid much attention to). In church I was impressed by Roger's pious and hypocritical behaviour. Butter wouldn't melt. Sonya sucked sweets and Toby asked loudly pointing to a stain glass window whether the man with ferns round his head was Jesus. The parson preached on the absence of God at the San Francisco conference† and the downfall of the League of Nations for the same reason ... My fancy strayed into visions of The Almighty in top hat and spats clamouring for a bigger say among the representatives of small nations.

Undaunted Colonel P. marched three miles in a Victory Parade in P-Z [Penzance] in the afternoon, coming back to tea undefeated. He answered my anxious enquiry with the retort that he 'wears out' three partners in The Flurry Dance so this was nothing. I love him ...

---

* Annie Maclean, Pauline's sister-in-law.
† The conference of fifty nations opened on 25 April and drafted the United Nations Charter.

Boskenna – 14.5.45

I'm glad of your letter of the 6th ... Your troubles come from crying in the Wilderness of Fascists. The breeding grounds in Spain, Portugal, Ireland and South America are [preparing] for the next war and the excellency of your opinions will be recognised as our children reach military age ...

I shall find a house to suit our means. How fortunate that I love cooking as well as you, and have practical tendencies. Darling I do so love you. I shall put up a small tablet in memory of Pauline in our house, in token of thanks that she enabled us to meet (even though we slam the door in her face!) ...

M.

Toulouse – 14.5.45

Mary, Mary ... this is all blowing up like a grotesque Russian tragi-comedy. It is known as 'the Siege of Toulouse' and I am sorry to say that – so far gone am I – it was an American colleague who drew my attention to its comical aspects.

The latest is that the French officer in charge of the [Allied] *mess went up to Paris and complained of my attitude to our Air Attaché who seems to be sending for and getting reports on me which strikes me as rather comic.*

I saw Bertaux, the Commissaire de la République *for the region.* * *He expressed friendship and approval of my work; but admitted that ... there was an 'atmosphere trouble' around me at Toulouse. And he'd obviously said so to the Consuls and spies who've been sniffing, which is as good as to say that he agrees I ought to go ...*

I shall arrive with exactly £30 in the world – which is stimulating.

---

* Pierre Bertaux, pre-war professor of German literature at the University of Toulouse, left-wing anti-Communist. In August 1944 he had survived a machine-gun attack on his car by a pro-Communist Resistance death squad.

The play is completely held up ... but 60 pages of notes for Is There a New France* *round themselves off nicely at the Capitulation ceremonies. I had luncheon yesterday with Julien Benda, the writer, and he greatly approved my title and subject ...*

Boskenna – 16.5.45

My Darling,

Another letter from you this morning was sheer pleasure ...

I think that everyone except the crowds in London who sound jolly enough felt a great flatness. To my children Victory has meant junketing, flag waving and holidays from school though whether this is due to St Buryan Feast week or to the Victory I have not yet fathomed. I heard a shout of 'Peace!' from Betty when I was out in the fields with Toby and said to him 'the War is over'. He went very pink and said 'It isn't'. His thoughts are his own. Roger is instilled with potted patriotism at school and fairly well informed. Toby prays fervently for the Japanese and Germans when he is annoyed with me. Most of the village POWs are back. They tell me they feel flat too.

St Buryan Feast bazaar was in the chapel this year. Colonel P. and I adorned the platform with the Minister (who is new and presumably uninformed as to my divorce since he asked me to make a speech). We sang jolly Methodist hymns, prayed impromptu and everyone made speeches, all of which started with 'It is my privilege, and I <u>might</u> say a pleasure ...'

Diana is here again, rather cross. Gluck and Edith left today. We sat round an emptying bottle yesterday afternoon and Edith discoursed on Yeats's funeral. I'm sorry they are gone.

News of houses is poor. Ronnie has ratted and won't part with his house. Betty is searching hard – but so is everyone else. We shall find one I know and am by no means desperate. I would like Gluck's

* *Eric was planning a book on the political situation in France.*

in Hampstead which is for sale freehold for £6000. It is Queen Anne and has a garden. Harry might buy it as an investment.

Ernest comes for walks and when I jog holds onto my hair with his beak for balance ... The trouble with him is that he makes no effort to fend for himself. He may be with us for life – and rooks live about forty years ...

Very warlike noises of exploding mines off the coast all afternoon. There is a lot of clearing up to do. I am now going to weed with Ernest. I have a theory that the reason Englishwomen are such keen gardeners is that they are sexually unsatisfied, so my enthusiasm is temporary ...

Toulouse – 17.5.45

Mary darling,

Your Victory letter came yesterday ... Your letters fill me with such joy ... I adore your three styles: narrative, jokes and 'bits' ...

As to victory, we seem to have had the same reactions, except that with my taste for paradox I celebrated by not drinking for the only time in my life ...

It is an unfortunate trait that I tend to exert myself only in trouble and I have never felt more vigorous or determined. I am manoeuvring the MOI and the FO rather along the lines of the Communist Party versus the Résistance here ... The game is to guide events through the following stages:

1. The Résistance are not necessarily against the Communists.

2. Therefore only those who are not against the Communists belong to the Résistance.

3. Therefore all Communists are of the Résistance.

4. Therefore all others are traitors.

... I have been thinking about our future and I am convinced that I must live in London ... Feeling that something must be done I have cut off my wife's allowance!

... We have spent less than a month [together]; and on that we are building our future ...

The elections here were Left in their results, although I believe the country is Right; but with 60 out of 80 municipal seats in Paris, to the communists, one can hardly imagine France taking part in what the communists (maliciously I suppose) are announcing as 'the war to liberate Germany [i.e. from Anglo-American rule] which is being prepared' ...

Love and courage (which I know you've got) –

E.

Toulouse – 19.5.45

First swim yesterday in the Ariège. The French told me with horror that it was snow-water, which would cripple me with rheumatism. But it wasn't too cold. The current is too strong, and one has to walk barefoot upstream, plunge in and come whizzing downstream with the current. A duck was treading a female duck underwater in a way I'd never seen; I didn't know if it was loving her or drowning her. He held her head well under the water ...

The expected attack has been launched and exceeds anything that might have been expected ... I am accused of antagonising Frenchmen, breach of confidence, drinking too much and even bad debts ...

By involving himself in local politics Eric had made enemies in the Foreign Office. In London, Eric's superiors in the Ministry of Information decided to terminate his mission. This was to be the first in a long line of jobs from which he managed to get himself fired.

Boskenna – 28.5.45

Little news but much love for you ...

Yesterday we had blazing sun and were able to toast in the afternoon and after dinner using Bill's leave petrol* but feeling extremely guilty all the same, we went to the pub at Sennan which was packed with singing fishermen. A competition between two crooning WAAF's was very funny to watch. Each had her following at one end of the bar and there was the makings of a real fight when they got back to their billet ...

I am anxious to hear the result of your fight, imagining that you are getting it about now. Prayers go up in little puffs ...

Toulouse – 30.5.45

Darling,

'Get out, and come back' is exactly what I'm doing. I shall leave here by car on Friday (1st June) and I hope to leave Paris on Monday ...

I shall have to see the Marines, as presumably I revert to R.M. uniform (captain) on July 1st: I don't expect they want me. It would be a bore to be sent to the Pacific – but convenient to get a job in Marine HQ in London (most improbable).

We cannot afford to gallivant; but we must have our reunion in comfort (possibly at the Mayfair, where I left my trunk) ...

I feel like giving the future a square look in the eye with you; an intimidating look. The wolf has been at my door before, but this time he is going to get a surprising reception ...

Darling, I adore you! Facing disaster with you is exhilarating. Let's make an end of disaster.

E.

---

* Bill Blackwood, RAF fighter pilot, badly burned in 1940, father of Nicky. His wife Diana had left him.

=====

Eric's suspicion that the Royal Marines no longer required his services was correct.

=====

Boskenna – 30.5.45

Colonel P. and I are looking forward to tomorrow when Bill Blackwood and Pauline leave – having a great craving to be free of visitors! Pauline has applied herself assiduously to the consolation of Bill, but I find she bores me …

I am being turned into a bureau for the search of lost prisoners of war by various anxious parents in the village. And there it is. I write for them to the Air Ministry, the Red Cross and to Alec. None of it's any use of course, as all the men were last heard of being liberated by the Russians – only to be thoroughly lost immediately afterwards. How infinitely better in these cases if they had methodical German minds. They are pathetically trusting people and I writhe at the empty words of solace I find myself giving out. One of them said, 'We parents feel it very hard that the R.A.F. have flown Lord Haw Haw* back and not our boy' …

The fathers are goaded by the mothers, all of which are having the change of life, to goad me. The fathers don't fuss as they go to the pub and let off steam and in take beer but it's not the thing for the mothers to go, so they let off steam at me.

I know I can do no good but am too cowardly to say so – it means votes for Alec, but I'm not altogether sure I approve of that either …

I am very sure I love you though.

M.

* Lord Haw Haw, nickname given to William Joyce, an American citizen and naturalised German who broadcast enemy propaganda from Hamburg. He was executed on a trumped-up charge of treason in January 1946.

Boskenna – 31.5.45

Pauline got very drunk last night, boringly so ... I am reading Thomas Mann, weeding the garden, keeping house and keeping sober and feeling well, in fact treading water until you come back. Ernest can now feed himself, and Toby has worn a false plasticine nose since the circus – but there is nothing new. Colonel P. a propos the visitors – 'What Devils!' We are gradually whittling them down ...

One thing about the visitors which startles me is that they toss the newspapers aside exclaiming 'How boring the papers are now, nothing in them at all'. I find them absorbing and it takes me all my time to get the faintest grasp of Polish, Trieste and Syrian crises apart from anything else.

Boskenna – 1.6.45

Delighted with your long letter of the 27th, pleased by the departure of the last visitor and contented with a bottle of claret produced by Colonel P. in celebration of our emptied house ...

I want to go to Provence with you. I loved Arles which I saw in September in a lemon yellow haze of heat after a long hot summer. I loved Les Beaux, unspoilt compared with Carcassonne, I swam in the river at Pont du Garde [correctly 'Gard'] instead of looking at the Roman Aqueduct and I loved Nîmes best of all. I went with John Pollock and the Macartneys in 1935 – we ate a lot of grapes.* I want to go again. I have a water colour of Edwin John's by my bed of a bit of country near Les Beaux. I remember disappointment at missing a bullfight at Arles I think, and being caught by a shocked Cook's Tour declaiming on the stage of one of the Roman theatres for John who, being an architect, was interested in the acoustics ...

A propos finance – to add to your impressive capital, don't you get £100 or £50 from a grateful King and Country on leaving the Marines? And you owe me £60 <u>not</u> £80. I have £140 most of

---

* John Montagu-Pollock, Mary's first real boyfriend; 'Trix' Macartney, a painter, was supposed to be Mary's chaperone but had allowed them to get on with it.

it to be spent on trimming the house when I find it, it won't go far either. But it worries me not at all.

Today Romie and I lunched at Mrs Grant's to meet the last girl friend of her generation, a Miss Dennison who is attractive with lazy drooping lids. We ate delicious turbot cooked in butter with herbs and cider and chocolate soufflé with lavish cream (I mimic your menus) and drank and laughed a lot. Afterwards I took Romie to Mousehole where we had tea with Jenny Heber-Percy* who is thirty-three and her lover who is twenty-one. He had a badly scratched nose and she two black eyes. Their conversation was of no interest and I left very soon. The children had been to the Corpus Christi Fair and returned satiated with roundabouts and ice cream, having seen a lion (asleep) and had a lot of fun with Alice's false teeth in the salle des glaces.[†]

I have given them a pair of bantams. Toby chose the hen leaving, generously I fondly imagined, the showy cock to Roger. But with a sweet smile he explained to me that the hen would lay eggs and hatch out little chicks which was beyond the powers of the rooster.

Alec telephoned with badly concealed anxiety to say he has two candidates to oppose him. One Labour and the other true Liberal, which will split the vote.[‡] I cannot think what he will do if he is not re-elected. He'll be a terrible bore ...

Yesterday I took Sonya, Roger and Toby to tea with old Mr Boscence.[**] They astonished him by their good behaviour and party

---

[*] Jennifer Fry, the beautiful muse of John Betjeman, Henry Green and Cyril Connolly – among others – married Robert Heber-Percy in 1942. He threw her out of Faringdon House, Oxfordshire, in 1944, preferring to live there alone with the owner of the house, Lord Berners. The 'lover' may have been a soldier called Michael Luke, who was aged eighteen and whom Jennifer once stabbed with a hatpin.

[†] Alice Grenfell's teeth had been removed at an early age. This was standard practice in Cornwall and many other parts of England to save dental bills, and was often part of a bride's wedding preparations.

[‡] Alec Beechman was a National Liberal MP. The National Liberal Party split from the main Liberal Party in 1931 because they opposed Liberal support for Ramsay MacDonald's Labour government. In 1947 they merged with the Conservative Party.

[**] Joe Boscence, a retired antiques dealer, formerly of Penzance, lived alone in a remote cottage at Sancreed near Land's End. He was a misanthrope who made an exception for Mary.

manners. Addressing each other with great politeness, spreading jam on their bread instead of their faces and piously saying grace. One should take them out oftener and it <u>might</u> become a habit.

Mr Boscence presented me with two enormous Bristol glass rolling pins – because the jewess his nephew married had once admired them, exclaiming 'She shan't have them though'. An iron gate fell on Toby's head, but it was a most pleasant afternoon. Roger shamed me. 'I see you've lost a tooth, Roger', 'Oh no. My mother pulled it out' – makes one look so brutal.

Boskenna – 2.6.45

If Harry <u>were</u> interested in Gluck's house it might be a blessing to be installed in something which had plenty of room for expansion from the first. This is putting the cart ahead again. Otherwise I had thought of something very small out of which we would have to move on expansion or prosperity. Diana will be giving up a furnished flat in a Kensington mews soon which is six guineas a week and small but might be a haven until we find something else ...

Hugh has become PPS to the Secretary of State for Air which he seems to like ...

Dear love, take care of your dysentery. I want you back in violent health and I love you as I shall show you. All of it –
M.

═══

Eric arrived back in London in early June. Mary invited him down to Boskenna to meet Colonel Paynter and to be introduced to her children. Eric, his war service nearly over, then returned to London and started to hunt for a job. He and Mary were unable to live together publicly before her divorce decree become absolute, which would be in October. They met discreetly, but Mary and the children continued to spend most of the time in Boskenna.

═══

Boskenna − 10.7.45

My Love,

I felt numb for an hour before you left and in violent pain the instant I left you at the station. No being busy in Penzance or lunching with Mrs Grant has done any good, the house seems very empty and the doors are banging. I am spoilt by five weeks of complete happiness and feel bereft ...

You have given me everything and crowned it by being so heavenly about Roger and Toby. I asked Mrs Grant what she thought about bursting into the open with my family and she says she thinks it's the only possible and sensible thing to do ...

I'm going to lie in the sun and think about you. The next best thing to contact.

My dear and only love, I miss you and love you.

M.

Boskenna − 11.7.45

... Toby seems to have enjoyed himself and has gone off again today to Truro with the Colonel to a County Council meeting and to see Tom Paynter in Hospital. The main attraction is I believe a fish and chips lunch with Muriel ...

As soon as you find out from Diana that we are getting that flat let me know as I will bring up a few things of my own to make it look less unattractive. Tell her to be <u>sure</u> and remove the goldfish!

... George Dawnay's* wedding is on the 23rd so all my family will be in London and Romie is having a cocktail party on the 24th so I suppose her Napoleon [Colonel Brinckman] is back at last. Mrs Grant breathed a sigh of relief when I told her as she said she felt sure virtue was getting strained ...

* A school friend of Hugh Farmar's.

I see now that never having wholly loved or wholly trusted before I was ungenerous in my silences and solitudes ...

M.

Boskenna – 12.7.45

... No letter from you yet but the posts are slow unless you happen to catch the country post. It's grey and quiet here. Mr Boscence did not turn up, put off by the rain. I had an agreeable afternoon with Roger. Toby turned up late from Truro and hungrily ate an enormous tea, later remarking that he had already had tea in Penzance on his way ...

Mrs Mitchell is doing your washing which I will post as soon as it's ready. Ask Biddy to post back any socks you can spare so that I can mend them. I've lots of time so grab your chance.

Claud's telephone if you want a bath is FLAxman 8034. He might be useful to you apart from baths. If you stay with Harry and are near a telephone in the evening or morning, ring me up so that I can hear your voice. (Not if it's a strain.) The children ask after you a lot and mind your having left ...

Boskenna – 13.7.45

My Darling Love,

I am just coming out of a terrible spin of gloom into which I plunged after talking to you yesterday. Except as an unnecessary proof that I love you I see no point in this odious separation! I hate living without you.

I trotted sulkily down to the sea by myself, sat on a hard rock and read a bad book. The sea was grey, there was a hot unpleasing wind and sultry atmosphere. Away flew my sense of humour on the breeze and I came back, seized the gin, thinking to catch up with you at the Savile, swallowed a large dollop and instantly felt ill and *épuisée* ...

I think I put myself into my spin with the thought that you were perhaps getting into a drunken spin without me and would make yourself ill and unable to work. I know I am gloomy because of reaction – being alone and missing you unbelievably.

I love you my darling and it's simple torture not to be able to leap into your arms and tell you so ... because I can't leave the children.

The sooner we can all get under one roof the better because although the pundits say one can get used to anything, I've never seen why one should. Colonel P. put on his pince-nez and remarked at dinner that he misses you too – and the chess. Your games gave him great pleasure ...

I have no news. I spend every breath praying for time to pass quickly – which it doesn't. From the way I feel any sane person would conclude we had parted for ever with harsh words. All this on one gin since you left.

I am so deeply happy when I'm with you that the contrast is altogether odious. Ugh. But write to me my love and telephone but particularly write, since that hobgoblin who chirps 'Your time is up' makes me nervous.* I love you.

M.

Boskenna – 14.7.45

My Darling,

It's deeply disappointing about Patrick's house. But don't worry, we'll find one eventually ...

I am sorry Mrs Mitchell gave you such a fright this morning. It was a dawn start with Colonel P. who was pure delight ... first losing his teeth, then his spectacles (tragic how everything become detachable with age) then selling a house for a thousand pounds

---

* Postwar telephone operators terminated the call after three minutes.

while he bought me a peach, and insisting that the car stop every time he saw a girl on the road; offering her a lift and on deciding she was not pretty, exclaiming 'Drive on, drive on, No room!' ...

Penzance was crammed, I met most of the neighbours. Mrs Grant's telephone was struck by lightning yesterday. All I can hear from her is baffled squeaks like some distant infuriated mouse.

There was a tremendous storm lasting hours. I was very frightened at one moment in the woods as Toby had gone off on his own thinking he would be terrified. I found him sitting on top of an iron gate simply loving it.

The sun's shining at last so I'm off to the rocks where I shall loll and think about you exclusively ...

Monday there is a circus in Penzance which I shall take the children to ...

Chelsea – 15.7.45

[Addressed correctly for the first time to 'The Lady Swinfen ...']

My darling,

... The order of events is to hear from the Marines tomorrow if the Admiralty wants me; then, if it doesn't, to decide quickly whether to propose something (a job) to them; I'm meeting Bob Boothby* on Tuesday, and he is a great friend of Bracken's† – so I'll decide by then ...

I have thought much about 'getting us all under one roof', and about how to tell your family and x-husband. I think you should get some new arrangement first; the Boskenna business

---

* Robert Boothby, 1st Baron Boothby, an influential Conservative MP and friend of Winston Churchill's. Lover of Harold Macmillan's wife, Lady Dorothy; he was bisexual and became involved in old age with an East End gangster, Ronnie, 'the gay Kray'.

† Brendan Bracken, 1st Viscount Bracken, ex-journalist and wartime minister of information, one of Churchill's most trusted advisers. As minister, Bracken was head of the Political Warfare Executive whose staff had been transferred into the Psychological Warfare Division, which Eric still wanted to join.

being, in essentials, unsatisfactory except for the one factor of the children's health ...

Your sad letter made me very sad ... This is the crucial period, so don't let's panic. I am frightened of cows but not of money problems. Unless they are likely to hurt you ...

On Earth, In Reality (chez Devos) – 15.7.45: 8pm

My darling,

The letter which I've just posted to you in Sloane Square ... left out essentials; for instance the children, how I loved them, and how I love you for loving them. Also, many small things; such as that I found an exquisite lunch of sandwiches in my parcel on the train ...

Darling, we have got to be very strong and realistic. After many dreams ... we are going to bump [to] earth during the next few weeks and find ourselves in reality – even harsh reality ...

As regards families, Harry's reaction to seeing me again ('You have confirmed your reputation of bringing calamity with you' – the garage fuses had blown!) serves as a warning of what yours may be ...

I'd better confess that I get into recurrent rages at your brother for having Carol as best-man (and for his letter), with the present arrangement at Boskenna which serves to victimise only you, at the lack of proper provision for you, and even at your attitude (for which, paradoxically, I love you). I am sorry – but I am determined that your rights should be stood up for; so you had better cool me down, before we take any steps 'envers les autres'! ...

I'll [mail you] Aurélien tomorrow. It's a rather depressing but brilliant ... satire on my generation, and is meant – I think – to tell what Aragon's life would have achieved in emptiness if Elsa hadn't pushed him into communism. Nancy [Mitford] told me that he caused annoyance during his recent visit by saying to somebody (female): 'Je déteste coucher seul' and then adding that he slept only with his wife ...

Nancy was slightly less strident, slightly taller, slightly prettier and much, much more ignorant (she couldn't understand about Benda) than I expected. Igor was there and another Etonian drunk and I resisted the attempt to drag me to dance at a Norwegian restaurant.

Gossip ... Boris's wife is now really a tart, and is being had by Edward Stanley who found Charles Sweeney* in bed with his own wife.†

Peter [Quennell] *– in connection with Betty, whom he refuses to marry – says Paul Ziegler‡ was Sonya's father. This is surely untrue? It was said long before your name had ever been mentioned between us ...*

Boskenna – 17.7.45

... I have never got used to being a parent and often find myself surprised and startled afresh realising that these two little creatures were born out of my body.

---

* Charles Sweeney was an American playboy whose first wife Margaret Whigham had broken her engagement to the Earl of Warwick in order to marry him. Following the above discovery, Margaret Sweeney started divorce proceedings and later married the Duke of Argyll. Their divorce case in 1963 became an international scandal; the duke provided the court with a very long list of men who he believed had shared the duchess's bed, including several Conservative ministers and three members of the royal family.

† Sylvia Stanley, née Hawkes, lingerie model, dancer and actress first married Anthony Ashley-Cooper, Lord Ashley, heir to the Earl of Shaftesbury, in 1927. They were divorced and in 1936 she married Douglas Fairbanks Jr. They were divorced and in 1944 she married Edward Stanley, later 6th Baron Sheffield. They were later divorced and in 1948 she married Clark Gable. They were divorced and in 1954 she married HRH Prince Dimitri Djordjadze of Georgia. They were not divorced and she died childless in Los Angeles in 1977.

‡ Paul Ziegler was Heinz's younger brother. During the war he served with the British Army in the London area as an anti-aircraft gunner. Before the war he had been an adviser to Warburg's Bank and had an affair with Betty Paynter. After the war he decided to become a Benedictine monk and joined the community at Quarr Abbey on the Isle of Wight – where he spent the rest of his life. Sigmund Warburg's son, George, continued to consult him from time to time on financial matters. Paul remained a good friend of Mary's and was for a time a strong influence on Toby.

The circus yesterday was a bad one but they enjoyed it immensely ... I went into a silent fury with the ringmaster who was brutal to two ponies and was not satisfied until I had telephoned the RSPCA who frothed with indignation and sent their inspector to the next performance ...

I am not surprised by Boris's wife, she always was a tart. Very good-looking but dirty. Colonel P. refuses to have her here. As for Paul Ziegler being Sonya's father all I can say is ... I know it is not true. Her father was a stupid good-looking Russian called Serge Federov ...

Boskenna – 18.7.45

My Darling,

... Phyllis should be getting your letter any day now. I'm praying steadily ...

I slept in the garden yesterday and then watched a mole digging for worms on the path. It was quite unaware, being blind, and scuttled round me and over my feet, staying by me for ten minutes.

It's still grey and stuffy in spite of a vile wind.

This time next week, God not interfering, I shall be on the train coming to join you. I have a great longing for your arms and close proximity. Alas (but possibly it's for the best), neither Hyacinth nor Dominick will be born next March ... *

M.

Boskenna – 19.7.45

In less than a week I shall be with you my Dearest Love ...

---

* Mary was pregnant and mistakenly thought that she had miscarried. Hyacinth and Dominick were the names they had chosen for their first child.

Tell Mrs De Vos* I am bringing eggs and vegetables and ration cards but <u>no</u> butter as there is a crisis on with the cows ...

Boskenna – 20.7.45

... Nothing is happening here ... The Colonel has a girl friend coming to stay today to go dancing with him. She is a recurring phenomena [sic] and of truly devastating gentility – wears long fake earrings and her hair in squiggles.

<u>Thank-God</u> you are not going to France again. I shan't feel safe until you are definitely out of the Marines ...

Claridge's – 20.7.45

... *Paul tried to commit suicide last night, didn't tell Sylvester and turned up 'for a quiet lunch' in such a state that I really thought she'd die. (She took 10 of his sleeping pills.) Better now. Quite nice. Loves you. Thinks we're no good for each other. Luckily, we're out of reach ...*

I love you. I'm sober but hurried.

E.

Boskenna – 21.7.45

... I couldn't hear very clearly about Pauline's suicide so keep me the details ... I'm glad she failed ...

I've been battling in Penzance ever since I talked to you ... I managed to get my hair washed and the children's cut. They look revolting. Lunched with Mrs Grant on my way home ... Nigel

---

* Eric was lodging with Mr and Mrs Devos in Smith Terrace, SW3. Mr Devos was the sommelier at the Ritz.

has sent her a picture which pleased her greatly. She was afraid it was going to be a nude of Margot but it's a bowl of roses ...

M.

Bagshot – 21.7.45

Darling,

I am missing you intensely, partly because I find myself in country surroundings again. The apples and pears are so thick on the trees that the branches have had to be propped up ...

We have amused ourselves by singing French songs ... Now Edith* I hear is playing 'Au Clair de la Lune' on, of all things, the accordion ...

I dined with Nora Oliver at the Gargoyle.† I was so disagreeable that she burst into tears and I had the embarrassing privilege of leading out a weeping, middle-aged woman under the quizzical eyes of David Tennant‡ and others.

Peter Quennell, who was there, told me that he just missed us in Cornwall and that Desmond Ryan is really quite intelligent but alcoholic. 'It's a very important distinction, Eric. There are intermittent topers, like you and me; and alcoholics. Ryan is an alcoholic.' I like Peter best of the London intellectuals; he was, as ever, with a new and ravishing girl ...

I told Edith about you and she is very pleased. She laments her husband being such a boor, because there is a wing of this house which we could have. I told her it would never work ... but it was a nice suggestion ...

I notice all sorts of things à cause de toi; the trees round the garden, the budgerigars, and the fact that the hen leads the ducks, which she hatched, about under the impression that she

---

* Eric's older sister, married to the Reverend Roger Bankes-Jones.

† The Gargoyle Club in Dean Street, Soho, was a private members' club. It closed in 1978.

‡ Founder of the Gargoyle.

is their mother ... I even distinguish between fox-glove and
delphinium ...

E.

Boskenna − 23.7.45

I'm getting very excited. Tomorrow I shall pack and Wednesday
thank heaven leave ...

My mother, father, brother, sister, niece and pregnant sister-
in-law will all be rampaging round Chelsea from tomorrow. Buy
me a mask ...

Oxford & Cambridge University Club, Pall Mall, SW1 − 23.7.45

Darling −

*I am waiting for Percival for lunch ... From the look of this
club, I daresay I shall get a rotten meal ...*

*After the week-end at Edith's ... a disaster greeted me: my
Reportage photographs have disappeared and I deeply fear that
I left them somewhere, as I had already rescued them from
Peter's club once. I regard this leaving things about as my only
bad habit ...*

31 Smith Terrace, SW3 − 22.8.45

*... The house is empty. How empty ... It's rather dreamlike, as
though I'd just seen a dozen you's crowding the hall and laughing
on the stairs, and then you'd suddenly vanished ...*

I'm lunching with Leonard Ingrams* at Boulestin tomorrow ...

* Leonard Ingrams was a banker who had worked at the Political Welfare Executive
producing black propaganda during the war. He had been chairman of the
pre-war Anglo-German Friendship Society and once flew his private plane
between the towers of Cologne Cathedral. He was the father of the writer Richard
Ingrams, first editor of *Private Eye*.

Irons in the fire at Rank; and I'll ginger up Harry (Courtauld's, Unilever) ... I shall see R. Hatt* in Bank ... David's departure might leave a gap at the D. Telegraph; so I'll see Muggeridge ... and I'll see Curtis Brown as soon as the play is finished.

British Museum – 23.8.45: 10am

... Mr Robert d'Alsace† called last night; <u>alas</u> I was out. That made two in one day, as Mr S. Smith‡ was limping about the restaurant where I had lunch. Is he a cripple?**

I had lunch with (and largely, on) Peter at a place called L'Hermitage, which I instantly joined (free of charge) as it is a 5/- menu and you can always get a table.

Chelsea – 24.8.45

... Lunch with Leonard Ingrams was interesting, without being directly helpful. He gave me some useful information, and confirms that 'people' are looking for 'political advisers' for overseas trade ...

I am seeing Hanbury Williams, head of Courtauld's, next Wednesday ...

Letter from my German relations in Zurich. They've got pots of money but no means of getting started again ... I shall write and suggest acting for them here!

Also from Zurich ... by the same post, a letter from my former Sancho Panza, a little Jewish journalist whom I befriended in

---

* Bernard Rickatson Hatt, director of the Bank of England.

† Parisian barrister, twice escaped from occupied France to serve with the Free French; wartime lover of Mary's.

‡ Apparently another wartime lover of Mary's.

** Early in their relationship Eric had insisted that Mary give him a list of her previous lovers. She had not asked him for a list of his.

Geneva and who is now Swiss correspondent for the News Chronicle. He ... says that he heard of me from Chester Purvis, an MOI colleague, whom he always refers to as 'Pervers' – in blissful unawareness of the verbal implication and of the fact that Chester is a well-known pédéraste ...

Mrs Devos' devotion takes the form of elephantine gambits on your behalf. 'I wasn't going to tell you,' she remarked, after the 'foreigner's' visit. (He [Robert d'Alsace], by the way, was fully aware that your departure was for Boskenna; so kindly report the latest.) Then: 'I think that's why they're jealous of her, don't you? Because she's pretty? They're all running after their men, but Lady Mary knows she can get whatever she wants.'

Today she asked me if I didn't think you would do well in the cinema. 'They' by the way in Mrs Devos' vocabulary are rapidly becoming a pseudonym for Betty; although there is a vague background in which are also lumped in Mrs Emanuel, the Duchess of Sutherland and Biddy ...

Give my love to Robert d'Alsace, and bear in mind a broken jaw if you see him.

I love you.

Eric

Chelsea – 25.8.45

Sat. 10pm

... The day began with a speech by Mrs Devos on equality, spoken through the bathroom door. This is not a moment at which I am abordable on that subject or any other ...

We had both better toughen up; because it is clear to me that we are in for the hell of a time. And I want my Hyacinthe-Dominic to be born.

Sun. noon

I met Antonia White (author of Frost in May*) and took her telephone number, as she was Tom Hopkinson's wife (one of her three
annulments) and is by now a mistress of money-making as a
freelance. Her eyes were even more glazed than they used to be
by the fear of being hurt; which in her case leads to lunacy ...*

*The newspapers are full of awful warnings about domestic
fuel. I've registered with Bull, and ... shall sing and dance about
returning soldiers, expectant mothers and god knows what not.
Likewise there is no chance of a telephone 'for months', unless
I get a word from Admiralty or MOI – which I shall try! ...*

*This week I've appointments with Courtauld, the Bank's press
man, and the Kemsley features editor ... I see Sydney Bernstein
is back in business – he's worth trying ...*

Boskenna – 26.8.45

My love,

　... It is yet another grey day with fog horns. I am in a fair way to
give up smoking. At least that's how I feel this morning. Nausea ...

Chez Devos – 27.8.45

Dearest love,

*A brief word because I am just going out to see Bull the Coal
Merchant: and Harry at the Bank to steal some typing paper ...*

Robin Fedden called (for the second time) yesterday, with no
ostensible purpose. His wife is in league with mine. Are we getting
action at last?*

---

* Robin Fedden was an academic and poet whom Eric had known in Cairo
during the war. Mrs Fedden was a friend of Phyllis, Eric's wife, whom he
was striving to divorce.

Boskenna – 27.8.45

... No letters from you this morning. I felt madly sick all yesterday ... I am slightly less sick today and ... I am thinking very hard about H–D. The more I think the more inconvenient they seem to be.* It isn't as you know that I don't want them, it is the problems we have already looked at. That it's very unfair on you even if you get started straight away with a good job. That it may turn out to be unfair to them. That thinking it over here I believe it might make things very much more difficult for Roger and Toby to be with us and I am sure that I should not be able to laugh off a bogus story about it.

At the moment I am <u>afraid</u> of the difficulties, probably because I am away from you and feeling ill. I want our children to have the very best start we can give them and this doesn't seem to be it! In a year or eighteen months' time when we've got established I would leap at it.

I have talked to Betty who is prepared to help and in such a case is a very loyal friend. She is naturally in favour of riddance as indeed I was for her in the same case. Nor do I blame her. Mrs Grant I also told. She was heavenly, and most concerned.

Please My Love, don't think I've been influenced or have panicked. I haven't. I've just been thinking hard and unemotionally. We are only starting our Alpine climb and I want to be a help to you not a drag.

Oh my Darling I love you ... Think about it too and let us decide when I get back to you on Friday night. Don't worry about ways and means as they are all set, safe and painless. I love you more than I ever imagined loving could be. I miss you dreadfully and you have made me happier than I ever dreamed I could be made ...

If I have worried you writing this please ring me up (reversing the charges).

M.

---

* Mary had not suffered a miscarriage after all, so had decided to have an abortion.

Boskenna – 28.8.45

... I saw Mrs Grant for two minutes on my way back from P–Z
... She was in *pleine déshabille* with her wig hanging on the bed
post. She sent you her love.

Yesterday all the children changed clothes. Roger truly revolting
as a female impersonator with his aertex pants hanging down but
Toby alarmingly pretty in a sun bonnet and wide skirt! The new
cook arrived at midnight and left again this morning having
received a summons that her children are ill ...

I worried all night about having written to you of what I am
thinking of H–D, i.e. putting them off. But I think I'm glad I told
you. I want to be in your arms to discuss it all. Writing is most
unsatisfactory and I writhe at separation ... Three more days.
M.

Chelsea – 28.8.45: 12 noon

*... Am I having this baby, or are you? My imagination is affected,
and I see babies everywhere. As I walk in Battersea Park they
sprout like mushrooms around my feet, in far greater numbers
than ever before ...*

*There is a beautiful poem by David Gascoyne (who seems to
be very good) which you must read me aloud:*

*Death died and Birth was born with one great cry
And out of some uncharted spaceless sky
Into the new-born night three white stars fell ...*
[Four more verses quoted]

*I've just had such a good lunch from Mrs deV (cod) that I've lit
the last of your cigars, except for two at luncheon tomorrow with
Rickatson-Hatt. I am also seeing John Hanbury-Williams, and
Antonia White is coming to dinner at the Phoenix tomorrow ...*

Robin has taken the house in Radnor Walk at the corner of our terrace ... I decided that he couldn't be an emissary. No reason why he shouldn't be an intermediary? ...

Try to sleep on the train. I shall be on the platform ...
E.

31 Smith Terrace – 28.8.45: 2pm

Letter 2 – <u>Read other letter first.</u>
... Half-an-hour after posting my letter about maternity, your letter [of 27 August] arrived. Which made me, I am glad to say, laugh ...

I agree that it looks – even if my circumstances improved – unfair on everybody. It probably can't be done. I shall hate getting rid of it; and I dread the personal experience for you. But it won't make any difference to us, nor hurt our relationship. All told I agree ...

I love you.
Eric.

—————

Mary's abortion was carried out illegally, in a private house in London, by a doctor who was probably unregistered. Many years later she said that she had lost her nerve and it had been a cowardly decision made largely out of fear of further family disapproval. Her parents' criticism of her divorce intensified when they realised that she had fallen in love with a married man who was, in their view, 'German'. Following this crisis, in September 1945, Mary decided to leave Boskenna after five years as a house guest of the colonel, and move into rented accommodation in London with Eric. Shortly afterwards he was recalled to the Royal Marine Barracks in Plymouth to be discharged.

—————

39 Smith Terrace, SW3 – 17.9.45

My Darling,

I am missing you. But I am not unhappy. This is something to do with the house. Having our own house ... It's turned into a hot summer day and I have the front door and all the windows open and warm air pelting in.

There is a tremendous brouhaha and a crowd of jewish children and their parents in the synagogue. A good rivalry from the Connolly's [an Irish pub].

Boskenna has sent me four huge cucumbers and a lot of sweet-corn. My parents were almost calm this morning and order is slowly emerging from chaos. I love our house ...

M.

Royal Marine Barracks, Plymouth – 18.9.45

... My dearly beloved Joe* was here, which was fatal. Joe broke the bathroom door, Joan (his wife) said she had always disliked me, and I fell tidily and politely on my head in the middle of a sentence. Then Joe drove me home ...

The Mess was bombed, but is still agreeable ... Colonels are agreeable, and people present arms wherever you go so that you have to salute backwards ...

Royal Marine Barracks, Plymouth – 19.9.45

Darling,

My transport is ordered and it is agreed that I should return to you by the Riviera [Cornish Riviera Express] tomorrow ...

I am having a very gay and friendly dispersal. They gave me £60 this morning because I get 56 days paid leave, and

* A fellow Royal Marine officer and drinking companion.

there will be more to come: and probably a full gratuity as a major.

Last night there was a farewell cocktail party for the Chief Wren. After she had had drinks she cried out 'I must meet Siepmann' – and confided to me that she was called Dicky and used to play the piano at the Gargoyle. Then an incredible amount of drinking in various clubs and rooms, but I went to bed sober ...

I'm glad you've seen Paul Ziegler. A demain! ...

Eric

═══

After six weeks in London Mary returned to Boskenna to look after her children.

═══

39 Smith Terrace – 13.10.45

Darling,

It turned out a beautiful day and now the moon is a yellow scrap of finger-nail in a luminous sky above the little houses with their lighted windows ...

I've just come back from job-hunting ... What do you think of the strike?* A split in Labour between the Trades Unions and the communists brings the Russian danger near. Pentman went to Hamlet at the Arts last night with the Tass Agency man and says that the Russian was 'against everybody (tout le monde était des salauds) and that they are determined to plough their own furrow, and paradoxically most suspicious of their allies.

---

* In early October the Labour government, which had been elected in July, was faced with a national dock strike. In response, the government sent troops into the docks to prevent an economic crisis. At one point 43,000 dockers were out on strike. The trouble had started in the London docks where the workforce was unofficially organised by Communist Party shop stewards. The 1945 dockers' strike revealed an ideological fault line within the political left that is still visible today.

I detest anti-rural materialism: but I find unfettered capitalism callous ...

9pm. Kippers arrived, and I cooked them while Christina* made a salad which emphasised your absence. So did her talk of goings-on at Boskenna in summer '44 – don't blame her, she is loyal! I am amused at her mother's notion of a you so undomestic that there would be no meals, as you'd be at the '400' every night ...

Boskenna – 14.10.45

Dear love,

I am rested and good tempered but I miss you. It is rather a nice day. Warm, absolutely still and grey. I spent the afternoon yesterday with Mrs Grant who was very sweet and sent you her love and begs you to come down in time to lunch on her birthday. I said it depended on how busy you are.

I sat by the fire after dinner with Betty and the dogs and she ceased being irritating. The dogs went frantic seeing a ghost and there was so much bristling barking and growling that we were driven to bed, I suspected a mouse.

The children are being very sweet. Toby claims to be 'very good' at what he calls 'figures' at school which he cannot get from me. I trust he will be – but he's an awful liar.

Paull [sic] Hill[†] is going back to India which seems to be his dream opportunity for trading – the RAF Transport Command does little else. Anyway he's left. He was fatter than ever, one of those rogues you really can't help liking ...

I love you and miss you badly and I can't think parting is necessary to make me realise it but they do rub it in. I miss this

---

* Christina Sandberg, a young lady lodging in Donne Place, familiar with life at Boskenna.

[†] Paul Hill, Cornish neighbour and a favourite of Mary's. He was a crooked solicitor who was running a black market in daffodils and butter in partnership with Colonel Paynter, who was a magistrate.

Sunday morning with you. Remember my last Sunday and the beauty of Battersea park in what was practically the dawn. It's not nearly so autumnal here in the country. London leaves are always the first.

Look after yourself my dear love and do not doubt me or my love which is with you and forgive the emotional storm I set going over my parents. You were so wonderful over it and I never said thank you properly.

I wish I were in your arms this minute.

M.

Boskenna – 14.10.45

I am sitting by the fire with the dogs by candlelight – this romantic inconvenience due to the eccentricities of the electric light plant. It is very quiet ... and the Colonel asleep in his library ... he made some remarkably filthy soup especially for me for dinner so I feel a little sick. The bulbs are already coming up in some of the flower fields and I saw several spring flowers

Boskenna – 15.10.45

... Paul Hill said the services voted Labour to a man purely on the grounds of quicker de-mobilisation, and that troops are being poured into the Middle East and particularly into Palestine because Turkey is so uneasy expecting Russian to pounce, and that out there war is expected at any minute ...

I must get the children installed in London – with Carol if we have no room for them – as it will be better for them after the winter than staying here. I look upon the village school as social education but they learn nothing else that I can see. Roger is a slow learner but once learnt never forgotten. Toby is capricious.

I should love to hear Christina's version of summer 1944. She behaved in a highly hysterical fashion because Dennis Bradley, who was here with a nervous breakdown, did not make a pass at her ...

39 Smith Terrace — 15.10.45

... I think your homecoming will be alright this time ... because the first time I was drunk, the second time you were brooding, and the third time I was greeted with all this stuff about your parents and Paul and Hans and god knows what ...

11pm. There has been an important development in my family finances. For the moment all I can say is that it makes our imme-diate future less uncertain ... It is all on a modest scale, so don't suppose that I've been left a fortune ...

I've taken seats for Noel Coward's revue for the 26th Ça va? Possibly Bentley's, followed by Wilton's first and Ritz afterwards? ...

Christina tells me that to all outward appearances you are a self-assured glamour girl with a Berkeley girl appearance sitting in the Ritz in a purple dress, and that Dennis Bradley was madly in love with you, at a period when Boskenna-ites went from bedroom to bedroom, but that you kept apart and were apt to 'snap people's heads off' ...

Boskenna — 16.10.45

My Darling,

I feel cheerful today and vigorous. I must be re-acclimatized. It's blowing a splendid wind and the sun is shining.

I fetched Gluck and Edith out to lunch yesterday. They were agreeable. After tea I read Keats to Toby who begged for more.

I miss you.

I have two bottles of gin and hope for another next week for our party and have written to Barbara to speed up the Cider.

Throw the cheese away. I rather suspected it had gone wrong before I left. *Je t'en ferai un autre.*

Salad Dressing

1 tablespoonful sugar, 1 teaspoonful French mustard, 1 teaspoonful vinegar, 1 tablespoonful medicinal paraffin. And a little chopped garlic. Churn it all up ...

Last night I took Colonel P. to the account's meeting of the Victory Sports in the village. They had £7–7-6d in hand [£7.37p] and should have been pleased but a lot of harsh words were bandied and muttered and I was hard put to it not to let go and laugh.

My prescious [sic] take care of yourself and eat something besides Kippers! How I love you. I won't nag – but come and eat some cream here if it's at all possible. I want to be gripped and feel very close, my sweet love, I love you.

M.

In bed – 17.10.45

... I met your father in the King's Road this morning; and we said good morning ...

Today I wrote a 2000 word article on Dostoyevsky, and I enjoyed writing it. This is probably the only subject on which I am reasonably well-informed ...

The development of a remarkable fruit – rhaspberries with an 'h' – is noted with glee; it is kind of rhubarbish and rheumatic, and it grows on me. I am also fond of autom – rather medieval and Latin; also burdon ... Darling, what a speller! Now you can attack my cooking ...

I cut out a ludicrous piece about finance by Beachcomber [celebrated humorous columnist on the *Daily Express*] *and took it to Harry and told him I'd written it (seriously) and got 3 guineas for it. He was tremendously tickled: he said 'It doesn't mean anything!' and proposed to circulate it* [round the Bank of England] *for comments. It never occurred to him that I hadn't written it, or that it wasn't serious. He was tremendously superior and jeering. Finally, Humphrey Mynors was called in.* * *He read it through and said 'Beachcomber'! Harry really is becoming absurd and inhuman. He made a disgusting speech to me about Jews ...*

Boskenna – 18.10.45

... I am surrounded by children at the moment. I love Roger best. He is at school bless him. Toby's ears are filthy in the bright sun ... How they all giggle. They mock me. It seems impossible for me to be both loved and respected by my children ...

39 Smith Terrace – 18.10.45

Darling,

Your letter is a great joy, and so too is your existence. Never was anything truer built up on the slim foundation (to most <u>outward</u> *appearances) of 'high-class prostitution' and drunken impotence! ...*

I have just seen John Myers at Rank's ... Also Tony Downing, his stooge, an international pansy whom (disguised as a Group-Captain) I had luckily entertained to an agreeable dinner at the Crillon in Paris. He had given me a personal letter to Madame Worth, Patou or Schiaparelli to get your scent I remember ...

---

* Sir Humphrey and Sir Roger Mynors were twins, and cousins of Mary's father, living at Treago Castle, Herefordshire. Sir Humphrey, a baronet, became deputy governor of the Bank of England. Sir Roger was a classicist of both Oxford and Cambridge Universities. He was Roger Swinfen's godfather.

Boskenna – 19.10.45

... I am amused at my father's oldest sister's request that I should pass on the family lace, veils and christening robe to Constantia. She is the Queen snob of that generation and was enchanted when I married a peer. With malice I have pointed out that the christening robe is really a Mynors' one and should instantly go to either Roger or Humphrey. I have made a bed jacket out of a lot of the lace and certainly shan't part with that. I think it's very funny ...

I have a chicken, a duck and eggs and cream cheese for us to take back, also gramophones and wireless ...

═══

In November 1945 Eric and Mary were able to live together in public for the first time, as Mary's divorce had been finalised.

═══

39 Smith Terrace – 12.12.45

Darling,

... Delighted that Toby accepts me as your lover. Don't read them any Grimm fairy-tales about wicked step-fathers, and perhaps I'll get away with it.

Most agreeable luncheon with Malcolm Muggeridge at the Authors' Club. I was greeted as the author of the 'Letter to Priestley' and met Hugh Kingsmill.*

I was immediately made a member of the Club which has a view of the Thames, a library and a Silence Room (with a coal fire) for writing, and this coterie of (right-wing?) journalists. It

---

* Hugh Kingsmill Lunn, prominent journalist, critic, parodist and wit.

is on the 11 bus route, and the cheapest club in London. It provides a solution to the problem of my 'study', and the children shall have an upstairs bedroom! ...

I heard Kingsmill – behind my back – inquiring whether 'Siepmann has a publisher for his French book?' An occasional push is most welcome.

Malcolm referring to his ravishing Parisian (who – you may remember named your scent), spoke of 'the disadvantages of going to bed with someone who hasn't read TS Eliot' – which is a not entirely senseless gag! (There had been complications.) ...

Boskenna – 12.12.45

... Colonel P. gave me a great welcome and produced a bottle of gin he had been hiding from Diana. This morning ... a walk over to the farm with Toby to buy eggs for Christmas ... He is beside me as I write, drawing with his left hand and cutting out with his right ... Alice is teaching the children carols. The resultant cacophony is most painful. The boys sing treble and the girls bass.

Boskenna – 14.12.45

... Roger's birthday is in full swing. Celebrations began at 5am and I am already exhausted. The other children are in tortures of jealousy ...

I am battling with all the Christmas presents I have to dole round here, and complicated arrangements for Christmas geese, eggs, vegetables and so on to feed the children in London. I have told Alice my plan to take the children away to London in the spring. Her eyes filled with tears at the prospect of parting with them. I have been so lucky having her to look after them and shall always be grateful to her for what she's done for them. She is a rare human being ...

Boskenna – 16.12.45

My darling,

I was glad to hear your voice last night, even though I couldn't talk to you properly as I had children, maids and Colonel P. milling around me ...

I finished the Mann last night. It is ... even better than the others and a great book.* The violence and guile, the sexual complexities and appalling deceit of the house of Israel and the great joke of good coming out of evil in thoroughly jesuitical fashion is fascinating, and Mann relates it with deprecating humour and apparent approval. I am inspired to read the Bible more thoroughly and with my eyes open this time.

Sweet love, Christmas is going to be fun albeit exhausting ...
M.

════

Mary took the boys to London for Christmas to stay with Carol in his house, formerly their house, in Ovington Square, Knightsbridge.

════

39 Smith Terrace – 4.1.46

... My brother gave a lunch at Frascati's for my father, Edith and Roger – to which I was not invited. We do not seem to be bien vu by our relations ...

I go to Arnwell Grove tomorrow. It will be exciting if I find you in the bath on my return ...

---

* Probably a reference to the *Joseph* novels.

Boskenna – 27.2.46

My dear love,

... I cannot get used to these separations ... I moaned in my sleeper which was very joggly. But I slept and arrived in good order into wonderful sunshine, warm and still. The country at its best, clean, rain-washed and smiling.

Greeted at the door by Toby and True who had been waiting for me. Toby ebullient ... True much slimmer and so pleased she came and sat primly by the bath when I had one ...

Carol is here, very much better and very amiable. Colonel P., no longer snotty, gave me a great welcome. Sam St Levan was leaving, having spent the night for a meeting. He is trying to get elected to the County Council and no one will have him ... [Lord St Levan, a county grandee, lived in his castle on St. Michael's Mount].

Carol, Toby and I went to the sea before lunch and sat in the sun. There are a lot more flowers ...

I see Harry figures in today's *Times* large and clear; as Carol remarked, my father cannot fail to see it! I shall write from here about changing my name.*

39 Smith Terrace – 28.2.46

... There is a reddish sun, and have had a late breakfast having drunk beer with gin in it from 5.30 to closing time with Voigt ...

---

* In order to make their life together easier Mary decided to change her name by deed poll from Swinfen to Siepmann. Eric then started to address his letters to 'Mrs Siepmann' instead of to 'The Lady Swinfen'. This change of identity was unwise since it enraged Phyllis, the real 'Mrs Siepmann', who had not yet agreed to give Eric a divorce, and caused Mary and Eric many years of unhappiness.

Lunched at club yesterday and saw Muggeridge and Kingsmill. The Tatler [magazine] revealed to me at last Group Cpt. Green in his full horror; a gross face and vile ears! ...

======

Under their new identity of Mr and Mrs Siepmann, Eric and Mary left the lodgings at Smith Terrace and moved into a rented house nearby at 29 Donne Place SW3. Following the move to Donne Place, Eric switched his hunt for employment to Paris.

======

29 Donne Place – 15.6.46

... I hope you arrived safely without being too bumped or frightened ... You have given me a year of complete happiness since you arrived back a year and ten days ago ... Hurry back and let's go on with the years ...

Hotel Scribe, Paris – 15.6.46*

Darling,
      ... I am just getting over my arrival nerves, when all concierges, waiters and even Parisians seem deliberately rude. This is made more complicated, and one's acclimatisation is delayed, by the fact that they really are!
      Good and frightening journey. They gave us sandwiches and chocolate and sweets. During the bus drive from Le Bourget one saw with the usual thrill the blue walls, the man sitting on the terrace café as if he had always been there, and peaches and cherries in the open markets.

* First letter addressed to 'Mrs Siepmann, 29 Donne Place, SW3'.

Very good room reserved, with bathroom. I am seeing Anouilh's Rendez-Vous de Senlis tonight; and Cocteau's Les Parents Terribles and La Folle de Chaillot later in the week – all alone, which I rather like ... I shall telephone to Colette and Darcy Gillie ...

Vernon Bartlett greeted me in the hall – first primrose of the Big Four's big spring: which looks as if it might harden into an early winter ...*

Love and many kisses,
Eric

29 Donne Place – 16.6.46

My Love,

... My cold being beastly I went to bed at six last night with hot milk, aspirins, books, wireless and True ...

I am enjoying Bechover Roberts's [Bechhofer Roberts] life of Verlaine – what an agreeable shit ...

Hotel Scribe – 16.6.46

Today I kept for myself, and I spent the morning sitting in the sun at the Deux Magots opposite St Germain des Près church, reading the papers and making notes ...

Yesterday as I flew off ... I realised that for the first time I was not flying 'away'. I had discovered in Tunis that my perpetual need to leave jobs, people or places was [a] centrifugal urge that went back to my running away from home as a child. Now I am not running away, even from myself; and I WANT TO GET BACK! That is your achievement and [a] great one ...

Women seem to wear long loose coats over long loose behinds, hats tilted backwards which only look smart when they achieve

---

* Vernon Bartlett, Independent MP, foreign correspondent and co-author of *Journey's End*.

a hunting-bowler effect, and bags on straps over their shoulders or between their breasts.

The Big Four, the new government, labour troubles and a wonderful fraud or 'black market' in bachot exam papers make the news ...

29 Donne Place – 17.6.46

... It must be interesting to be in Paris at this very moment with the Big Four meetings and de Gaulle popping up like a jack-in-the-box.

With a view to joining you on future wanderings I went to Cook's this morning to get forms to fill up for my passport. I sneezed my way from shop to shop looking for a black dress, an unobtainable rarity, and had a long gossip with Nina Le Clerc in Fortnum's. Her office was strewn with garments chewed by rats in the night. 'They don't usually like black,' she murmured, turning over a ragged black coat with her toe ...

Jan Masaryk* has gone to Prague but may come back this week.

I am delighted by an announcement in the Court Circular of Col. and Mrs. Napoleon Brinkman's new address at Ascot. Yehudi Menuhin played last night but I fell asleep in the middle ...

29 Donne Place – 18.6.46

... I am writing this in bed, where I have been all day ...

Once I had made up my mind to spend the day in bed and not to see the little boys I felt much better. The last two days they were horrid, and it is bad for them and me that they should torment me

---

* Masaryk, the first foreign minister of post-war Czechoslovakia, had been the leader of the Czech government-in-exile in London during the war. He had become a friend of Mary's through his own long friendship with Heinz Ziegler. On 10 March 1948 he was found dead in the courtyard of the Czernin Palace in Prague, beneath his bathroom window. The Communist government said he had committed suicide, but it is accepted today that he had been thrown out of the sixth-floor window by Soviet secret police.

into a frame of mind where I cry in the night because they are naughty! Also ridiculous to be blackmailed and bullied by them. A holiday from their temperaments is lovely, selfish little pigs that they are!

I am rejoicing in Verlaine which I read with left eye, the right one waters. Like Blunden's *Life of Shelley*, which was about Byron, Bechover Roberts's *Verlaine* is about Rimbaud. He, as a character, is a joyous discovery to me ...

When you say in your letter that you have always been running away I realise that I too have been a fugitive, usually frightened and sometimes defiant. Since we have loved I have gained courage and with your help can say Boo to many geese ...

19.6. – No news this morning. I slept very well after saying 'Boo' to my mother on the telephone. She stuck her neck out too far so I chopped it! ...

Hotel Scribe – 19.6.46

... I have a luncheon party for Jean Cassou, *Vernon Bartlett and Darcy Gillie on Friday ... It's lovely here but pointless as there's not much work to be done ... I've had lunch with Claud Cockburn†* *(the communist) and his wife;‡ and today* [there is]

* Art historian. Founded the *Musée de l'Homme* resistance group in Paris in 1940. Was appointed Commissaire de la République in Toulouse in 1944 before Eric's arrival, and had survived a lethal attack by retreating German troops.

† Claud Cockburn, a contemporary of Eric's at Oxford and a school friend of Graham Greene. In the 1930s he founded and edited an influential political news sheet, *The Week*, in which he coined the phrase 'the Cliveden Set'. He joined the Communist Party of Great Britain, travelled to Spain during the Civil War, and filed carefully constructed reports to the *Daily Worker* about imaginary Republican victories.

‡ Patricia Cockburn, née Arbuthnot, born into the Anglo-Irish ascendancy, was presented at court in 1931, married a wealthy businessman and travelled through the South Seas, India and Africa. On returning to London she kept a pet cheetah, divorced the businessman and married Claud. She and her husband went to live in a tumbledown barracks outside the town of Youghal, Co. Cork, where she bred ponies and made shell pictures. She once broke a Bakelite telephone receiver over the unwelcome grasp of Malcolm Muggeridge.

a press luncheon at which Leon Blum* is the guest of honour. So I'm getting around. My former colleagues welcome me back to the fold ...

29 Donne Place – 29.6.46

My Darling,

It is a windy, sunny day and I have talked to you on the telephone. Also I have pulverised [thoroughly exercised] True ...

Although, as my former wife says, neither you nor anyone can be my 'solution', you give me a basis to work out my own solutions (which I prefer to do; I can't bear her interferences with my 'soul') and that basis is that I love you deeply, as I have never loved nor thought that I ever could.

True is in good spirits, but looks for you in the bedroom ... I bring cigarettes and Marsala, and bangers ...

I love you.

Eric

* Socialist politician and pre-war prime minister of France.

PART TWO

The Crisis: 1947–50

*E*ric's job-hunting proved successful and he took up a position as a press officer with British European Airways (BEA). Meanwhile Phyllis Siepmann, reacting angrily to Mary's decision to change her name by deed poll, decided in July 1946 to refuse her husband a divorce. At the same time she started a campaign of stalking and persecution, following Eric around London and into his office at BEA. In October, she managed to get into the house in Donne Place carrying a suitcase. Eric had to return home and throw her out of the house, assisted by Mary.

During the winter of 1946–7 the crisis with Phyllis worsened. In November, her letters to the management of BEA took on a more sinister tone. She said that she was in urgent need of money and that if she did not get it she would create a scandal. She feared this might result in 'harmful publicity'. In April 1947, Mary decided to take temporary shelter with a friend who lived in Scotland, Joan Hamilton.

═══

Westercroft, Symington, by Kilmarnock – 10.4.47

My Dear Love,

... We nearly missed getting to St Pancras as Carol's carburettor was leaking ... Miss Mitchell [Carol's housekeeper] gallantly chased us in a taxi with bits of the children's luggage which had been left behind ...

The Third Class was clean and we ate all meals in the restaurant car ...

There were lambs and magpies to look at and astonishing beautiful bleak country in Cumberland, huge hills with masses of snow and brilliant sun. In the low ugly Midlands were dirty floods. What black sinister towns are Leeds, Chesterfield etc. stark, wicked, evil – black. The country round is tainted.

I read Peter Q's article on Ruskin in the *Cornhill*. I see Ruskin wrote *Harry and Lucy*, the first book I ever read. My father bribed me ...

We <u>must laugh more</u>. We haven't laughed enough lately ...

Away with this to you. I love you.

M.

Westercroft – 10.4.47

... This country is rather bare and beautiful. Three miles away is the sea ... We all, Joan, myself and six children, went for a beautiful walk this morning. True in paradise! Pebble* fearfully urban pranced round the cows ... True chased a rabbit deliriously and then got stuck down a hole ...

Please my darling let us never live in a large house and be worried about the servants. Joan and her husband seem quite old with worrying about servants, it seems to be a terrible thing. They also wonder 'what the country is coming to ...'

Pebble has a dachshund friend of his own age. True is livid. Joan's husband simply hates dogs and wasn't told we were coming until just before. He is trying to be nice to them. They yelp quite suddenly under the table at meals, and Joan sneaks the dachshund into the bed when he is asleep ...

Joan is a bully. I like her ...

---

* Mary had a second dog, a large mongrel, one of True's puppies. Both dogs had a lifelong habit of escaping and disappearing into the landscape so that search parties had to be sent out.

I am looking forward to Curtis Brown's letter.* If possible I would like to re-write the 'bad third'. While re-writing the bad third I would brood on the next book ...

Westercroft – 14.4.47

... Joan's husband who is a very stupid man [but] ... fond of children, and who refers to the cook who is under notice as a Bolshie! ... [is] a pompous ass exactly your age called Adam Hamilton ...

Westercroft – 16.4.47

... I was glad you rang up in the middle of Dalton's budget speech.† Joan's husband was verging on apoplexy. Afterwards he let off a great spout of rage and indignation and it was quite endearing ... It will be so wonderful to get home ... Pebble is a beastly bed fellow in a snuggle bed. We struggle all night ...

I certainly don't want to live up here. The Scotch are horrid. Madly nationalistic, soon they will be wearing tartan shirts and shouting 'Heil!' They detest the English. The country is very clean and bare, like a scraped pig ...

=====

Shortly after Mary returned to London, Eric flew to Rome on BEA business.

=====

* Mary had sent her first attempt at a novel, *The Glass Bugle*, to the literary agent Spencer Curtis Brown.

† Hugh Dalton, Old Etonian socialist Chancellor of the Exchequer in the Attlee government. His budgets were designed to fund the welfare state by redistributing wealth. He raised higher rates of tax and death duties and strengthened exchange controls.

29 Donne Place – Tuesday 29.4.47

... No letter from you yet. Nancy* is sending this for me on tomorrow's plane ...

I sat in windy sunshine while Roger and Toby ran with other children in the park yesterday. Pebble and True played with a lonely child in woollen gloves ... The other children ignored her brutally.

Nancy and Ronnie [Emanuel] came to dinner ... Afterwards we went to the Curzon where we saw *Le Déserteur* in which Corinne Luchair† [sic] never changed a bovine expression except to tidy her hair when her young man committed a murder ... It was remarkably bad and the Curzon audience thought it was wonderful and were angered by our laughter.

Today I am lunching with Carol, to hear about his amours I suppose. In the Berkeley Grill ... I miss you abominably. Pebble slept on my stomach and True on my feet. They were most comfortable.

Harry forwarded a letter from PKS [Phyllis Siepmann] to Charlie, sent without comment by Charlie to Harry. The usual poppycock – You are mad, your insanity vouched for by Strauss,‡ and I am a 'woman of bad reputation'. Apart from feeling a little flattered I mind hardly at all ...

Time drags on leaden feet so I try and fill my days with this and that but it doesn't work ... I badly need a hug ...

M.

---

* Nancy Gow, Eric's secretary at BEA, was one of the few people capable of standing up to Phyllis. When Phyllis suggested that 'no little boy in Cairo had been safe there during the war' due to Eric's presence, Nancy commented that this seemed 'implausible'.

† Corinne Luchaire, French film star of the 1930s once hailed as 'the new Garbo'. She was the daughter of Jean Luchaire, Vichy government apologist and minister who was executed for treason in 1946. Corinne was sentenced to ten years' 'national indignity' four months later. During the occupation she had been a prominent member of the Parisian beau monde surrounding the German ambassador, Otto Abetz, and had a child with a German officer. *Le Déserteur* was made in 1939.

‡ Dr Eric Strauss, prominent psychiatrist, who was treating Phyllis; author of *Sexual Disorders in the Male*. He also treated Graham Greene.

In May, while Eric was still away on company business, Phyllis got into the office and frightened a young woman working there. Eric felt embarrassed and humiliated and Nancy Gow noticed that his health had begun to suffer. Fearing that he would be sacked, Eric resigned from BEA in June 1947. Encouraged by this, Phyllis started to write to Mary's former husband, Carol Swinfen. In September 1947, she warned him that his little boys were not safe in Eric's company. She said that she was bringing an action against Eric for separation on the grounds of drunkenness, cruelty and unnatural vice, and repeated her claim that in Cairo during the war he had several times made advances to little boys in front of witnesses. Carol was not impressed and invited Eric to stay with him and the boys whenever he wished.

Following the loss of his job, Eric decided to make writing fiction his full-time occupation. Mary wanted to do the same. Spencer Curtis Brown had been encouraging about The Glass Bugle. He offered to send it to Collins, the publishers. Eric thought it needed more work.

'Some bits are so good,' he wrote, 'that they show that you have it in you to do something really good ... The chief point and the ultimate effect is that you have written a novel that is well above the average, beautiful and amusing in parts (funny and beautiful is, I feel sure, your line) ... and full of promise as a first novel. I am frankly amazed!! ...'

Then, referring to Phyllis, he wrote: 'Do you know I am glad this woman persecutes me – it keeps me alive, and balanced (this memento of how not to live) and <u>drives</u> me to write! I am only sorry that it should affect you.'

In August, Mary and Eric decided to head to the West Country for a holiday with the boys. They went to a hotel at Pinchaford, near Newton Abbot in Devon. But Phyllis, who was a talented amateur detective, followed them to the hotel where she threw a glass of water in Eric's face. She agreed to leave if Eric would return to London and talk to her. Then she waited until Eric had boarded the train, returned to the hotel, walked into the dining room where Mary was lunching with the boys and struck Mary violently in the face. The police had to be called.

Mary and Eric continued their flight. They took the boys to another hotel, the Beverley at Chagford in the middle of Dartmoor, where the holiday continued a more peaceful course. In September, the boys returned to live with Carol in London and went back to school. Mary stayed in Chagford and started to rewrite her novel, by now called Henrietta. In October, Phyllis tracked her down again. Phyllis picked out one of the hotel guests, an elderly lady, and wrote to her out of the blue.

'The woman posing as "Mrs Siepmann",' Phyllis wrote, was not married to Mr Siepmann, and the latter was 'a violent, adulterous, alcoholic, wife-beating child molester … [but] it is wrong to blame or condemn him [as] my husband is irresistibly compelled to ill-treat all his women owing to a deep and unconscious mother-fixation which can only be cured by psychological treatment.'

Phyllis next took to tapping on the hotel windows calling Eric 'a Bluebeard and a sadist' and denouncing the hotel proprietor, a Major Hughes, for running a hotel that was being used for 'immoral purposes'. Major Hughes emerged to eject her from the grounds, whereupon both Phyllis and her dog bit him on the leg.

Major Hughes then summonsed Phyllis for assault and battery and she was bound over to keep the peace. If she caused a disturbance in Chagford again she would be locked up. As a result, the village and parish of Chagford, reputed to be one of the most haunted settlements in England, became a safe haven for Mary and Eric.

But beyond the parish boundary, the struggle continued.

In November 1947 Eric finally sued Phyllis for divorce on the grounds of her wartime desertion. This move interrupted her campaign of persecution. Eric's father Otto, a distinguished teacher and linguist, had died in January 1947, and with the small amount of money Eric inherited he and Mary were able to buy a house with ten acres of land in Cornwall. They moved

into the new house in the spring of 1948. The property, called
Peakswater, stood three miles in from the coast at Lansallos,
between Looe and Fowey. It had no electricity. In later years
Mary remembered that she was happy there, learning to be a
writer. In the late summer of 1948 Eric wrote to her frequently,
from Chagford, where he had retired to write a novel.

———

Chagford – 8.8.48

Darling Mary,

I left [Peakswater] *feeling sad and sore. Mrs L.* said pointedly
several times, 'We'll do anything for <u>Mrs</u> Siepmann'; and one of
the boys said 'are you leaving for good?' ...

All this is exaggerated, and my telling you of it in direct
contradiction to my resolution ... to write gaily and say nothing,
and to wait six weeks by which time I shall have forgotten the
stings of horseflies and tenants. But ... in my present mood, I
wouldn't be prepared to live at Peakswater again without a
guarantee of good will as well as good behaviour from the L's ...
Alternatively ... I should like to raise their rent, limit their
gardening activities, or get them out ... Why should I be upset
and tormented by the stupidity of others? ... I did not escape an
office, to be pinpricked by bumpkins ...*

Chagford – 12.8.48

*... I am happy here. I have polished Part I for the typist,
which makes 30,000 words ...*

*You have nothing to reproach yourself with, except choosing
me. And the disadvantage of me is that work must come first,*

* Mrs Littleton – the Littletons were their tenants at Peakswater.

and that I came to it late so that I have more difficulty than others in concentrating. I promised you a life, and I shall be in a position to give it to you about 1951 ...

We will be alright; but it may be a bit drastic for three years. Thank you for your faith in my talents ...

Chagford – 17.8.48

Darling,

No letter from you today, which is a disgrace and fills me with anxiety. I am playing for Chagford at cricket tomorrow. (Their plea in inviting me was that the N.U.R. – National Union of Railwaymen – should be represented: an allusion to my blue trousers.) ...

I am having my shirts patched with their tails, but there is nothing to patch my pyjamas with! Is the third pair, which I left at Peakswater, so torn that it would serve?

The cellist from the Hersch Quartet is at my table; so I am learning a lot about music. He agrees that Myra Hess is wonderful and Harriet Cohen awful. He says la Cohen plays everything slowly because she can't play the piano.*

It has occurred to me that Jack McDougall, who took my first novel, will come in useful when it comes to making 'an arrangement'. (I want £600 for three books ... spread over the next year.) It would be logical to follow him from Chatto ... The point about Jack McD is that he knows every character of whom I write; and knowing me might be easier to discuss terms with.

I reckon we'll be £150 down by the time I sell my book (exactly your money from Carol for another year!).†

All my love,

E.

---

* Among those who did not share the judgement of Eric and the cellist were William Walton and Ralph Vaughan Williams, both of whom appreciated the professional talent of 'la Cohen'.

† Carol was supporting both Roger and Toby, and paying Mary an annual allowance.

Chagford – 19.8.48

... I am going to the [Agricultural] Show with my cellist. I can't tell you what it means to have an artist at my table. It makes me realise what specialists we all are. I have <u>nothing</u> in common with anyone else in the house. We listen to the Proms together, and he is helping me to enjoy Sibelius and even Dvorak – but I am doubtful about the latter. He (the cellist) was in the RAF and played at the Potsdam conference, and says the Russian back-slapping was sickening and that when Stalin came to dinner with Winston he brought his <u>own</u> guards six deep ...

PK menace abated my foot. She is telephoning and writing to everybody saying that I'm 'in prison again', adding as a post-script to ... my informant: 'Are you by any chance coming to the Mental Health Congress?'!

Chagford – 22.8.48

Darling –

Yesterday was such a day of wind and rain that one could enjoy nothing ... The days are now unbearably long, pending your arrival. But your visit has already had one desired effect, and I shall have finished Part II. (50,000 words altogether.) I have done 3 chapters in the last 4 days! ...

The book on Dostoyevsky was crammed with interest, and you must read it. The story of how his young wife cured him of gambling, and of their married life generally brings the tears to one's eyes. I am now reading I. Compton-Burnett with delight. I wonder if you will. It is a narrow but highly original vein which I find exquisitely funny and beautiful, but it isn't easy to read. Nor am I sure that I want to read another ...

I should like to be licked standing up, and then to have you on all fours from behind, and then to whip your bottom with a lash and then to lick you till you came in my mouth and then to fuck you till you came on my cock. Some portion of this programme, at least, we should be able to carry out!

All my love,
Eric

Chagford – 23.8.48

My dear Love,

You will find me with a red nose and bleary eyes and, which is worse, untouchable as I have caught a cold ...

Allow me to add that my pyjamas are falling to pieces, and that if there are any coupons I might get some winter pyjamas at Gale's? ...

Chagford – 30.8.48

Darling –

... It was wonderful to have you and, if I fail to make you know how much I wanted and always want you, that was my failure and all I can say is that it was due to being tired and <u>not</u> to any lack of feeling!

You looked forlorn and even angry with your cup of tea, so please be gentle in your thoughts about me and forgive me for being difficult to live with. I really believe that I shall be better, as lover, husband and companion when I have achieved a little belated recognition ...

I love you,
Eric

Chagford – 31.8.48 [postcard]

The old lady occupied the bathroom from 6.30am onwards and I have LEFT! ... Your note <u>very</u> welcome, as you looked so angry on the platform.

 All my love,

  Eric

═══

Eric moved from the Beverley Hotel in Chagford – where the other guests were making too much noise and monopolising the bathroom – to the Easton Court Hotel, a mile outside the village, which was used by many well-known writers. Patrick Balfour (Lord Kinross), a contemporary of Eric's at Winchester and Oxford, had introduced Eric to Carolyn Cobb, the American owner, who gave writers preferential rates. During Eric's stay, the hotel very nearly closed down when it was removed from a hotel guidebook. Mrs Cobb told her guests that she was on the verge of bankruptcy and so her many distinguished guests put their names to a publicity campaign.

═══

Easton Court Hotel, Chagford – 31.8.48

Darling –

 At first sight, this seems a very good move indeed. I have a room in a sort of shed, away from the hotel, a solid table and chair, AND the silence is complete ...

 I wrote you a long letter last night about your tears and my bloodiness and your terrible threat to fall out of love (with house or me?) ...

Your note was a relief ... I WILL make it all up to you. You've born [sic] all the brunt so far.

All my love,
Eric

Easton Court – 1.9.48

... It is in fact a very good hotel with at least six servants and no more guests than Beverley; and I have at the moment my wing to myself. I sit in a sort of glass cage, which gets all the sun, with a view of thatched roofs and a friendly hill covered with bracken and walls, and a gay flower garden and lawn. No one is tiresome ...

Easton Court – 5.9.48

... I must say I am most comfortable and quiet ... Moreover, in the singularity of wanting to be quiet, one is not alone. Apart from the Master of a Cambridge college, I have an ally in Elizabeth James, who has had one novel accepted and is now writing another ... She has a scarred face, two Pekinese and declares that she loathes children, so that I took her for a frustrated spinster till I discovered ... that her lover had arrived for the week-end! (She is the daughter of Lord St Germain whom you might have met in Cornwall?) ...

All my love always to you –
Eric

PS Did you see the Su. Times *photograph of Masaryk? He has Toby's eyes so exactly that I wonder if you are quite sure what bed you were in?*

Easton Court – 6.9.48

... *After lunch*

Elizabeth James' boyfriend turns out to be Maurice Hastings, who looked like a guardsman at Oxford but was trying to become a parson. I remember discussing Christianity with him at luncheon. However he changed his mind and took as his Bride not the Church but an American heiress ... [then] he took a large house near Oxford and sent Rolls-Royces to fetch Maurice Bowra & Co. out on Sundays ... He is writing a book about Exeter Cathedral and calls E.J. 'lovey'.

Interesting statistics: Alec Waugh works 5 hrs. a day and writes 2000 words. H.E. Bates works four hours a day, five days a week. Elizabeth James works three hours a day, and writes 1000 words. Eric Siepmann considers four hours a good day and writes 17,000 words every 4 weeks ...

Darling, I must work ...

Easton Court – 10.9.48

... I sat up till midnight reading Waugh's The Loved One. Fashionable as ever, he succeeds in being as fashionably unpleasant as Sartre himself, without sacrificing his own nauseous style. Quite a technical feat.* It is about an American Undertaker's and Burial Ground and 'cadavers'. The girl the hero falls in love with trims the corpse's nails and hair.

Old Mr Baumer† shows me his paintings. He and I are the only people in the hotel without a title ...

---

* Evelyn Waugh had stayed at the Easton Court Hotel in 1944, writing *Brideshead Revisited*. Eric and Waugh had been on hostile terms since their days together at Oxford.

† Probably Lewis Baumer, *Punch* caricaturist and portrait painter.

*Rather suicidal the last two days. I am LAZY, and neuras-
thenic. Also, I find we need £500 to last us six months, only! This
book slump is the devil.*

*I need your encouragement and faith and joie-de-vivre. I do
rejoice in life, when I think of you ...*

Easton Court – 12.9.48

*... I am boiling with ideas like a dog with fleas; and I pray for
stamina. I decided in the night to re-write my Balkan satire as
The Fall of Budapest ... I can do it in three weeks ...*

*Was it Paul Hill ... who sold two stolen Mosquitos and four
Beaufighters* [wartime RAF fighter-bombers] *to a crook?! ...*

*Glad to discover that other people are even worse than I
am about noise. That sensitive flower Beverley Nichols found
even this room too noisy – because of the crooning of the
cockerels ...*

*My memory of your body is vivid. And as for 'feeling randy
after five days' ... I found myself singing at the top of my voice
as I swung down the lane the following entirely impromptu
song ...*

*Oh we went for a wonderful hunt
And we stopped and I showed him my cunt,
And he taught me a curious stunt,
    And I came and I came and I came.
Then I reached down and opened his flies,
And it fell like a bird from the skies
As it stiffened and started to rise,
    And I came and I came and I came.
Then I thought it was decent to pause,
So I put on shoes and my drawers,
When it rains it invariably pours
    And I came and I came and I came.*

… What about the [marriage] *Licence?! I have two baths a day as a precaution …* *

Easton Court – 16.9.48

… I am glad that my crude verses tipped you over; and I look forward to tipping you over myself. On the other hand when you refused to read Ulysses as an aphrodisiac you said: 'All this lust isn't love.'

Kindly let me know if you commit any infidelities in London, as I shall then purchase a whip and the choice will not be between love and lust, but between aphrodisiacs and sheer pain! …

Easton Court – 19.9.48

Darling,

This is written to the strains of Brahms' violin concerto and my window looks out on a green lawn where Pebble is sitting in the sun, and I feel that I have much to be thankful for indeed.

This feeling is enhanced by the fact that tomorrow (having been consulted) I shall be alone in the Annexe with the corpse of the old American lady whom you met and who died here this morning. Mrs Cobb had brought her to the hotel these last days, and I believe that she is a kind woman …

How one ignores Death! Donne said (which I love): 'We die, and yet we sleep!' (I like the mild surprise.) I shall have an opportunity to think about it … Old Mr Baumer, the White Rabbit, lingered beside my table in the dining-room to discuss my methods and said: 'Well, you're lucky to want nothing more than your work and your walks.' I was surprised, and I realised that my wants are, in fact, simple; as long as I have you. Then he added – and I am afraid he did not think that he was being

---

* This is a reference to the popular belief that hot baths rendered the male less fertile.

irrelevant! – 'You know, William de Morgan began writing his novels at sixty.' He intended, I think, to be encouraging.

I think of you today, having packed much earlier than necessary, and everything neat. Am I wrong?

Your hips contain a mystery which I shall not weary of exploring, and I send you a sharp, if unwelcome, nip of your nipples.

All my love,
Eric

═══

In September, Mary took the boys up to London. They all stayed with Carol at 12 Ovington Square, SW3. Toby was to join Roger as a boarder at Summerfields prep school in Oxford, a feeder school for Eton. Carol was meeting the fees. Mary was very upset that her younger child was leaving home.

═══

Easton Court – 21.9.48

… Toby's departure is indeed an ordeal … In other words it is a milestone, marking the passage of time; but you have everything to rejoice in, when one considers that you've brought Toby triumphantly to this point (the vital years, according to psychologists) an outstanding little boy – and that nowadays they enjoy school! So dry your tears, and hurry to my consoling arms.

Our conversation last night left me disturbed. I was (paradoxically) hurt that you should be ready to give up our home, as you were probably hurt when I was! – and it made me feel that I had failed to settle into and appreciate the home you'd made for me.

But today I feel that in present conditions we might be very happy here [in Chagford]. For one thing the only real home to me will be one bought by my own efforts – for you and the children. Not acquired by a windfall, in which you and Carol played the major part. That is a matter of pride, and does not mean that I am not grateful. Also I think running a place as remote as Peakswater is too tough ...

As to affording it, we can't afford my being here and we are well in the soup already ... I reckon we are about £200 on the wrong side. I am going to ask £1000 for my three books; for which I shall probably be offered £150.

So I bought a bottle of champagne to buck you up and cele-brate the last days of our (illusionary) prosperity ...

Pebble has taken to waking me six times a night; perhaps he doesn't like corpses. As for the madwoman* she, too, gave me a bad night. But, what the hell ...

Easton Court – 22.9.48

... Of course I never said in Chagford or anywhere else that 'the boys drove me mad with their noise'! You might tell Carol, in case he believed it. I suspect Mr Cox† – a grotesque oaf – as the remarks about looking for a room at home were so circum-stantial. What the hell? Don't let's worry.

While you spoke to me last night she [Phyllis] rang up Mrs Cobb, who had had several drinks and a row with Major Ritchie (who demanded a postponement of the funeral because he is having his sale today) and who had a funeral on her hands. La P.K.S. was told that I'd left, and on asking rudely to know where I'd gone, I gather that she ran into an American tornado! Tant mieux; and, as usual, she climbed down when the Cobb turned tough ...

Hurrah for having the children at Christmas! ... I shall write letters to greet them on arrival at school ...

---

* Phyllis had tracked Eric down to Easton Court and was renewing her perse-cution by telephone and letter.

† A Chagford resident. Eric had a habit of falling out with his rustic neighbours.

Easton Court – 23.9.48

... *I hope that the arrival of the fateful day hasn't been too much of a shock. I am sure Toby will be alright; he is so lucky to have Roger there, and he will love you more than ever in the 'hols'!*

I am ready for you, having eschewed thoughts of sex, smoking and drink as a sort of purification before you arrive (I will <u>not</u> have a hang-over this time) and having written a great deal, so that my novel will be finished in a fortnight ...

All my love,
E.

━━━

In December 1948 Eric finished his novel, which was turned down by the Bodley Head and he became severely discouraged. He decided that he would have to get another office job but was worried about the possibility that Phyllis would resume her campaign if he did so. His doctor was concerned about his mental health and noted that Eric was in a state of acute worry and insomnia, the result of 'the persecution he was suffering at the hands of his wife and his concern as to the effect it was having on his ability to earn a living'. Then in February 1949 Eric and Mary dined with Malcolm and Kitty Muggeridge and Muggeridge recommended Eric to the Sunday Times. Eric spoke good German, Spanish and French. Ian Fleming, the foreign manager, offered him the position of Berlin correspondent. This was a key post since the Berlin airlift was still in operation and many considered that Europe was once again on the brink of war. Eric took up his post in March and set off for Berlin. His first letter was written while he was en route and still in London. Mary, who had also finished a novel, replied from Peakswater where, during the school holidays, she was caring for two small boys and a number of dogs, pigs, geese, ducks and hens. After only a year the property was back on the market.

━━━

Authors' Club
2, Whitehall Court, SW1 – 24.3.49

... *I have given your MS. to Westaway Press ... so you should hear directly from them.*

I go, probably on Wednesday, to Berlin, and back via Hamburg to Frankfurt and Dusseldorf ...

Germany is critical, and – I gather – grim, with Allies at loggerheads and Germans loathing each other. 'Assignment in Hell' was how someone described it. Most interesting! ...

My employers are delightful. After filling in questionnaires I have ideas about getting you out there quite separately (via War Office – Stopford*) not using my office facilities! ... I'm sure we'll find a solution ... When asked I say I've no idea if you (my wife) will join me or not ...

Love to the little dogs,
E.

Authors' Club – 25.3.49

... *I am lunching with Rutherford† today, and perhaps a plan of campaign will emerge. I doubt if he thinks the case worth bringing at all, but Counsel may and we must get that opinion ...*

Harry came to lunch, and laid on his German expert whom I interviewed at the Bank; and they are providing me with important contacts, on the understanding that I provide them with intelligence. My only doubts are my technique in dealing with the cruder news ... Everything has to be 'human'! ...

---

* Richmond Stopford, wealthy bachelor and wartime officer in MI6, had been dining with Mary at the Ritz on the evening she first met Eric.

† Edwin Rutherford, Eric's laid-back divorce solicitor.

I am much taken with the idea of you as secretary-chauffeuse; seriously! ... They are most excellent employers, on what Fleming calls an 'adult' basis of doing things ...

Junior Army & Navy Club
Horse Guards Avenue, SW1 – 27.3.49

... My club is shut on Saturdays ...

I am beginning to get worried. I gave Edwin Rutherford lunch on Friday, and he violently urges that I should do nothing which might bother Kemsley,* say nothing about my private affairs and generally lie low until P.K.S. attacks – if she does. Then Edwin can help because he is a friend of one of my directors.

The implication of all this is that you and I should remain apart until the divorce, on the chance of winning it and getting married. This is all very well for Edwin, but I don't like it ...

Authors' Club – 28.3.49

... I do not mean to leave you for six months. I can't ... So let us be very pliable and wise and resourceful and quick and cunning and discreet. I rely on you, because you can be all these ...

You must write

c/o A. L. Hutchinson, Kemsley Newspapers Correspondent
British Press Centre, Press Services Section,
318 R/B Det., Mil. Gov. Dusseldorf
B.A.O.R. 4.

(Would you believe it?)

---

* Owners of the *Sunday Times*.

Peakswater – 31.3.49

My Love,

Especially at night I miss you, longing to lie close against you and fit my body to yours along its whole length. Physical loss and missing sets in later than the mental which begins even before you have left. It is the pain of loving which is all part of it …

The children are very happy. As we ate Lord Nelson [pet gander] (who was rather tough) Lady Hamilton [pet goose] was brought to bed. A rather long and difficult accouchement with Henny-Penny playing midwife. The first gosling wandered out and died. I helped two, partly out of their eggs, while Lady H. savagely bit my fingers. The mortality or survival rate may be known by tomorrow night. I hope some of them live, poor little things …

Toby consistently wins at chess which infuriates me. His smug smile of nonchalant triumph as he snitches my Queen is odious …

I long to hug you and lay my tongue on yours and press my breasts against you. *Tu vois? Je suis randy après une semaine.* What a frolic we will have.

I love you,
M.

Berlin – 31.3.49

… Stayed in billets where I write, and drinks at the press club … A typical Berlin quarter, trees … quiet roads, and the drone or roar of the Air Lift continuously to give a weird impression of abnormality and effort and war. Ruins are tidied up, and Germans well-dressed, but Berliners bothered by food e.g. no hot drink, tea or coffee, perhaps just bread before they go to work. The Allies utterly isolated and insulated, too comfortable or too neglected …

Dinner in the only place where Germans can go 'out', an incredibly dreary black market restaurant with a band ... No choice at that hour. Berlin shuts at eight. Lights out, streets dark. All electricity off at 10. I borrowed a candle to go to bed ...

There is no limit between sectors; you just walk in and out. In the Soviet sector you can eat cheaply and legally at plain non-ration restaurants ...

The play [I see tonight] is said to be brilliant, about the 30 Years war ... by Brecht, of pre-war fame, with his wife in it. I chose the Soviet sector because I want to see Germans and not British.

Look out for photos of the Archbishop of York. I was photographed with him as we left the plane ...

Peakswater − 1.4.49

... An East wind for April and poor Bassett [local handyman] here to mend the pump which he found had something broken inside but he was able to solder it. I hope to have no more trouble. He is <u>very</u> kind ...

Poor Lady Hamilton's hatching has been a disaster, only one hatched out and died, the others died in their shells because the dry weather has made them so hard they can't get out. Everyone else is having the same trouble ... We are all very disappointed. Meanwhile we chew away at Lord Nelson in the most heartless fashion ...

When I wake in the morning a feathery softness waves gently across my face. It is the plumy tail of the terrier asleep beside me, head downwards on his back beneath the counterpane with only his tail and sometimes his feet exposed ...

I am going to bed with Mirabeau. I am still reading him. In the latter half there is less fucking and more politics so I go to sleep sooner. In the beginning his skips from bed to bed left me breathless and admiring! ...

Berlin – 1.4.49: 9am

... *I have had my ride round Berlin, which is just like the City of the Dead outside Cairo, where empty houses are kept as a memorial to the departed. Only here the empty houses are tidy shells ...*

We went to a film, Berliner Ballade ... very good humoured about the grotesque city which greets the returning soldier, guying both the Allies – east and west – but the west-end audience laughed most at the anti-Russian jokes. Then to supper at Intourist, in the Soviet Zone. Only there is a separate room for Russians, and another separate room for Germans, so you sit among Czechs ... Shabby people, smoky room, tango band. But I had caviar and vodka ... No ill effects ...

The German girl friend of my host was dour, offered me English cigarettes, and told me that she didn't like the English. Why? Oh, she likes them more than the Germans, of course! ... But ... we have lost India etc. This reminded me of the German in London who warned me that they dislike the Americans, but 'despise' the English!

Berlin – 1.4.49: 6.30pm

It is a heavenly evening, blue sky going mauve, birds chirping, even the airlift is momentarily still ... This street in the Grunewald is quiet, villas among trees; and I have a huge desk in the large sitting-room, with double windows ... The bare wooden floors, and the large centrally-heated room ... have a strange atmosphere. Once a German businessman lived here with his family, or perhaps an artist. Voices echo under the pine trees, and children shout; but one wonders how – having been conceived among horrors, and grown up among ruins – they will turn out ...

I am giving a dinner party tonight at the Club for the Howes ... Ted Howes is a dear, slow chap and 'Robin' his wife is red-headed

*and of the Raj ... She spent the war in Jamaica, and so knows
how to treat German servants ...*

*They gave me a fabulous lunch yesterday and I must be polite.
So I have greased my hair, and put on my grey shirt, and off I
go. I would like to do things to you ... which would surprise the
military censor and even you ...*

I love you.

E.

Peakswater – 3.4.49

... I have been reading Alan Moorehead's second article on Berlin
in the *Observer*. I pray you are now safely away from that hopeless
place ...

I had a visit from an agent from Looe to whom I had written,
who on hearing that I could not give him sole agency said, 'Then
I won't bother. Then I won't bother!' Detestable Keltic Fringe! I
have written to fourteen so some of them are bound to bother ...

Poor Lady Hamilton still sits hissing on two addled eggs and
there is nothing left of Lord Nelson but soup. The passage of time
blurs memory. I can now look at the bacon and ham on the kitchen
racks without thinking of Bentham and Hooker [two pet pigs] ... *

Hotel Reichshof, Hamburg – 3.4.49

*... After Berlin, Hamburg is like an old fairy-tale book's picture
of a clean, busy,* gemuctlich *[gemütlich] German city ... But I
am going today to see some 5 miles of demolished buildings which
one 'doesn't notice' at first.*

* On the last page of this letter below the signature Eric has made cryptic notes
in which he refers to 'Occupation forces ... police ... code name ... Vocke ...
Czech ... + Cz./id. Papers ... I disagreed with regime ... Unusual witness! cp
US secret service? ... Brought report of 2 days. Paid 4/500 crowns plus marks.'

Ricardo* rang up promptly ... My first impression was that he was Jewish, but I don't think so. A German business-man, going bald, with the family double-bend of the nose, but in a little German piggy nose. Light blue aggressive eyes, self-assured manners.

His wife Dindi ('Dietelinde') is beautiful and distinguished, and I proved to have a delicious little niece of 15, with merry eyes and good manners, most pretty ...

Ricardo has a large, rather tasteless flat, while other Germans live in one room, because he is on such good terms with the British. His Control Company is agent for the Marshall Plan! ...

He offered me five kinds of drink before dinner, and some brandy afterwards. It was marked 'Naafi' and he said that he had paid a very high price to a British officer for it. We had a merry little family meal with Moselle, and discussed money and Anouilh and money ...

Ricardo bullied his wife in the German manner, and although she stands up to him I thought she was a little frightened. He has the arrogant violence of the German without a gleam of humour, and all my father's violence without his charm; but all this is latent because he is well brought up (his mother, my Tanta Gisela, was an aristocrat as well as a snob) so that one can enjoy oneself, or even join Dindi in teasing him. He looks like a pig, and I believe is one ...

But he can do everything for one. He has an office and friends at Dusseldorf, and he is arranging for me to go round the harbour here in a boat. But the great thing is that they assure me that Dusseldorf is with Hamburg the most civilised of the bigger cities, with an intelligentsia and an especially good theatre with Gustav Grundgens (a homosexual actor of genius whom Erika Mann once married).† With introductions from them ... life should be alright, and I plump for Dusseldorf.

* Ricardo Siepmann, a Hamburg businessman and Eric's cousin.

† Gustav Grundgens was perhaps the greatest German actor of the twentieth century. His career prospered throughout the Nazi years.

*After dinner they had invited a German film actor and his wife, both elegant and speaking perfect English, and the actor being temporarily debarred from work having been a Nazi. He was exquisitely good-looking and polite and worldly. (When Ricardo heard I'd been in the war, he said: '*We *didn't think it worthwhile to fight for the Nazis, so we stayed at home.) And I smoked a whacking cigar and enjoyed myself thoroughly and made up my mind to exploit my cousin to the utmost. Today he fetches me at noon ...*

All my love,

E.

Peakswater – 4.4.49

... I am longing for news. I hope my letters are reaching you.

Crocksford, the agent from Fowey, visited me this morning. A nice old bozo – no 'fringe' about him. He liked the house very much, said he thought we would get £4000 for it and that he had several people asking for a place like this whom he would inform at once ...

I am only going to deal with people who know the wants of the upper classes who are the only people likely to want this house. The others are waste of stamps.

Dunstan appeared on the doorstep with Mrs Goetz* just before tea. We gave them a huge tea with poached eggs and what Roger calls 'poor piggy'. Mrs Goetz is a slightly faded blonde quite pretty and shakes hands limply ... I quite liked her. She has teeth, large slightly drooping breasts, is Australian and a sociologist, whatever that is ...

Darling, this will never do. I had an erotic dream last night about Rutherford clasping me consolingly in his arms and wearing pin striped trousers! You must hasten home *ou bien je me soulage moi-même* ...

Toby takes on all the long words he can. He asked at lunch 'Is this lemonade paralysed?' meaning I found 'diluted' ...

* Neighbours in Cornwall.

I have finished Mirabeau and sent *La Nausée* back unread. I cannot read Sartre without you being within hugging distance ...

Hamburg – 4.4.49

... I have provisionally agreed to 'take over' at Dusseldorf on May 1st; and I shall have to begin without you, that must be faced. Even correspondents' wives cannot get out here (it means months of red tape and delay) ... anyway it takes several months to get a flat ...

Ricardo makes me feel that the 'assignment in hell' phrase has its full moral significance! (He is, I think, the worst kind of German, and I am studying him. We are great friends.)

Peakswater – 5.4.49

Two letters from you to break the silence. I needed them after a bad night fretting over some remarks of Dunstan's as to the nearness of war this summer ...

The only thing I am <u>afraid</u> of is being parted from you ...

Your cousin Ricardo sounds revolting! ... I am jealous of your good talk ... especially so since I have no one but the children to talk to ...

The bloody pump has gone wrong again and I have had to appeal to Bassett. He is so nice about it but I feel a fool ...

Hamburg – 5.4.49

... We dined and wined again, this time at an old-fashioned restaurant and at a night-club. The word has gone round, and I was repeatedly assured that this was not characteristic, and only available to the 'upper hundred'. The girls in the party were excessively pretty, and one wore a dress cut so that you saw her breasts, which

were also pretty and made me want you badly. It has all been rather gross but quite interesting: and I am looking forward to a good dose of politics and economics in the next 2 towns ...

Dusseldorf – 6.4.49

Darling,

This is the end! We motored for seven hours across dull country to find the worst kind of transit hotel in which a bare small room with a bed in it is supposed to be bedroom, sitting-room <u>and</u> office. The taps fall off, the food is foul, the view is ruins ...

I have hired a woman (thrice married) who belongs to one of the Dusseldorf 'families' to help me through the first days ... I (must) short circuit the British billeting system, whose aim is to keep me in this hell-house – a typical brothel, minus les girls – for 6 months or so ... Her father was one of the big magnates, and she knows all the theatre people and so on; but above all she can translate my newspapers for me! Everyone by the way understands my German and says that I speak with a French-Swiss accent. Alas I don't understand theirs ...

The Germans in the offices across the road have been at work for an hour and a half, and the English around me are waking up or breakfasting ...

—————

Eric returned to England, arriving at Northolt Airport on 13 April. In May he was advised to abandon his divorce action against Phyllis and accept the fact that he had wasted thousands of pounds in a legal wild goose chase. Phyllis was now free to resume her persecution.

He next returned to Germany, this time as a staff reporter for the Kemsley Press news agency, most of his work still appearing in the Sunday Times. As was frequently the case, his first letter *to Mary referred to his recovery from the fear he almost always experienced when flying.*

━━━━

Dusseldorf – 2.5.49

... I rather like my room, which is austere with two solid desks and sun coming through the window with birds chirping among the ruins outside. A good journey ... and I am quite recovered.

It rather looks as if Western Germany was losing its import- ance. Interest has already switched to Berlin. Moorehead, though pompous, was well-balanced yesterday. If the political parties play for 'a united Germany' and postpone a West German elec- tion, that may lead to a quieter time here, and make a move elsewhere in the autumn more likely ...

Dusseldorf – 5.5.49

... I have got into a panic ... Hannah [the woman hired in Dusseldorf] *turned out to be quite, quite hopeless; and my German even worse than I feared!*

So I am rushing up to Frankfurt, to find Frau von Heydebrecht, the really efficient secretary whom I'd reserved up there ...

They want me to drive into the blockade when it's lifted (I mean across the road into the Soviet sector, the moment they let us) ... What a bore!

Frankfurt – 5.5.49: 9pm

My darling,
A letter arrived from you at lunch time and I feel less lost. I dashed up here with Hannah's lover in his Buick station waggon

which looks like a Zeppelin ... He knew Ronnie Emmanuel ... and has a 150 acre farm in Somerset ... He has little red tufts over his cheeks, and seems extremely clever ... Then I got hold of Frau von Heydebrecht, who is ready to join me anywhere within a fortnight which spells relief to me. She even does <u>English</u> shorthand. Now the embarrassment is to sack Hannah, who is taking it pathetically ...

I must, tomorrow, pick up some news to send. I haven't sent a word yet ... What a life. My German is so bad!

The airlift drones by, the beggar picks up a fag-end, and the US military police sergeant makes fun of his prisoner as he parades him up the street handcuffed ...

My call comes through. I am to write a 'colourful story' when the Russians lift the blockade! Well, well ...

You give no news about the Nicholsons.* I hope they haven't fallen through, as they seemed such promising customers ...

Dusseldorf – 8.5.49

... I feel much better now that I've sent my first messages: one on Friday, and three last night including a gruesome murder. I wonder if you'll see anything in the Sunday Times; I made a mistake about Bavaria, but it doesn't matter.

And I feel much, much better for a very fine letter from you here on my return. You lay naked and will grow brown. Which reminds me, oh but I found a house at Frankfurt! It may be awful but to find a house is miraculous ... [and] you can transform it ...

Just off to Bonn with Terence Prittie [Manchester Guardian], Mann of D.T. [Daily Telegraph] and Norman Clark of N-C [News Chronicle] ...

---

* The couple intending to buy Peakswater.

Dusseldorf – 9.5.49

... *I am in a rage, having had my first slip up. I rang the German news agency at midnight, and so did that ass Hannah and we were assured that there would be no vote on the German constitution until Tuesday. Actually, the vote was taken at midnight and everyone else will have it. The only consolation is that ... our newspapers pay small attention to the details; all the same Germany's new constitution went through, and I missed it! I am sacking Hannah this morning, and my war-horse from Frankfurt begins next Monday.*

Actually, it was quite interesting and I'd written my message leaving a blank for the votes. (Curse her). I went to Bonn ... learned quite a lot and saw the Germans at their organised politics for the first time. My colleagues seem to think that Frankfurt will be the capital; in which case I am the only one to have captured a house ... But the chief likelihood is of some compromise, and they all expect to go back to Berlin by September.* That would bring my job here to an end.

So I say come out as soon as you can. Come for <u>Voice and Vision</u> (not Vogue) as that means you would get a room in the businessman's hotel across the way ...

Tomorrow I motor off to the border to see the blockade lifted. That means a story at midnight from the border. Then on Thursday (you mayn't motor at night) I drive up to Berlin through the Soviet Zone ... There are going to be millions of journalists and it's going to be hard to reach or reserve a telephone ...

All my love,

E.

---

* The expectation was that Germany would become a united democratic national unit in 1949. When the arrangement eventually broke down in October, the British, French and American zones of occupied Germany became 'West Germany' – the Federal Republic of Germany, while the Soviet zone became the German Democratic Republic.

Dusseldorf – 9.5.49

... I feel much, much better. I have spoken to my office who noticed no great lacuna; in other words, they don't care a pin about Bonn! ...

*PS Fish being in soup anyway, after yesterday's S. Times 'She' has no doubt written to editor, and received a raspberry.** *

———

The Soviet blockade of Berlin ended in May 1949, and the airlift finished on 12 May.

———

Dusseldorf – 16.5.49

... No, the blockade story was <u>not</u> amusing. I couldn't think of anything to say, to begin with. Then I picked my car and driver so that we whizzed past every other car at a steady 85 mph – only to leave the road by accident, and spend the night dodging Russian police posts in Potsdam! ... It was of course quite funny, but oh how disastrous. My driver wept.

The result is that I am doing thoroughly badly. There have been two stories since I came; Bonn and Berlin; and I missed both, through accidents. I don't think I can do very well because of <u>a.</u> language, <u>b.</u> new country, <u>c.</u> lack of news sense. (I can do features better than news.) So I am now in an un-nerved and disgusted state, feeling that my job may not last. So ... I think you'd better come. Firstly, you can help me, secondly, if I am to be here a short time, we may as well be together. So, I shall send

---

* Eric assumed that Phyllis would have noticed his byline, unleashed her next assault and been rebuffed. His first two assumptions were correct, his last optimistic.

my wire to Beddington tomorrow ... Berlin rattled me, and when I panic I drink, and then I panic more ...

Glad you stopped Carol's money* ... Grab at £4000 [for Peakswater] if you get an offer ...

Dusseldorf – 17.5.49

Darling,

... I have now faced up to my situation, and I am completely calm. The fact – which knocked me off my balance – is that I cannot do this job. It is a matter of 'news', and I am essentially a writer of leaders or commentaries. I cannot even do 'popular' features well. And I don't know Germany. All this, quite apart from the intolerable living conditions, means that I ought never to have taken this job. But I had to jump at it for the sake of having a job at all.

Having you, I have no intention of chucking it without consulting you. I will do what I can, and we might use it to try to guide ourselves into congenial work.

An alternative is to face things squarely, tell Fleming I can't do this job (he may guess it already) and come back to spend two months with you at Peakswater. Then, if we sell the house, to go to London and take – if necessary – a few months to find something literary and congenial, if modest, which would enable us to live in Chelsea or somewhere and try to do our own work as well. This appeals to me, by its existentialist element of choice and renunciation! But it wouldn't help my chances of finding congenial work to have thrown up this job ...

I have an idea, though, for the future; and I hear this is the very moment to find a job on the Observer.

Let me know what you feel. I am tempted to chuck up and come back. I have made a bad mistake. It's foolish to go on. I lose prestige every minute ...

---

* With Eric once more employed, Mary had told Carol that she no longer needed his allowance of £150 a year.

I am sorry to fail you, but I love you dearly ...
E.

Without you, I would now be in the soup. With you, I feel like
fighting it out ...

═══

In June, Mary joined Eric and they moved from Frankfurt to Berlin.
By September Phyllis's aggressive intrusions had caused such havoc
in the foreign department of the Sunday Times *that Ian Fleming*
suspended Eric, whereupon he resigned and returned to England.
In October, Eric was offered a position in Paris for the Observer *but*
by December Phyllis had bullied the editor, David Astor, to fire Eric
from this job as well. Dr Whitcombe noted that 'his condition has
worsened and he appears to be developing into a nervous wreck'.
Eric was suffering from depression, severe headaches and a tremor
of the hands. He was approaching 'a state of acute nervous break-
down'. Harry added that he was worried that Eric might become
suicidal. Eric had been paid off by the Observer *with £500. He and*
Mary moved back to the Easton Court Hotel in Chagford where
they spent Christmas with the boys. After Christmas, Eric decided
to write a play for the West End. In January Mary took the boys up
to London to stay with Carol before the start of the new school term.

═══

Chagford – 19.1.50

Darling,
*   What a sad departure. I felt very badly about it all yesterday ...*
*   Today there is white ice and a blue sky, and I have decided*
that we __must__ stay here ... I have made a scheme for paying our
way, but I need 3 or 4 months.

Whenever I pour out my troubles in terse and bitter terms to Mr Bowden, he yells with laughter and says: 'Eric, I love your wit.'

Chagford – 20.1.50

<u>Mary,</u>

I am coming up on Monday, because Harry and Rickatson-Hatt want me to lunch with them on Tuesday ...

Will you get me a room for 2 or 3 nights at the Hyde Park, Basil Street or some cheap but comfortable hotel? The Observer will pay for one night, so why should I not be near you? ...

It is freezing cold, so I hope you have bought some woollen drawers! If not, please do. Rather old-fashioned and exciting.

I see Fry's play has a poor notice in the Times, so perhaps Olivier will need another play.* I am sure he would see himself as Don Juan ...

Chagford – 8.2.50

My pretty,

... Herewith an envelope full of disasters. Never mind! I believe, on the contrary, that we're about to weather the storm.

I am sorry I was a trifle sharp on the telephone; the letters had made me nervous ...

All my love,

E.

---

* Christopher Fry's verse play *Venus Observed* had opened in the West End, directed by Laurence Olivier, with Olivier in the leading role. Denholm Elliott and Rachel Kempson were also in the cast.

Chagford – 10.2.50

... *I am busy on the Orwell article**

Thank you many times for Venus Observed *which I liked all the more for you sending it to me ...*

My views about your legacy are: it now strikes me as absurd to borrow £600 and pay £26 a year interest ... And we don't, of course, want to sell for £750 unless you absolutely have to. We have till June on my money to decide that. So we can breathe and talk. And that cheers me ...

E.

---

* Eric and Orwell had both been in Spain during the Civil War, and George Orwell had died on 21 January.

PART THREE

We Shall Be Rich!: 1950–54

*I*n the spring of 1950 Eric was still staying at the Easton Court
Hotel, attempting to finish another book (Foxy), while Mary
was staying with a friend in Mecklenburg Square, WC1. She
was determined to find some means of making a living and had
an appointment at the offices of Vogue, hoping to interest the
magazine in her plans to start a business making cheese. On the
back of an envelope from Eric she wrote a recipe and a marketing
strategy for home-made cream cheese: 'A Good name – plain
cartons – labels – weighing machine, basins, muslin, string, salt,
pepper, paprika, onions, chives, fennel, vinegar.'

Meanwhile Harry Siepmann and Bernard Rickatson-Hatt had
found Eric a promising job. This was as overseas sales manager
for Portals, a company that manufactured paper for banknotes.
The position demanded a talent for languages, political aware-
ness, a feel for public relations and some business experience. It
could have been invented for Eric.

═══

Chagford – 7.5.50

My darling,
      ... This is a gallant effort of yours, and it makes me feel that
I haven't done enough to make our future secure. But, to be
plain, I do believe that if you can earn £5 a week in the first
months, and I can do a few articles, we <u>can</u> just pull it off – if
I sell Foxy, and I think I will. So I no longer think in desperate

terms of a superhuman effort as needed, either in cheese or literature, but of a joint effort which could succeed. So let's add our faith, and move the mountain ...

Chagford – 8.5.50

Darling,

... I rang up Harry and reversed the charges – he refused the call! Family manners ... *

Portal's† need someone urgently, so I wondered if I could commute taking long Friday to Monday week-ends here as a trial period of 3 months. I could stay at Whitchurch, Mondays to Fridays, and work on Foxy in the evenings. Then in 3 months we'd know where we were, including cheese. I know you're against it, but it would fill up the till. (Say nothing of this project to Harry.)

Chagford – 12.5.50

Darling Mary –

... By getting a 2lb order, you have got £10 of your capital back in the first year ... Don't let it worry you, but if you can work it up to six or seven pounds (£) a week, you can live at Easton by that alone ...

I am not worried at all. If Portal's make me an offer, we shall be – for us – rich. That is, we shall soon have that £1,000 in the bank. The good thing about it is that I like him: very quiet, precise, small and not at all lacking in sensibility. (I decided that

---

* It was entirely typical of Eric that he should ring his brother at the Bank of England, and ask him to pay for the call, just when Harry was trying to place him in a responsible position.

† Portals was based in Hampshire. Its customers included the Bank of England but overseas sales were critical for the company's growth.

*Wykehamist manners really are best – and a relief.) The others
are toughs (introduced by nepotism) or technicians; but I can
always get on with him.* *

*I read with shame in the guidebook at the pub where I stayed
in Whitchurch that* [Cardinal] *Newman had spent a night there
and written a hymn, and* [Charles] *Kingsley had written about
the Queen Anne ceiling. Because all I had been thinking about
was* tes fesses.

Chagford – 15.5.50

My darling Love,

*I have thought it over, and accepted. I feel sure we could
not do better. I hate the separations, perhaps more than you
do … but there is a big compensation in our being able to live
here, and for me to return here, instead of living in London
again. If I stay more than a year, I am equally sure that we
can wangle some pretty voyages together. All told, we have no
choice; and I prefer it to 'public relations' and to Paris, which
is poison to me since all the Toulouse hangovers have installed
themselves there …*

*And it will be nice to have some money! We both need
clothes etc., and some security is essential. I have thought it
over seriously and extremist-ically from a writing point of
view, and it fits …*

*Frankly I think it's a lucky break, and I like my Chairman …
Sooner or later we'll get a play done.*

*I love you, and I love your efforts re cheese, of which I take
a rosy view as long as you have time and occasion to develop it.*

---

* Eric 'liked' the chairman, Sir Francis Portal Bt, an exact contemporary of his
at Winchester. The 'toughs' in question included General Lord Ismay,
Viscount Monck and J. V. Sheffield. Eric overlooks the fact that he too had
been 'introduced by nepotism'.

So I send you all my warm love, and long to hold you by the hip bones.

A toujours,

E.

Chagford – 16.5.50

Darling,

A cold bare day without a letter from you. Warmed only by the news that Freedman, the best agent in America, has taken up my play. He isn't wildly optimistic. He writes:

'I was amused by the play, but whether it will prove caviar or not, I don't know. However I would like to take a shot at it. I think it might do better in England than here, but there is a slight chance for it and I would like to go after it. It is a very capable job of writing. It is just a question of whether the material will sell at this time. Maybe I can find an actor for it.'

Cautious, but I'm told he handles only top-notch playwrights and that this is a good omen. My idea is to use his interest to work up the Shekels at this end.

By the way, don't tell anyone about my job or salary. Don't tell Carol; I believe that Miss Mitchell may be, indirectly, a leak; by overhearing etc. I usually find secrecy too much of a nuisance, but there's no harm in discretion – against which I'm usually the offender. It's only a matter of time, but I thought we might give the lawyers a start this time. If you've told him, no matter. But I mistrust la Mitch, who hates me and is a bit crazy!

Five midsummer days, followed by two cold ones, and the heating's off. I pray for more blue weather at the week-end, as the buttercups are thick and above my ankles in the field towards the salmon pond, and the hillside blue with bluebells ...

═══

Eric's new job required him to spend weekdays living in lodgings near Laverstoke Mills, Whitchurch, Hants, where Portals was based. Mary, having sold Peakswater, now took up residence, in her turn, at the Easton Court Hotel in Chagford.

═══

Laverstoke Mills, Whitchurch, Hants – 2.8.50

My Love,

All sorts of pussy-cats popped out of bags at luncheon with Harry yesterday; the story of his failure to become Governor.* I see now that he is a bitterly disappointed man. Also he has had much to put up with from his dear ones – me, as well as wives. (Cobbold cruelly reminded him that when the night clubs in Budapest played 'Goodnight, sweetheart' they sang the words 'Goodnight Siepmann, Goodnight, Rodd' – a saga of my own come home to roost!) ...

Oakley – 27.11.50

Darling,

... Quite a lot to read and plan at my office. I spoke to the Jugoslav Commercial Counsellor, and he foresaw no difficulty about getting a Visa quickly ...

The Simplon express takes me from Paris to Belgrade in 36 hours via Switzerland and Italy. It sounds rather fun ...

---

* Harry Siepmann had set his heart on becoming governor of the Bank of England. His intellect and independence of mind made him a strong candidate for the position. But in 1949 the deputy governor, Cameron Cobbold, later Lord Cobbold KG, an Old Etonian 'lifer' at the Bank, was appointed instead. The anecdote about the Budapest nightclub was cruel since it suggested to Harry that his brother Eric's notoriety, and Eric's close relationship with the rakish Peter Rodd, would have counted against him.

I am going to London tomorrow to meet the Bank expert and then lunch with Harry and Marsden* at the Athenaeum ...

The only thing that keeps me spiritually buoyant in this squalid pub is the moral and physical vigour engendered by Chagford. Look after yourself, and do write about animals.[†]

My firm is most odd and eccentric ...

You are a great joy to me, and you have transformed my life, and I delight to think of you in your cafay-oh-lay condition, and in spite of my recent lack of lubricity, I love and desire you, always –
Eric

Whitchurch – *30.11.50*

... I've booked at Montalambert [comfortable Paris hotel] *for Tuesday and Wednesday. Thence by Orient express via Lausanne, Milan, Venice and Trieste: but I can't get out! A little Jug.* [Yugoslav] *is lunching with me on Monday, he sounds nice.*

I hope you enjoyed yourself with Carol, and I look forward to hearing about it ...

A demain,

E.

Easton Court Hotel, Chagford – 5.12.50

My dear Love,

You should now be arriving in Paris and I will cast this ahead to Belgrade hoping to catch you but if there are no aeroplanes the mails will perhaps be slow? ...

It is still very cold ... Yesterday I had to unfreeze the icicles on Pebbles' whiskers with a warm cloth. Today we bussed to Chagford and went to see Mr Sadleir who is a useful aide and

---

* A director of Portals.

[†] Mary's first novel for children, *Speaking Terms*, about animals that spoke to each other, was eventually published in 1969.

adviser à propos Roger. He is going to write to the Eton housemaster and he says that if Roger were his, he would send him to
a crammer. I have already written at length to [the] crammer and
hope to go to meet Carol with a clear head and proposals ...

I wish I was with you. I would love to see Yugoslavia again. I
remember the scarlet leaves of the wild pear trees among the pine
forests in the autumn and rushing rivers. It must be lovely now ...

Easton Court – 6.12.50

Much colder and no baths this morning as the pipes froze ... Pebble
and I have just skated perilously back from Chagford by the lanes,
solid glass in places. There were fat piping bullfinches and yellow-
hammers and flocks of redwings and fieldfares. Fat piebald ponies
down from the moors munching along the hedgerows and staring
with mouse-like eyes from under deep fringes ...

Harry has sent you a volume of Proust's chronicles ...

Easton Court – 8.12.50

... I accepted a lift into Exeter from Mr Bankes [fellow hotel
guest] yesterday and went with him to the antique shops where
he exhibited a lot of bad taste and as a revenge I took him to a
bycicle [sic] shop and after buying a very fine bycicle for Roger,
watched a dreadful Marxian [brothers] scene while Mr B and the
boy from the shop battled to get the bycicle into the back of the
car. At one moment poor timid Mr B. got pinned underneath it
onto the back seat. He left this morning with Norman [Norman
Webb, Carolyn Cobb's partner, and hotel manager] and twenty
pieces of luggage to Southampton ...

There was a crisis day yesterday with pipes bursting, Miss
Holmes' [fellow guest] nose bleeding, unexpected visitors arriving
and Ina [staff] having a heart attack. Oh! And the sweep inexorably
sweeping all the chimblyes so that there were no fires ...

Otherwise no news. The sweep has managed to block the mouse hole with soot ...

Penelope Sandberg* has announced her engagement to a gentleman in the Guards so no doubt the Sandberg family are in full squawk. It will give them a new impetus for their annual Christmas row ...

I miss you all the time, your arms, your company, your mind, your jokes ...

On being asked when it was announced that we were coming to stay and what were we like la Russell [another guest] said, 'Oh yes, I know them very well. Not what you and I would call cosy.'

I will write next to Paris.

M.

Paris − 8.12.50

... I am just off to Belgrade ... Most enjoyable and interesting luncheon today with Cassou and his wife and daughter, and we have been talking ever since ...

(Everyone says how well and happy I look, and that is you) ...

Basingstoke − 26.12.50

In bed! 9.30pm

My darling,

My gloom was <u>a.</u> disappointment, at our 'slightly spoiled Christmas', <u>b.</u> self-reproach at showing my annoyance with Toby, and on Christmas day: − resulting in an utter sense of failure, with you and with the children. Forgive me.

I feel better now, although the black cap fell over my eyes, for a moment, as I entered my public house bedroom, and found myself alone. I am afraid of my dependence on you. 'I am afraid to lose you, I am afraid of my fear' ...

* Sister of Christina, Mary's lodger at Donne Place.

But I had a good [train] journey with Nancy [Gow], two living sandwiches of luxury (my metaphors are odd, tonight) between Bank Holiday hoards [sic] who shrank from invading our [compartment] cold, dignified, middle-aged and offensive solitude – they invaded everyone else! Then the landlady was courteous, the fire was lit, the sheets are clean and I have washed. And there is, of course, the chance that one will wake up an utterly different person tomorrow; or at any rate, Next Year ...

I love you, and the boys. Goodnight.

Eric

=====

At the end of 1950 Eric changed solicitors and instructed the experienced firm of Gordon Dadds, which had handled Mary's divorce case. After hearing his account of his wife's behaviour they quickly advised him to sue Phyllis for divorce once again, this time on grounds of cruelty.

=====

Easton Court – 28.12.50

Dear love,

... You are good and good to the little boys. When Toby is odious it wrings my heart because he should never be odious to you, only to me. Only perhaps by including you in his cruel net he puts you above all others ... This morning when you left I saw two large tears and said, 'Why are you sad?' 'I don't like Eric to go,' he said and hid his head under the bedclothes ...

I went to the village and saw Glyn Hughes.* He will write his statement but does not want to be put in the box. I said he wouldn't

---

* Major Hughes, owner of the Beverley Court Hotel in Chagford, a potential witness in Eric's second divorce case.

be. Few will step in willingly. I think perhaps of all of them only Ronnie [Emanuel] and Nancy will be unselfish. A sweet letter from Nancy. She has had a request for an interview from Gordon ...

I have arranged tea parties for various days ... so the last week of the hols will be busy. How fast they go, already half-way. I shall be very desolate alone when they are gone. I must get busy and see the crammer ...

Enjoy yourself and do not forget me, when you smell the roasting chestnuts of the street vendors, when you sip your ouzo ... when you fly up the Gulf of Corinth, when the waiter corrects your pronunciation, remember me, for Athens was ours together ...

Park Lane Hotel, Piccadilly, W1 – 31.12.50: 8am

Darling,

Herewith cheque for £65 ... My ration book* is missing, but will turn up. The secretary at Portals has car papers ready for us; if you __must__ have them before my return, please write privately to Marsden ...

Your letter was wonderful.

__All__ my love,

E.

Chagford – 16.1.51

... I bathed Pebble in Lux and we walked up to the point ... The view exquisite, heavy browns, greys and purples under a cloudy sky and a wet west wind blowing in from the sea ...

I have laid aside Sitwell and am reading Turgenev. So funny sometimes and so clever always about dogs.

Pebble points at his bag of biscuit and today when I have moved it up out of sight he 'points' at the basket where it was before smiling and wagging to show that he is making a joke ...

---

* Food rationing was still in force and Mary needed Eric's ration book to supply the necessary coupons for the family larder.

Chagford – 17.1.51

... We seem to be dogged by delays with poor Uncle Charley's trust ...

In his last letter Leest says he knows I want the £1500 advance in cash, less £200 to himself and £400 to Rutherford, and that he is finding out how much more money there is to come to me ... I do not wish to show Gordon any of his letters as each one makes some remark or an allusion to something already obtained, and I do not consider this any of the old Shylock's biz! On the other hand I think he is fully entitled to assure himself of his costs.*

Chagford – 22.1.51

... In a way PK did us a good turn getting us out of Berlin ... I feel loving and strong. We have gained a lot of ground during this last year. Come what may I think we won't lose it again ...

Chagford – 23.1.51

I have begun. By this I mean that I have transported in rough order the notes for my book from my mind to paper. A few days of note making and then I can write that hideous first paragraph after which it will be easier and a very suitable task for me ...

Did the book arrive safely? How glad I am that you are writing again ...

It is raining and blowing and Elizabeth who brings the tea ''ates January' and 'longs for a lighted ballroom with an

---

* The 'old Shylock' was George Gordon, their new expensive divorce solicitor, who had written pointing out that the £500 they had repeatedly promised to pay remained outstanding. 'We have done and are doing everything possible for your protection and the preparation of your case ... As you know, with your approval I retained Mr Geoffrey Lawrence KC, to fight your battle at the hearing.' The delay was due to a late payment of an inheritance to Mary by Leest, her family solicitor. Rutherford was the amiable solicitor who had failed in Eric's first divorce case.

orchestra. There's nothing in Chagford.' But I love it when there's a fire and even Pebble does not want to go out. I have nearly finished the Turgenev and loved it. He so ably describes the Russian utter irresponsibility and foolishness and indifference to human life ...

Laverstoke Mills – 24.1.51

Another of your best letters today. They give me joy and inspiration ...

Last night I rejected all but chapter one of Foxy, and had to wonder if it was worth starting again. I've started again. It needs to be much harsher and less nonsensical ... but I've got a plot and at least one Character ...

I am lunching at the Ritz with Francis Portal and a Bank man tomorrow, and I have announced my plan to attend here on Mons. to Thurs. and to go to Devon on Friday mornings. The Chairman quite agreed ...

Hurrah for your book. I believe in it. Learn from me, and write for pleasure without a thought of 'success' ...

Laverstoke Mills – 29.1.51

... A huge mail ... some of which I enclose.*

There was also a friendly note from Bernard R–H saying he was ready to give information to the lawyers ...

Also a screed about David Astor saying he shows animosity on the ground that I wasn't frank with him about the reasons I

---

* Among the letters was one from Jean Cassou, dated 26 January: he thanked Eric for writing to him after his 'too brief' visit on his way to Yugoslavia and for keeping him in touch with '*ce grave et passionnant problème*'. He added that he hoped they could renew the cordial dialogue they had maintained since Toulouse – '*dialogue de deux hommes libres et de bonne volonté, et, si vous me permettez de partager ce titre, de deux gentlemen!*'

left Kemsley's, i.e. I told him about Germany, but not about PKS' scenes. I have sent Thomas enough facts (e.g. his remark that one could be what one liked on the Observer, even homosexual) for Counsel to be able to keep him strictly to the point! Fleming returns at the end of February; and I have decided to see Edith's ex-boyfriend Billy Mabane* who was nice about me to Harry. Thus, I can fix Fleming before his return.

I am giving Zilliacus† lunch at the Ritz tomorrow; a good move, as Djilas,‡ a very important Yugoslav, is here and I might meet him. He is addressing Chatham House and I am getting very interested in Tito-ism! How Spanish Cassou is – this business about 'gentlemen' (caballeros) is the Spanish half of him ...

Hotel makes me more than a guinea reduction, and finances just work out, for the time being. If I get the £100, as I will, we can pay Easton and car (or polish off my tailor's?). Your £50 is now automatic, into Lloyds Pall Mall.

Chagford – 29.1.51

My Precious,

Another most exquisite day. I took the car to the village and walked back all the way by the river. Pebble's molehills were all frozen into iron cones, otherwise the walk was a fine one ...

Last night I listened to the Haffner – not very well played – and read Kitto's The Greeks which is written for me, just exactly what I need ... I loved our weekend ...

---

* Eric was going to see Sir William Mabane, a director of the group that owned the Sunday Times and a former boyfriend of his sister, Edith. This was in order to dissuade Ian Fleming from giving evidence against him in his divorce case.

† Konni Zilliacus, left-wing Labour MP who spoke nine languages and published a biography of Tito, Tito of Yugoslavia.

‡ Milovan Djilas, Yugoslav dissident Communist and onetime heir to President Tito.

Laverstoke Mills – 31.1.51

Darling,

I have fixed to see Whitcombe on Tuesday, and I shall rope in Liz Marsden too. Also, I've discovered I've only <u>this</u> week-end for my article, so please clear the desk and set me to work on arrival till it's done.

Lunch with Zilli was amusing. <u>We shall spend our next holiday at DUBROVNIK!</u> I'll fix an office journey, and arrange for you to come, too. Zilli will lay on the Mayor, and a couple – a sculptor and his wife, both of whose parents were English. He spent last summer en famille with Tito. He is just off to Yugoslavia, and will invite us both for a soirée with his American wife on their return. (Maybe to cheer us up during our case? Thomas now estimates 'end' of March.)

I spent an hour at the National Gallery. To my surprise, I find it quite easy to admire pictures. I loved Titian, and saw also Poussin (which I don't like), French moderne, Italian primitives, and the sensational Velazquez and Grecos. We must go together..

I love, and long to get my fingers (and whip, but I'm not allowed) about you ...

A demain.

E.

Laverstoke Mills – 5.2.51

Darling,

I have completed and sent off the details for Gordon Dadds. You achieved a masterpiece. Without you I couldn't have done it. I haven't flagged, as you expected, but I positively didn't remember a lot of it, which must be my subconscious at work! Anyway it's a good job.

Mary Farmar, aged 24 in 1936, shortly before her engagement to Carol Swinfen.

Eric Siepmann, aged 20 in 1923, a scholar of Corpus Christi College, Oxford, shortly before abandoning his studies.

10 - 7 - 45

My love, I left numb for
an hour before you left
and in violent pain
the instant I left you
at the station. No
being busy in Penzance
or lunching with the
Grant has done any
good, the house seems
very empty and the
doors are banging

Mary writes from Boskenna in July 1945.
(See corresponding letter on page 78.)

Mary and Eric's correspondence was in manuscript. Mary
invariably wrote her great looping hand in pen and ink.

Tel. Chagford 3183

THORNWORTHY HOUSE

CHAGFORD

DEVON

21/ix. Sunday.

My Pol,

The sun shines bleakly and I shall think of you in your train across the Worcestershire plain. Give Emily much love.

I took them all to Dartmeet and at Iza (at The Forge as I missed the Two Bridges; I also lost my way to Dartmeet); and last night Christian invited them to the Kino. I hope there is a connection; anyway, everything downstairs this morning was perfect. They are now having breakfast. Billy woke up at 6, but I kept him going.

Peckett sent a nice letter and £100; and Victor Haggard confirms that Billy's name is down again. I like the sand of that school. I must now make an effort to pay for it by books, in spite of lessons. It could be impossible, except that the Pentecostal flame licks me now and again.

We are off (à trois) to Mass. All my love, Eric.

I am TRIUMPHANT over the results of your interventions for Toby, and it makes me happy that Harry was so nice and so favourably impressed.

Eric writes from Chagford in September 1958.

Eric usually wrote in pencil, in the neat, exact handwriting in which he wrote all his books, until the inevitable moment arrived and he destroyed them.

Mary kept all their letters in chronological order, in shoeboxes, until the year she died.

ABOVE
Twelfth of May 1937: Lord and Lady Swinfen, robed for the Coronation of George VI.

RIGHT ABOVE
Some of the children of the wartime nursery at Boskenna: (l.to r.) Toby, Ann Bailey, Nicky and Roger.

RIGHT BELOW
Colonel Camborne Paynter JP on the lawn at Boskenna in West Cornwall, with Paul Hill, second husband of his only child Betty. Together the magistrate and the solicitor ran the local black market.

Heinz Ziegler, alias 'Flying Officer Henry Zetland' of RAF Bomber Command, rear gunner and professor of economics, secretly Toby's father.

Wing-Commander 'Paddy' Green DSO, DFC, night-fighter pilot and one of Mary's wartime lovers.

ABOVE
Father Paul Ziegler, Heinz's younger brother; banker, anti-aircraft gunner during the Blitz and finally a Benedictine monk. The Ziegler parents were deported from Prague to Auschwitz.

RIGHT
Going into battle – Eric's first wife, Phyllis, arriving at the Divorce Court in July 1951. She was a champion skier who drove Eric out of three jobs, punched Mary in front of the children and bit a hotel keeper in the leg.

July 1954: Eric at Broughton with Pebble and his son Billy, born in 1953.

Toby, Sonya and Mary. Sonya Paynter found refuge from her mother's rackety life with Mary, who loved her as a daughter.

Toby, Roger, Mary and Eric, the golden days before the crash.

Roger, a regular officer in the 1st Royal Scots, leaves Mary in 1959 to join his unit.

Mary, alone and broke in an unheated cottage on Dartmoor, after Eric's death.

Cullaford Cottage, Dartmoor, last home of Eric and Mary. The thatcher said that Mrs Siepmann paid him in cash, and was the only customer who always paid him on the nail.

Mary Wesley, on a summer holiday during her years of fame.

Bogan Cottage, Totnes, where she wrote *The Camomile Lawn*. The shelves by Mary's bed in the room in which she died.

Mary and Sonya at a publication party in London in the 1990s. They are in the arms of David Salmon, a good friend and Dartmoor neighbour, who Mary could always count on for a Christmas joint.

I shall see Miss Marsden tomorrow, and I am lunching with Patrick [Balfour] at his club (St James'); then Dr Whitcombe at 3.

I am well behind with my article ... So I'll probably do it for March (the April number) ...

Laverstoke Mills – 7.2.51

Whitcombe sat me down in his chair and told me that he knew all about it from Barbara. He proposed to write to the lawyers saying emphatically that he had treated me for colitis and insomnia in October '49 which he attributed to my wife's persecution on losing me my jobs. All this without my saying a word.

I suggested – after clearing my throat and blowing my nose – that he had treated me at other times. We looked in his books and found that he had treated me in '46, '48 and '49. So he proposes to testify to my insomnia, colitis and nervous state throughout the period. He said: 'I will do everything I can, because I so want you to get married.' He sent you his love. You make good friends. I put the medical evidence, now, as 25% of our case (plus Harry and Nancy)!

... Patrick – hoist with his own gossipy petard! – is in a stew in case la PKS brings up the 'little boys' story and attributes it to him, which she may be able to prove if she has got 'Patrick's letter to Pauline'! (Cats out of bags.)

We agreed 1. not to call him; but if she brings it up, 2. exactly how to treat the whole thing; as a stupid joke, maliciously seized on by her. He is solid on our side; but of course afraid for <u>himself</u> (where the accusation is true, but not in mine!). Actually, G. Dadds may want him, as this explains and explodes the homosexual story! – but I didn't tell him so! He made a good statement to Thomas.

All told – much cheered by Dr Whitcombe. So important ...

Laverstoke Mills − 14.2.51

Thank you for this morning's letter − and the boys'! Roger's is a masterpiece of conscious self-improvement, and a step forward, genuinely, too. Toby needs kicking, tell him from me.

Thank you, too, and a million times, for paying the lawyers and the car ... I think your income's been bigger than mine ...

Chagford − 19.2.51

This to wish you *Bon Voyage* and success in Paris ... Give my love to Boris [Melikof] if you see him.

I bear you company in spirit and sit greedily beside you in the *Petit Riche* and wherever else you pause to eat. Do not let this spoil your enjoyment though!

Hotel Meurice, London SW1 − 19.2.51

I sit in my neat little room and miss you badly ... Journée bizarre d'un commis voyageur ...

Frances Ll. G. * has flu; she says the beginning of March will be the 'earliest date' for London; but we might go over there some week-end (I need her for Kemsley) ...*

Sykes and Berteaux in the news. Please <u>keep</u> *the Berteaux cutting for me; I have an account for him storing up.*[†]

=====

In January 1951 Roger was taken away from Summerfields and sent to a boarding school in Cardiganshire to be coached for

---

* Frances Stevenson, secretary and mistress of David Lloyd George, later his second wife.

† Commissioner Berteaux of Toulouse had failed to support Eric in 1945 when Eric fell out with the Foreign Office.

*Westminster School's common entrance. After three weeks, Mary
went to visit him.*

━━━━

Wales – 3.3.51

I miss you terribly so lovely was our week together. I pray time
will pass fast until we are together again *en permanence*. Last
night I slept in a double bed with Pebble and two hot water
bottles ...

This is fantastically beautiful country more like the Pyrenees
than any other place I've been to. The whole of my drive yesterday
was wrapped in mist and quite thick fog on the Cotswolds so that
I drove with my lights on and then after Hereford when I reached
the mountains it changed – I will lift up mine eyes to the hills –
and the Glenlimmon [correctly 'Plynlimon'] pass was of incredible
beauty. I reached Machynlleth and was soon here after. A little
mountain village on the road by a big waterfall. Roger sleeps in
another house just up the road and the school is a hideosity perched
up on the hill. Roger looks blooming and appears happy. He had
supper with me last night and I am having him from lunch time
onward today. I shall stay until Monday because he would like me
to and it seemed silly to come so far for so short a time ...

I have talked to Mr Cross about Roger. His verdict is that he
has quite a good brain and is intelligent but that he is very lazy ...

He says that he cannot agree with Carol that 'what Roger needs
is praise, praise, more praise and encouragement'. He thinks he
shouldn't get his praise until he has done something to deserve
it and is driving him and making him buck up. I think he knows
his job ...

I'm in lodgings with a good fire in the sitting room and arctic
bedroom but very comfortable bed and no bath – at least like
chez de Vos there is a bath but no hot water ...

Laverstoke Mills – 5.3.51

I wrote to Boothby and Quennell,* and told Thomas our dates (first two, or last week of Easter Law Term look best to me) ...

Laverstoke Mills – 5.3.51

Your letter and your telephone call gave me immense delight. This is to greet you chez Mrs Grant, with my love to her ...

Be good and don't let Mrs Grant corrupt you! I know she encourages you to flutter your eyelids and laughs at the size of your men ... She ought to know better. In fact, you had better tell her about the joys of Virtue ...

Laverstoke Mills – 7.3.51

I shall miss you on Thursday night and your visits to The Brothel [i.e. Mrs Grant's house, Trevatha in Newlyn] are accompanied by hallu-cinating visions of your running into the ghost of the French flier, pebbles against your window thrown by Colonel Vavrin (escaped from gaol) and enticing encounters with that ultra-charmer Don Smith or that ultra-vulgarian Pip Holman! Etc. Etc. SO BE GOOD ... And tell Mrs Grant that I do not really grudge you now you are there, bad influence as she is, as I know that you love her ...

Most amusing and satisfactory talk with Sheffield yesterday. It emerges that their only doubts are that I may get 'suddenly' fed up and that they are very pleased with me. House alright ... but 'if Portals bought one they'd expect a Service contract'. What is a Service contract? A sort of a life-tie-up. Suits me. Especially as I discovered that Harry [Monck] gets my salary, and Marsden

---

* Robert Boothby and Peter Quennell had agreed to act as witnesses against Phyllis in Eric's second divorce case.

only £3000! I said that I'd like to be a director, and I intend to get my next £500 tax (and maybe PKS) free. Also, a pension. But we want a nice house! ...

Just heard from Harry [Siepmann] that the Persian PM* has been shot dead. If by a communist, <u>anything</u> may happen. Also, my man will probably take power.

Laverstoke Mills – 13.3.51

... Fleming has the same lawyer as Astor, who has advised him not to make a statement. I can't see that it matters. Rather the contrary, as the facts must emerge from obviously unfriendly witnesses. And Bob Boothby has recalled that she asked him to bitch my job at Kemsley's!

I don't know what happened on Sunday. I have been wondering if you were not genuinely shocked and jealous, in spite of yourself, about my going to Rome?! ... The reaction to 'go to Boskenna' struck me as suspect. Now, of course, tell me that it was all my fault.

I get depressed, sometimes, about this case; Fleming and Astor sadden me ... But this is very pusillanimous ...

———

The divorce hearing took place in the High Court in July. It lasted three days and was widely publicised. The court heard of the extraordinary determination of Phyllis's campaign. She had extracted information from the Passport Office, arranged to have a question asked in Parliament, persuaded the Ministry of Labour to investigate Eric's business affairs, driven her husband out of three jobs, intimidated two naval officers – one a director of

---

* Lieutenant General Ali Razmara, the appointed prime minister of Persia, was shot dead while attending a mosque in Tehran. Contrary to Eric's hopes, the assassin was a Shiite fundamentalist.

military intelligence, the other a decorated member of the Special Forces – carried out three criminal assaults, persuaded Mary's parents to put her up for the night and harassed a director of the Bank of England. But the judge was unintimidated. Referring to 'the malice and hatred' Phyllis had shown against her husband, he granted Eric a divorce on the grounds of his wife's cruelty.

This meant that Mary and Eric could at last live together openly. They bought Knoll House in Broughton, near the Portals office in Hampshire and were married in April 1952.

In the autumn, Eric set off on a two-month business trip round the Far East. Mary took advantage of his absence to visit some of their old friends in Hamburg.

===

Gloucester Hotel, Hong Kong – 7.10.52

At this moment … I sit sweating in my pyjamas, fan at full speed, balcony open on mountains, skyscrapers and harbour …

The heat coming out was staggering; at Damascus, Bahrain, Karachi, Dacca, a soaking (sweaty) night at Rangoon, and Bangkok, and here we are at 20 degrees less (a mere 75–80 F.) [c.25° celsius, down from 35°] …

I was met here on Sunday evening by Lines, the agent, a delightful very tall youth, with hard-bitten Somerset Maugham wife … The entry by plane is not only the most dangerous in the world, but as beautiful as any I'd seen … The Chinese are nice. The Far East is delightful compared to the horrors of the Middle East …

Within this kaleidoscope, the British keep up a jolly good imitation of themselves. I found a bottle of gin and bottle of whisky laid on in my bedroom (both are and will remain untouched – you can't drink in this sweat-heat) and I found two RSVP cards formally inviting me to dinner-parties to meet 'the Colony'. Sir Arthur Morse has invited me to his 'box' for the Saturday races … and I've been made an honorary member of 'the Club'.

108, Edinburgh House, Hong Kong – 18.10.52

I've dined with 'les boys' [MI5] here (as slinky and sinister as usual) and my host shared an office with Ann Glass* in London: name, if Richmond asks, Michael Handley.† Their chief is Courtney Young,‡ Gerry's almost equally irresponsible brother!
…

Now back to my news.

Your instinct is always right. The money which Beazley kept on repeating he has 'inherited', was stolen – in China! His name stinks. As for DLR (De La Rue),** even their agents agree about them, and I found them trying to sell COINS in Manila versus the very rates [i.e. banknote values] they knew I was out for; and arguing coins 'more durable, even if more expensive'!!! That isn't the half of it. My dossier is growing, discreetly, fat.

Manila is an awful place. Like a flat slum of Los Angeles, with no sea except a dirty harbour, higher prices than New York, no inland except some cardboard mountains, grey grey skies and sheets of rain in heat so steamy and intense that you dodge in and out of 'air-conditioned' – ie frozen – rooms, from appointment to appointment … Bell hops jumping to it with cries of 'yes, sir!' … £5 for a bordel-type room, and Corruption and Insolence everywhere.

At night a small diplomatic colony goes to 2 or 3 parties every night. I was taken up by Bank Manager with lovely Spanish

---

* Ann Glass had been recruited by MI5, aged 18, at the same time as Mary, in 1940. She stayed on after the war as an intelligence officer. A brilliant linguist, with a sexy, deep bass voice, she became an expert in Soviet counter-intelligence.

† Michael, later Sir Michael, 'Jumbo' Hanley rose to become Director-General of MI5 from 1972 to 1978. In 1952 he was a member of 'E' Branch – responsible for colonial subversion. He was D-G at the time of the 'Spycatcher' fiasco, when a group of MI5 officers became convinced that the prime minister, Harold Wilson, was a KGB agent.

‡ Subsequently head of MI5's Soviet counter-intelligence section. Young was a friend of Anthony (later Sir Anthony) Blunt, and – hindered by alcoholism – conducted several ineffectual interrogations of Blunt and investigations into his contacts with fellow Soviet agents Burgess and Philby.

** The firm of De La Rue were direct rivals to Portals.

wife, and British First Secretary (Clinton-Thomas) with mad Italian wife – he, a gentleman, member of Travellers, mutual friends etc – so I joined their quartet and went to parties every night, and I must say I enjoyed it.

The routine of all Filipino parties is Phase 1: Women sit, apart, Men stand, apart, drinking whisky. This lasts 2 hours. Phase 2: Buffet supper. Food may be good. Sexes mix. Phase 3: Guitar, colour films or merely radio.

Hong Kong seemed <u>Paradise</u> on return, with its trim British tidy streets and monuments, immaculate Victorian Club where I drink (milk and soda), with a view of a green bay crowded with craft from liners to junks …

Be GOOD (even if I was gay in Manila!).

I love you –

Eric

Hamburg 13: Nonnenstieg 9 – 27.10.52

It was really wonderful to be met by Meg [an English friend] yesterday saying there are two letters waiting for you from Eric. Six days from Hong Kong, just before you left for Tokyo …

I am still tired from the journey which was long but comfortable. Everybody was sick on the boat except me …

Richmond and Roger saw me off from the filthy inferno of Liverpool St. and the scene changed at once on reaching the clean tidy Hook – and German trains nothing but smiles, helpfulness and good manners …

In London Richmond was the kindest of hosts and looked after me well. He has taken fishing for Toby who, he says, can go alone whenever he wants and is going to fix Roger up to learn to shoot with a keeper through his own keeper in Essex who comes from near us and knows everyone in Broughton …

I've run out of ink. I hope you can read this …

Harry was sweet to me in London and gave me a further introduction to a Dr Karl Blessing* who is now Unilever and used to be banking, who is a present day big noise. Harry says Schacht† is getting old. Meg tells me he's been refused permission to start his bank here but is starting it in Kiel, I hope to meet him ...

From what I've seen today Hamburg is very prosperous and Harry told Richmond who was consulting him about doing business with West Germany that there is a lot of money to be made if you are prepared to put in the capital ...

Meg is making me very comfortable ... I forgot to tell you Dunlop is now Consul as well as Land Commissioner. Dindi has just rung up. I am lunching with her tomorrow ...

[In London] I was rung up by Pauline which profoundly upset me, ridiculous as I know you think it, to me she is like an intoxicated crow, the harbinger of evil ...

Remember me constantly as I do you, not only as your dear little wife but most loving mistress, lover, friend and company, existing like the fork without the spoon until your return ...

I missed Nesta Obemer in London who was only there ten days to clear up her affairs and turn her cousin Miss CoOptimist out of the house as she appears to have gone off her top proclaiming Biddy slept with every man who came to the house and with Felix Green [sic] especially and that I did too – with Felix Green!‡

---

* Dr Karl Blessing, a director of the Reichsbank who was dismissed by the Nazis in 1939. In 1958 he was appointed president of the Deutsche Bundesbank.

† Dr Hjalmar Schacht was a Nazi supporter who was president of the Reichsbank until he was dismissed in 1939 for opposing German rearmament. In 1944 he was sent to Dachau concentration camp. In 1945 he was tried for war crimes at Nuremberg and acquitted but subsequently convicted and imprisoned on lesser charges. He was an old friend of Harry Siepmann's. Following the lead of the British High Commission, none of the British community in Germany wanted to have any contact with him.

‡ Felix Greene, first cousin of Graham Greene, left-wing idealist, Buddhist and pacifist, worked for Charles Siepmann in the pre-war BBC Radio Talks Department, and spent the war years in California.

Biddy very upset as she said the chief recipient of these attacks was poor Elena Green.* Nesta said Miss CoOptimist had always been known as 'Sexy Annie' and Biddy was not to mind. Nesta's gone to live in some other island for a year ... Samoa I think.

My sweet precious love, remember me even when dancing with Spanish ladies. I am <u>very</u> jealous as you never dance with me, and remember me with loving lust as I do you. Thank you for eight lovely years. I pray for eighty more ... I put in what was said about Mr Green because I had a <u>pang</u> when you said you 'were gay in Manila'.

Je t'aime,

M.

Hong Kong – 31.10.52

... Tokyo proved to be totally without interest, a flat alternation of shacks and shoddy skyscrapers ... I went straight to Jardine Matheson, who are the Kings out East (or were) and met Erik Wates, the managing director, who had a lunch of 'notables' ... I was invited, and driven there in a grey Rolls-Royce. The 'high-ups', most of them 'of the blood' (imperial), were pleasant... My man is called (Viscount) Kano ...

Three days later at Erik Wates's invitation, I moved into his (and Jardine Matheson's) house, the most comfortable in Tokyo, and had the grey Rolls put finally at my disposal ...

He is a strange, lonely interesting man ... some of Richmond's bachelor 'tics' and mystery ... His love seems to be Vi St Aubyn, who has married someone else; but it doesn't seem to matter too much ... I said you probably knew her. There was an Augustus John of her on the writing table; and she 'knew all

---

*Elena Lindeman, of Mexican-German descent, married Felix Greene in California in 1945.

the gypsies from Penzance to Polperro' ... *We made friends, and he interests me. An 'old China hand' whose father is still inside China (he never mentioned this to me – highly characteristic), whose uncle rode a famous ride out of Pekin in the Boxer rebellion, and whose own heart is still inside China (where he ran mines with 60,000 employees) and therefore probably broken. He was <u>marvellous</u> with his servants, laughing with them and not at them ... His Chinese servants here, in Hong Kong, I've discovered, refuse to work for anyone else (he left 3 months ago) so he goes on paying them! ...*

It is 6.30 and there is a mother of pearl sunset behind the islands ... Do not worry about typhoons and wars, which are powerless because I love you. (And anyway, they're interesting.) ...

Further instalment tomorrow ... includes the Kibuki [sic] Theatre – a staggering experience where the leading <u>danseuse</u> was a man of over 60 ...

Key to photo: Eric and 'Kikki' (Baron Kikkawa, Master of Ceremonies of the Imperial Household) ... taken inside the Imperial Palace ... to which no one, Japanese or European, is admitted ...

Hong Kong – 1.11.52

I have packed in my 3 cases comfortably, and blessed your name. (They now contain 3 new suits, 12 new shirts, 1 new pair of shoes!) But it has left me no time for the promised Japanese saga. I must go out to dinner with John Keswick and his wife, née Elwes, and get up at 5.* So this brings you all my true love, and a further promise to write from Saigon ...

---

* Sir John Keswick, *taipan* of Jardine Matheson and friend of Zhou Enlai, married to Clare Elwes, daughter of the tenor Gervase Elwes. Shortly afterwards the Keswicks were put under house arrest in Peking.

Hamburg – 3.11.52

Last night Meg, Michael (Parker) and I went to *Fledermaus* ...

It was all very *hommisch* and the singing was quite heavenly. As the Opera refuses to divulge more than three days ahead what they will present, it's difficult to know what more I shall see. Michael took us to the Rathaus for dinner afterwards and it was prima. *Carp au bleu* ...

No response alas from the Schacht. He is in Kiel. He is reported to be universally unpopular and suspected by all and sundry but I must find out more when oh when I meet some Germans!

5.11.52

Schacht has written that he will telephone when he gets back so he <u>has</u> responded. [Marion] Dohnoff* [*sic*] not yet back from Luxemburg and if she were she would be writing editorials about Eisenhower's landslide, oh dear oh dear I had so hoped for Stevenson.

I lunched yesterday most deliciously at the Four Seasons with Bridget Bernsdorf who is most extremely nice and a <u>good</u> person. She says the Germans are afraid of Schacht because he is so clever and that when Bismarck said the Germans fear nothing except God he really meant they fear everything but not God. She is so moved by the Godlessness that she made a vow to go to church every Sunday not just at Christmas and Easter. She says it's very boring and no one goes except the refugees. She's going to ask me out to Schloss whatever it is. She had a cosy war as her husband was a raging Nazi. She has two children. The eldest is at Salem.†
They are Protestants.

---

* Marion Grafin von Dönhoff, one of an aristocratic family of East Prussian landowners, was a journalist and a member of the wartime anti-Nazi resistance. She had been the political editor of *Die Zeit* since its foundation in Hamburg in 1946; she later became its editor-in-chief.

† Salem College, founded by Kurt Hahn.

Last night Meg had a party and I put Michael Parker and Ingeborg [Siepmann, Dindi's daughter] together. She also made a great impression on Doctor Dunlop who was so captivated that he wouldn't leave. I made him talk to her in French and his French is terrible, Swiss accent. He got rather mixed up, or perhaps his drinks did as he ended up by asking whether I was born in Hamburg and when I said mildly that I was English he was deeply puzzled ...

Hamburg – 7.11.52

Tonight I am dining chez Grafin Donhoff who beguiled me into putting off the Siepmanns until Monday on the grounds that <u>she</u> couldn't alter her parties. I gladly connived, to the fury of the Siepmanns who have, on receiving this kick in the stomach, organised a huge dinner in my honour for Monday instead ...

Prince Zoln, whom I've not been allowed to meet again as his wife has pink eye ... says that now Schumacher* is dead there will be a coalition at the next election ...

Bridget Bernsdorf says the habit of work which has supplanted religion is so deep that now after fifteen years in Germany she cannot play tennis on a weekday without a deep feeling of guilt ... She says she is ashamed and shocked at the way all the Germans have just dropped their English Occupation friends the minute the necessity to get bottles of whisky and lifts in cars stopped. Bridget being English is I think extra sensitive on this point.

Chez Donhoffs we had a very good dinner, Blue Carp again, and met the banker Eric Warburg† in whose bank Paul Ziegler worked, a very clever international jew, Michael Thomas ‡ (who

---

* Kurt Schumacher, leader of the Social Democratic Party and of the West German Parliamentary Opposition, had died in August 1952. He had spent ten years in a Nazi concentration camp and once described Communists as 'Nazis painted red'.

† Eric Warburg, prominent member of the German-Jewish banking family who settled in the United States before the Second World War.

‡ Michael or 'Michel' Thomas was a successful businessman and language teacher. He once wrote a book claiming that he had escaped from the Treblinka concentration camp following which he had arrested 2,500 German war criminals. The Los Angeles Times eventually exposed these bogus claims.

we met and distrusted in Berlin), who talks English better than us and has now English nationality and works for 'Big Steel', is domiciled in Italy but travels all the time like you, and a charming couple whose name I never grasped but will be easy to retrieve as he is the chief of the Anglo-Iranian Oil here ... I liked Marion Donhoff very much, she is rather of the superstrata and was feeling refreshed by a visit to Luxembourg where everyone was dealing on a high international plane. She got rather distressed when a shouting match developed between Thomas (who does not ring true to me) and Oil who took up a blatant dictatorial capitalist attitude over the new concessions made by Adenauer to the Trade Unions, and said that neither he nor any of the big companies would do other than cheat and circumvent!

Marion D. is a very great friend of Kurt Hahn's and is helping him found the new schools over here. He, Hahn, is having a nervous breakdown ...

They all talked a lot about the American elections pumping Warburg who lives there ... I was able to give a perfectly false impression of knowledge by murmuring that Nixon was the danger and Warburg says that is exactly it. *Pourvu* that nothing happens to Ike.

I got the impression that Marion Donhoff enjoys and rather trades on her sense of power from *Die Ziet* [sic]. 'I have not denounced him in my paper,' she said of Otto John.* 'Of course, if I did, he would be thrown out of his position [censor's orange crayon].' I told her what John had said to me during the Manstein† trial and perhaps she is now a little less likely to denounce than before ...

Write next my treasure to Broughton ...

---

* Otto John was the head of the BFV, the West German secret service. In 1944 he had been involved in the 20 July plot to assassinate Hitler. When the plot failed he escaped to London but his brother, also in the plot, was executed. Otto John assisted Allied prosecutors at the Nuremberg war crimes trials and acted as an interpreter during the trial of Field Marshall Erich von Manstein. In 1954 he defected to East Germany. He reappeared in West Germany in 1955, claiming to have been kidnapped by the KGB. He was nonetheless tried and convicted of treason, the victim of plotting by the ex-Nazi US *protégé*, and rival intelligence chief, Reinhard Gehlen.

† Field Marshal Erich von Manstein, Wehrmacht commander on the Eastern Front in 1941 and 1942, was tried in Hamburg in 1949 and sentenced to twelve years' imprisonment for war crimes.

Unusually, the following very long letter from Mary attracted close attention from the British censor who suddenly woke up. His orange crayon accompanied the <u>underlined</u> sentences.

Hamburg – 10.11.52

... At last this morning your letter of the 1st greatly delayed because the Germans lick off the stamps (and probably steam it open too). Both your letters have been treated so and the English authorities then make enquiries and fill in forms before delivery ...

How fortunate we are to have Harry. Tomorrow I am lunching with Doctor Schacht whose secretary came through on the blower this morning and said in accents of awe that Dr S. wanted to speak to me. There was such a long pause that I got cold and rang off, instantly to be rung again. 'Mrs Siepmann, you are <u>very</u> difficult to get hold of, please hold on, Dr S. wishes to speak to you,' whereupon I replied tartly that I wasn't used to being kept waiting and the old gentleman materialised instantly. Report tomorrow ...

Yesterday I had tea with Dr Dunlop. A *bon enfant*, more Hamburger than the Hamburgers. I put him through a brisk catechism and he talked for three hours. Very interesting but strictly limited to his <u>own province</u>. After leading him through every subject I wanted him to hear about he suddenly asked anxiously whether I was going to write articles when I got back to England and was obviously reassured when I said not.

What I <u>do</u> appreciate is that both Germans and English alike look down their noses and positively click with annoyance when I say I am to meet Dr S. To begin with <u>none</u> of the English have met him except Dunlop who he goes and teases occasionally, and to go on with the Germans, all behave as if they were afraid he might 'put something over on them'. The press hints that he is off to Mossadegh* [sic] again.

When you get this I shall be home again. Leaving here the 18th and going straight through to Pebble and Broughton ... I must go on with my reportage of how I see things here. To begin with what we know already is forever in the foreground. The intense materialism and complete Godlessness of the people. The gap between rich and poor is far too large and very few of the people who could and should, concern themselves with it.

Even the Socialists have to a large extent ignored the working classes and their living conditions and meléed themselves with foreign affairs instead. The intellectuals are largely returned emigrés or east german emigrés who in consequence of their floating position carry less weight. There is no new literature, no new painting. Any creativeness there may be goes into building and industrial design and here there is splendid opti-mism for the new buildings are nearly all of glass. Those precious [sic] few like Trügel and Donhoff are working for something more but they too are surrounded by far too many emigrés ...

The young are still holding back and keeping out of politics. Old Dunlop, like a prep school master who thinks it a good thing the boys are so keen on football and so do not masturbate, says the young men are keen on sport and sailing and leave politics to the old and the trade unions.

To me this is the eagle head of irresponsibility being reared again ... Even Donhoff says 'oh the Nazis were dreadful common people, we had nothing to do with them, we kept away'. A

---

* Mohammad Mosaddeq was the democratically elected prime minister of Iran. He introduced a programme of social reform and nationalised the Iranian oil industry which had formerly been under the control of the Anglo-Iranian Oil Company (later BP). His government was overthrown by a *coup d'état* organised by the CIA and MI6 in 1953.

coalition is expected at the next elections ... the Internationals [press] predict what you predicted three years ago – a close pact between America and Germany leaving the rest to go hang.

11.11.52

... Another letter from you this morning, no licked stamps this time and I am just returned exhilarated by lunch with Schacht. Lunch lasted from one till four and not a dull moment. Of course I shall love him for ever because he laughs at my jokes. He is also a fearful old flatterer, beginning by saying as we sat down in the restaurant after the waiter had exclaimed 'Ach! Herr Doctor Schacht and Frau Schacht', 'All the same I hope someday you will meet my wife because like the Siepmann family I cannot tolerate anyone unintelligent near me.'

As I am both inquisitive and indiscreet I made him talk. He was nothing loath. He is very good company, very spry for seventy five, he has a young wife and two little girls of ten and twelve in Munich, also very funny. I enjoyed myself thoroughly, ate a large lunch and drank a very good Moselle which was just what I needed after tottering to bed at three from the Siepmann party of which more anon.

He, Schacht, is just finishing writing his memoirs ... Harold Nicolson [reviewed] the first book kindly and justly apparently, and Schacht now says he will ask him [to translate the memoirs].

A propos Persia, he says that when he got back some six weeks ago he went straight to Dunlop and asked whether he could make a reportage of his visit with the suggestions he had made to Mossadeq to Kirkpatrick.* Dunlop was evasive and nothing was done at all. I said he should on future occasions write to Harry. He loves Harry and adored Norman.†

---

* Sir Ivone Kirkpatrick, British High Commissioner for Germany.
† Montagu Norman, governor of the Bank of England, 1920–44, personal friend of both Harry and Eric Siepmann.

He sent you salutations and says he hopes to meet you.

He is an extraordinary man with tremendous vitality and an enormously wide outlook, deeply suspect on all sides because he is obviously cleverer than anyone else and most uncompromising. He has a slight persecution mania as he has been harried and imprisoned quite a lot, but I would rather be with him than against him and I took a fancy to him so that's the safest Bismarck Herring [private code for German lover] there could be!

Last night the Siepmanns had a dinner party of twelve for me which I enjoyed ...

Ricardo looks about seventy from overwork and is just starting Menière's disease like Charly [Charles Siepmann]. He (Ricardo) makes twelve thousand pounds a year* of which he spends four, saves four and four goes in taxes. We had a sumptuous dinner and oceans to drink ...

Apparently I have done a 'good' thing by introducing her [Ingeborg] to Michael Parker as she was quite *éprise*. I rather like Ricardo as everything pours out and he has no pretentions [*sic*]. The party was I suppose rather dull except for this intelligent woman but I enjoyed it as one enjoys an American musical. All the women were very pretty and all the men jolly unattractive. I drank enough to say what I really think which was fun and not enough to be really rude – only a little ...

Any tiny toys for Christmas stockings greatly appreciated. German toy shops rotten this year and if you do not bring me a ruby and a length of Chinese silk bring me back your love intact because mine grows and the appetite too and I love you most deeply and with joy.

Tonight I am going to hear *Fidelio* and I shall listen for you. *Je t'embrasse avec passion* ... take care of yourself, for me, with extra care –

M.

---

* Today's equivalent would be over £300,000.

Hamburg – 13.11.52

... My visit which began so slowly because every single person I wanted to see was away is ending on a far higher note. In my letter yesterday I wrote of Dr Schacht, who is wonderful ... I was told yesterday that he would die for a bon mot and it is obviously true. I am bewitched by the old rascal. I am making notes for you as I did in Berlin, for your return ...

Last night Harry's friend Blessing and his wife took me to hear the Vienna Philharmonic conducted by Clemens Krauss. I who have <u>not</u> a musical soul sat through the Seventh Symphony with the tears spurting, a feeling of fearful joy in my heart and nearly clapped my rings off my fingers!

At the end the crowd roared and would not go away and shouted and clapped and stamped and cried and Blessing says they <u>never</u> do this in Hamburg – so Krauss came back and for sheer fun gave us 'The Blue Danube'.

We tottered into the (Unilever) Mercedes and dined at Halali. I thought the other guest, a Herr Getchman, was going to have a fit. He has just been released by the Russians and looked as though he would burst with emotion. However, liberal doses of Moselle to wash down oysters and pheasant calmed him a little ...

The Blessings are charming. Very civilised people with lovely manners, he is devoted to Harry ... Blessing says that no one has any legal right at all to prevent Schacht starting his bank and they only do it because they are afraid of him.

Hamburg – 16.11.52

... I am furious for you that you are being made to come halfway home to Karachi and then back to Bangkok. However, even though you work for idiots there are times when you have leisure. Here the German business man is at his desk at eight, leaves it at seven, has practically no time for lunch, pays 70 to 80 per cent income tax, and is always on the move, rattling off to Cologne, Dusseldorf, Munich, Frankfurt or abroad on a non-stop conveyor belt of exhaustion. Blessing says it's terrible. Ricardo at 50 looks 70 and the only person who seems to thrive is Schacht for whom, as you may have noticed, I have developed a strong taste ...

I spent all yesterday recovering from the effects of being trotted around the night clubs by Dindi and Ricardo who under the mixed influence of a variety of drinks ending up with pink champagne quite unbuttoned and we had a very jolly evening contradicting each other.

Tomorrow I am spending the day at Rosenberg chez the Bernsdorffs. I like her very much. She is intelligent and observant and has a sense of humour ...

I miss you so much for <u>jokes</u>. Ricardo who, as we all know, reeks of money and works like a black said that Charlie had complained bitterly ... on the subject of his abject poverty. I said, 'Quite ridiculous. He isn't so rich as Harry perhaps or Eric who does very little work and gets enormously paid.' 'Enormously paid!' said Ricardo. 'Naturally,' I said. 'What else do you expect?' Ricardo looked very thoughtful and sent me an expensive book next morning about Mount Everest.

He says that news from the East Zone [East Germany] where he still has offices, and from Roumania, is of ever increasing restlessness and of some cases of open revolt against the Russians. Last month's desertions to the West of the East German police was the highest ever.

Bridget Bernsdorf says that in the event of Germany being reunited there would be very little 'going back to the old home', most refugees have got settled there, so the people shoved into the farms and businesses they previously owned would remain put ... She is a very level-headed, impartial girl. Married to Hugo Bernsdorf in January 1939. H was an early member of the Nazi party in '32 and quarrelled with them in '35. He was SA during the War, wounded and had trouble with the allies after because he had won a *proces* against the Nazis and had not been put into a camp. He is a large landowner and has just had a flaming row with Burgermeister Brauer.

My treasure, you are far too far away ... Tender and provoking kisses *partout* for the next hug ...

M.

Broughton — 20.11.52

I got home yesterday lunch time after a fearful bouncing across the North Sea. The boats after mine failed to make port and I held on with both hands so as not to be thrown out of my bunk — with one to be exact as I was reading Joyce Cary's last book which is frightfully good,* as good as *The Horse's Mouth* ...

I left Germany ice and snow bound under a black sky, blew home in a gale and nearly died of cold when I got here ... My last days were busy ... I was lunching with Marion Donhoff fifteen minutes before I caught my train. I like her very much and I think she is very much of the élite, which she collects ...

Of course she loved Adam Trott who was hanged after the July '44 [assassination plot]. Her flat is <u>full</u> of his photographs.

On Monday before I left I spent the whole day at the Bernsdorffs who have a heavenly Schloss, 18th century and Bridget has made the part they live in quite lovely. I like her very much, she grows upon one rapidly. He is delightful too. Terribly wounded in the war and poked his eye out with a ski last winter and though not of the elite not stupid. He was originally a Nazi. Although they only live in a small part of their house it is still immense and in great comfort with lots of servants, horses, lady dachshunds who live in your lap and several motor cars. The rest of the schloss is inhabited by refugees who work on the farms and one or two old Lady Bismarcks. They also have a bullfinch in a cage in their bedroom whose pipes reminded me of my childhood.

---

* *Prisoner of Grace*; Joyce Cary had been a pupil of Eric's father, Otto, at Clifton.

Safe home, the house is in order. Nothing has changed ... The leaves are off the trees and winter is come ...

Missing you atrociously ... I love you,

M.

Comet (between Singapore and Bangkok, en route to Rangoon)
— 27.11.52

I found the whole Hamburg saga at Singapore ...

You can hardly imagine the delight with which I lay on the bed and read through your adventures. Most amusing and well-written so that I gloated. I have rarely had such a thrill. It was sexual and intellectual ... [It] is my delight, and brilliant.

Kindly state clearly, at once, with whom you went to Fidelio and who made the fourth when you Tarantella-ed with Dindi and Ricardo ...

I was met in Indonesia, to my surprise, by a polite and slightly dour Dutchman, and his very pretty and cultivated wife; and they took charge of me ... They are condemned to live in Djakarta, which is AWFUL ... We played Beethoven Piano Concertos on the gramophone, and I was made to dance. By a miracle, the style in Djakarta is 'Savoy Ballroom 1923', smooth and even with outside steps etc — ie my stuff! I gained confidence, and fairly glided around, partly with la petite exquise who danced badly, and partly with a lewd, very old trout who — as these lewd old trouts do — danced perfectly ...

My host encouraged me in my fell scheme — to spend a week in Bali, a mere 500 miles. And I did, staying with Mr Pandy, an art dealer, who 'lets a few rooms in his studio on the beach'.

As you reach Bali there is a huge notice forbidding tourists to photograph Balinese women with naked breasts, as this is derogatory in the new Indonesian republic. These breasts are brown and very lovely, but 70% of the girls wear drab blouses since the war. I am glad you did not see the young men, who swim naked on the beach, brown ... brown-shouldered and thin-hipped and bien dévéloppés. But the hatred of the foreigner is being installed by the Javanese, and you don't feel quite happy even in a Balinese village ... and I was massacred by mosquitoes ...

After luncheon, at Bangkok: A most agreeable Englishman, of the Richmond type (most solid tweeds ... feather appurtenances in hat) has promised to post this in London at 2pm tomorrow ...

We are moving off ... so love and love ... Vibrations due to Comet, not lunch.* It's a marvellous plane. We're going up runway. Soon!

E.

Karachi – 9.12.52

Karachi is awful, and I have been prostrate for 3 days ... Money and cruelty are the keynotes ...

Burma was unexpectedly delightful, and – one guessed – beautiful outside town, where one cannot venture. Even in town, very green trees and shrubs round huge lakes, bougainvillea, frangipani, hibiscus; and I lolled swimming all one Sunday with an unusually nice British group. Then, of all things, an Asquith! The old man's grand-daughter,† whose father (Brigadier and VC)‡ and mother (a Manners) I'd known. It opened the flood gates: I dined with them – her husband called Boothby,** wholly obliterated in this same influence, so that I realised how special, how isolating it is – and we talked Antoine and Elizabeth and Puffin ...

---

* The De Havilland Comet, the world's first commercial jet airliner, had entered service with BOAC the previous May. In May 1953, the first in a series of unexplained fatal Comet crashes occurred. After some time it was discovered that the aircraft had broken up during flight. These accidents were eventually attributed to structural failure caused by metal fatigue – which would have been accelerated by vibrations.

† Susan Asquith, daughter of Arthur Asquith, third son of the prime minister H.H. Asquith, 1st Earl of Oxford and Asquith.

‡ Brig. Gen. Arthur Asquith, D.S.O. and 2 Bars, was not in fact awarded the V.C.

** Evelyn Basil Boothby, at the time British Consul in Rangoon.

*I've got that feeling of exhilaration ... really because in SIX
days I shall be hugging you. You have been a dim, un-nourishing
ghost in my bed, nightly, around Hong Kong, Tokyo, Manila,
Saigon, Singapore, Djakarta, Bali, Rangoon, Karachi ...*

*Darling, I am indeed lost without you ... So much to tell you
... A toujours –*
Eric

═══

The years at Broughton were the happiest of their marriage and
their son, Bill, was born in December 1953. Throughout his four
years at Portals, Eric frequently made long business trips around
Europe and across the world. He found these an increasing strain
and the final journey ended in disaster. Eric set out in the spring
of 1954 for a six-week tour of the Middle East that took him back
to Karachi. The region was in a ferment of actual and threatened
revolution; the secret Anglo-French partition of 1916 was being
challenged by 'Arab nationalism'. It was not a promising moment
for the arrival of a salesman from Hampshire bearing samples
of banknote paper. His letters to Mary describe the international
crisis and hint at the personal crisis that was brewing inside. He
started in Beirut.

═══

Hotel St Georges – 1.3.54

*... I was met by a nice young Lebanese who instantly diverted
me with the double crisis of Neguib* and of the Syrian dictator†*

* Mohamed Naguib became president of Egypt in June 1953 following the
military coup that overthrew King Farouk. He was deposed by Colonel Gamal
Abdel Nasser in November 1954.

† Adib Shishakli, the military dictator of Syria, had been overthrown by a
Communist-led military coup shortly before Eric's arrival in Beirut.

... Everything is still attributed to British macchiaveleism [sic] (hooray) and ... every crisis raises the question of a possible union of Irak-Syria-Lebanon. This might be Irak-led, and more friendly to us than an Egyptian-led Arab League; but none of it is likely to take place. One cannot help being pleased at Neguib's personal success, a moderate man, though a collapse of the 'revolutionaries' followed by a revival of party politics might have been more malleable. I hope Damascus has quietened down when I get there, but it is all most interesting and I derive a shameful joy out of the messes made by all these nationalists when we leave them alone ...

2, Mary Road, Karachi – 7.3.54

It is 5.30am and the old turbaned 'bearer' is finishing my packing. I hope to give this to somebody on the aeroplane, which goes on to London ...

I leave Karachi with joy ... I have been dogged by the DLR [De La Rue] chief – who plied me with liquor and impertinent questions, so that once or twice I was rude to him ... It all ended amicably in dinner-jackets and politeness, and hatred underneath! ...

Now I am in the aeroplane [Eric is back in a Comet] ... the vibration rouses my senses, and I think of you in accommodating positions ...

Karachi is odd. The British shout 'bearer' and talk to their servants like dirt and drink gins at the Club; but they are polite to the ruling Pakistanis, Civil Servants etc. which I suppose they weren't in EM Forster's day ...

———

Baghdad, when he reached it, was 'awful!' Then came Damascus ... In his final report to the chairman of Portals, Eric wrote:

Please excuse the slight scrappiness of my reports ... It has been a tiring and beastly tour ... the conditions have been so foul in most of the Arab countries that pen, ink or table ... have been totally lacking even in the 'best' hotels.

He then referred to the problem directly:

[In Damascus, Syria] I visited the permanent head of the Ministry of Finance ... one of the few consistent factors in a country where a revolution had taken place a few days before my arrival ... I had a foolish misunderstanding with the British Council, of all people, about some indiscreet remarks which I was alleged to have made about Arab Nationalism, within hearing of Arabs. They took it up with the Embassy, and I shall have to report to you privately about this ...

When Eric got to Tripoli he was joined by Mary and he told her the full story. He had found the trip exhausting and had started drinking to keep going. Then in Damascus, as Mary recalled, someone had given him 'some pills' which, mixed with whisky, had robbed him of any discretion, so at a party at the British Embassy, he had predicted 'trouble and war in the Middle East between Jew and Arab'. 'The Foreign Office are very angry and they are going to report me,' he said. 'I'm going to lose this job.'

Which is what happened. Phyllis had driven him out of three good jobs, and he had lost two through his own errors. He never held a regular job again. The war he had prophesied, the Anglo–French–Israeli attack on the Suez Canal Zone, broke out two years later.

Twelve months after Eric was fired he and Mary were forced to sell Broughton House. The roller-coaster ride had begun.

PART FOUR

The Making of a Writer: 1957–67

*I*n May 1955, one year after Eric had been fired by Portals, Mary took a lease on a tumbledown farmhouse high up on Dartmoor. The house was called Thornworthy. Life had not gone smoothly following Eric's departure from his well-paid position. Further attempts to hold down regular jobs in advertising and public relations had failed, but there had been an unexpected success when he completed a book. Confessions of a Nihilist, an account of his early life, was published by Gollancz in November 1955 to mixed reviews. He continued to write novels and continued to abandon them halfway through. Mary was also writing fiction, but she did not feel confident enough to send any of her work to a publisher and was mainly occupied in looking after her husband and their young son, Billy.

In August 1956 they were both received into the Catholic Church after taking instruction from a Jesuit based at Farm Street, Father Richard Mangan. The novelist Antonia White, author of Frost in May and a former girlfriend of Eric's, was one of their godmothers. The circumstances were unusual since both were remarried divorcees and their conjugal life was illicit under Roman Catholic canon law.

In the summer of 1957 Eric started to work as a summer relief sub on The Times foreign desk. He intended to take cheap lodgings in London, writing fiction in the mornings before starting his evening shift. Thornworthy had already become a financial burden but Mary loved the house and did not want to lose it. She decided to turn it into an asset; she would take in foreign students as paying guests and teach them English. It is clear from Mary's first letter that Eric has just abandoned and destroyed another book.

Authors' Club
2, Whitehall Court, SW1 – 31.5.57

Darling,

... *The tiny club is awful as usual ... Pens and writing tables reduced to two! ... Luckily there is the London Library.*

I am not to be deterred from my book which is ... inspired by you ... I wonder what you'd write, if you told our story truthfully? I fear I have been a great trial to you ... But I love you more than ever.

Yours is a courageous venture, and I'm sure it will succeed ...
All my love,
Eric

Authors' Club
1.6.57

Good morning my love,

I do hope you are not too lonely ... Je te regrette. I slept not too badly without pills, but still fitfully and nightmarishly ...

I've found a good writing table; if I can bag it early enough! ...

Johnny [unidentified], *warned to be sober, said he was too broke to be otherwise ... He besought me* [to write] *down in 60,000 words 'How I became a Catholic' ... Second person to ask me: Gollancz having done so. It would take a year ...*

Nat Micklem* is in this club almost daily! Great news. 'A good influence.' I rode on his back in 1907 ...

Thornworthy – 1.6.57

My Darling,

Lovely to get a letter from you so soon, I wasn't expecting one until Monday at least ...

---

* Nat Micklem CH was a theologian and a Liberal Party politician who became president of Mansfield College, Oxford.

Overslept this morning as the usually fast clock was two hours slow. Got bogged down in the Chagford 'shopping' ...

A lot of correspondence a propos PG's. Takes ages. The Spanish pain in the neck now wants to send a nephew instead as her own child has ratted [i.e. *raté*'d – failed] his 'bachot' [French slang for school leaving certificate, the baccalaureat] or whatever you do in Spain.

Tomorrow to Mass armed with the jumble and then I must get the house in *ordnung* ... Mrs Wonnacott* says the signs are pretty good. Marjorie [a cleaner] wishes to come too and Valerie is standing by so I certainly won't be left alone so <u>please</u> don't worry ...

The Master of Hounds has had to tour every farmer to <u>apologise</u> for the numerous foxes. One farmer is poisoning the foxes and threatens to poison the MFH and hounds too if they come near him. The smith came up last night to shoe the ponies so a lot of local news leaked out ...

On reading this I see I had better brush up my English or my little visitors will return to their mamas belching fearful slang ...

I am very glad you are writing a happy book, not only because it will sell but because it will be better for you to write about something you enjoy. The manuscript of *The Lovekiller* choked the boiler – this one won't ...

Authors' Club – 2.6.57

... I am off to The Times. It is 4.30 and hot.

I went to a church off the Strand ... 'No confessions till 5'. But a down-at-heel Irishman with a hard [luck] tale took 10/-†off me (well-known place for rascals and thieves, was Father Mangan's comment) and took me to a French church off Leicester Square – where confessions are heard 'at any time'. I rang a bell in vain and then an angry French priest bustled through the church and said rudely he was just coming ...

* The Wonnacotts' farm surrounded Thornworthy House. Mrs Wonnacott and Mary became firm friends.
† 50p – today's value £20.

When I unloaded my tale of seven weeks, he questioned me fiercely and rudely and said it couldn't be so and 'she is not your wife' and he couldn't understand and better go to Farm Street and no priest could accept ... etc. How had I been received? I said by the Charity of the Church. This shocked him (and made Mangan laugh) and he gave me an angry absolution and THREE ROSARIES (105 Hail Mary's, I think). To be continued. I go to work ...

———

When Roger was filling in his application form for Sandhurst he did not know what to put for his mother's religion and asked Toby if he had any information on the subject. Mary and Eric's conversion to Catholicism was part of their private relationship, and a mystery to Roger and Toby. Bill, on the other hand, was brought up as a Catholic.

———

Thornworthy – 2.6.57

Such a wonderful hot day and you not here ... I have divided the day between long sunbathing and getting the house very clean. The little dogs and the geese giving lots of *gesellschaft*. I still have the posh Sunday papers to read in bed.

Mass this morning and the Archbishop of Canterbury got a sharp rap in the sermon. The little dogs sat outside and then ran up the lane on the way home. I thought of you, probably in Westminster Cathedral. On Saturday next I am having my hair washed in the morning at Torquay calculating that there will be confessions in the afternoon (when I can let it down). If you wander to Farm Street give my love to Father M. who is a good man. Good to us anyway. Tomorrow the geese are to mow for Miss Varwell*

* An old lady who lived with her sister in Thornworthy Cottage, nearby. She owned the Thornworthy estate, including the farm.

but they will come home if they don't like it. I wired them in to
eat round the pond and they crawled under it and went back to
their own pen. I had fits as I thought they had *disparue* down the
drain under the tennis court.

I love you, do not be afraid.

M.

Authors' Club – 3.6.57: 7.30am

... I am too early for them so I have come back to my bedroom ...
The Times *was delightful. I got there at 5, and 'as it was
my first day' I was allowed to go home at 10.30. At 9 or so we
all retired to the canteen for half-an-half. I had two mutton
chops piled with peas and potatoes and a cup of tea for – I
think – 2/9d. The colleagues were helpful, and I was able to
read the whole of the Otto John trial in the cuttings book besides
mastering the elements of the trade which vaguely came back
to me ...*

*Father Mangan whom I also saw (and who gave me absolution
in his room then and there) said God is better than A.A. [Alcoholics
Anonymous] and much better than psychiatrists ... I do think
that the need to communicate weekly, or more often, is a very
strong inducement and a great help. I didn't feel this so much
at home but without you I now feel it and MUST take communion
each Sunday which deters certain obsessions (sex) and irrespon-
sibilities (drinks). So cheer up; but I will do the others, and I'm
getting Strauss* free, it seems. He was tres chic with semitic grey
waistcoat and chains etc. and very friendly.*

*Nat is the new Chairman of the Liberal Party, by the way,
and most keen and understanding on the Jacko case† and
Mental Report ... He is also moderate – seeing that he is one*

---

* Dr Eric Strauss, who had formerly treated Phyllis.

† see Note on p. 211.

of the Heads of the Evangelical Church (he knows Dibelius
and Niemoller*) – and has written decent pamphlets on
'Romans' as he calls us. I'm going to get him together with
Woodruff?!†

Thornworthy – 3.6.57

... Found a delicious printing works – would fit into your study –
at Morton who are going to print us writing paper. The old owner
too busy reading the *Western Morning News* and too deaf to attend
to me he said, but a nice young man did. I stopped to ask a man
where the butcher was and before I could open my mouth he
cried, 'For God's sake tell the butcher we've killed the pig and to
come and fetch it!' Meekly I did ...

The son of an Italian *professore* at Milan is coming. I referred
him to Mario Praz ... If everyone comes who is supposed to there
are now <u>far</u> too many. It will be *interessant* where they all sleep.

A wail from Thora‡ – don't breathe it – her gentleman who
is fifty and safely married has declared himself. I wrote her a very
sharp letter on the declarations of safely married men and gave
her the push to get rid of him before he gets rid of her, which
will help her morale and her reputation. Very glad about Johnny.
He is so literal that he will probably do just exactly what you say.
I pray so. I expect you have saved his life ...

---

* Martin Dibelius, an iconoclastic Lutheran professor of theology at Heidelberg
University, had died in 1947. Martin Niemoller was an anti-Nazi Lutheran
pastor who survived Dachau and became a pacifist and nuclear disarmer.

† Douglas Woodruff, author, publisher, dominant Catholic journalist and wit,
editor of the *Tablet* for over thirty years, one of the many friends Eric had
in common with his enemy, Evelyn Waugh.

‡ Thora Bernsdorf, a cousin of Hugo Bernsdorf, with whom Mary had stayed
during her visit to northern Germany in 1952. Thora lived on a family estate,
Wötersen, in Prussia, adjoining the new border with East Germany.

c\o *Mrs Sloan*
75 Grove End Gardens
Abbey Road, NW8 – 3.6.57

... *The room is nice, the Abbey Road traffic is less than 20 yards from my nose. All I can say is it's better than Whitehall Court which had Charing Cross bridge and steam trains as well ...*

<u>Please send me £10</u> *as the Times are subtracting MAXIMUM tax and anyway I can't get any money until Thursday week. I'll return the £10 <u>then</u>, sans faute, and I have <u>not</u> been extravagant ... we can't have Hughes* more than one day a week next year; we'd save £100 ... Rent of £250, as it is, is uneconomic ...*

I've been trying out various routines: today I went to London Library, quiet but dirty and crowded tube ...

I live for your letters ...

Now about that priest ... He refused to accept the position and nearly refused me absolution and gave me THREE ROSARIES to say and advised me to go to Farm Street. Fr Mangan said the only sensible thing he'd told me was to go to Farm Street! But I was afraid, glimpsing automatic excommunication (if I were refused absolution). Fr Mangan said not. If one refuses, go on to the next one! I said according to our consciences and against our instructions we'd made love for a few weeks after 5 weeks' sexlessness. He thought five weeks very good. As I'd cursed the priest, and fallen into despair (not drink), he gave me absolution again. He is a fine, brave man ...

Thornworthy – 4.6.57

... I laughed for hours over your confession. Just like a Frenchman! How nice about Nicky Charles. Nice too that Father Mangan

---

* Odd-job man at Thornworthy; no relation to Major Glyn Hughes, proprietor of the Chagford Hotel, and later, briefly, Eric's landlord in London.

consoled you and very nice that you met Eric Strauss, that the *Times* were agreeable, in fact your news cheered me. We have good friends.

I too feel the need for communion but I am choosing to confess in the rush hour at Torquay when it will be Whit Saturday and hope to avoid 105 HM's [Hail Marys] though I would not mind. Did I tell you that when I sat so boringly for the painter last autumn I said my prayers? I found it a very good way for stillness though the Catholic painter exclaimed at intervals that I was drooping.

The reconnection with Nat Micklem must be lovely …

Ann Ruegg [a neighbour] came to supper and cheered up quite a lot. Three nice nieces came to have coffee afterwards. Apparently Marjorie has been with the Rueggs nineteen years except for four years during the war when she was 'lent' here [to Thornworthy]. Lady W.* constantly interfered with her work and on one occasion screamed at Marjorie who was laying the table 'I seem to be doing more and more of your work', to which Marjorie replied, 'You will soon be doing it all, My Lady.'

The Boy from Madagascar is coming for six weeks on July 30th. Monsieur his father wrote a very nice letter. The geese contrary to my fears are <u>most</u> popular chez the Wallers but have discovered that if they sit outside the hall windows they can listen to <u>all</u> the fascinating telephonings, so they sit riveted, gazing in through the window – Animal Farm …

I am now in the position to pick and choose my pg.'s. They are nearly all boys but the Ruegg girls have promised to come and play tennis with them. They say the court is quite alright and that they played on it last year … a lot.

Frau Bentinck also has the pg.'s but charges I think less than me. Next year I shall charge more and work less hard.

Viva your book. I'm afraid for you for the noise. I was noticing last night how excessively quiet it is here which makes you the more vulnerable. Pills?

I love you and miss you. You may be irritable but you have cause – you are tender my love and I dearly love that!

* Lady Waller, sister of Mary's landlady, who had previously occupied the house.

I must take the little dogs out. There are sighs, groans and nudgings. I alarm myself to get up, and do so at 7.30am, getting back into bed it is true with my breakfast ...

Thornworthy – 5.6.57

... Alas I read your letter when the postman had gone so I shall trot down to Yeo and just <u>pray</u> you get the cheque in time to cash it tomorrow. I have no car, it is at the garage. Feet will do. Douglas at the P.O. says it is <u>fatal</u> to express letters, delays them no end!

Don't worry about the cross French priest. Even Tom has popped from one box to the next in the Oratory and we were warned this would happen ...

OK for the ten pounds but must have it back as you say Thursday week because of the wages. My first lodger arrives July 1st and then I can start paying my way ...

A propos the French priest, it seems to me we undertook to love God not the French priest and if loving one another and consoling one another are not according to the preaching of Christ I will eat my hat salted with the technicality of unmarriage in the eyes of the church. When I was very worried about lapsing into loving, we know what Father Mangan said. He's our spiritual advisor damn it ...*

With all my love,

M

London NW8 – 11.6.57

My darling,

I left you with a pang, and I wondered if one's ability to feel pain decreases with age ... I was 'glad to feel sad' because I love you ...

---

* Father Mangan's briskly empirical approach to the 'technicality of unmarriage' stands in sharp contrast to the clanking public debate on the subject within the Catholic Church today.

Times *is a long stiff pull until you are used to it (if you ever are) ... Card there from Bridget, suggesting we meet tomorrow. I hope to gigolo a lunch out of her: maybe see Patrick, whose American inamoratus (masculine) has arrived ...*

Here I am at my table. My hostess is clean, but even here dust drifts and settles; traffic ROARS. I don't know if I can stand it ...

My book is a problem (the 'I' narrator method is failing me) but I have more faith now that I know <u>what truth I want to tell</u> (not just 'write a book to make money'). This applies even to a funny book. I think I can do something true and funny by September ...

I have much faith in your heroic enterprise, because I feel you have just the gifts for it ... I'll see G. & Thring about an extra pupil ... and I'll write eventually to Bowra and Livingstone, too. *

All my love, you have helped me immensely ...

Thornworthy – 12.6.57

I went and suffered at the hairdressers' where they said of Pebble – 'That dog has been coming in for years and years!' ...

I love you most dearly my darling. I think that now you have realised at last, after a lifetime of trying to persuade yourself and others to the contrary, that you are a naturally good person your books will flow. A lot more Rouge et less Noir. *Pour moi tu es presque toujours Rouge. Je t'aime* and Billy shall prove it to you.
M.

<u>Afterthought</u> ... I wrote a note to Miss Varwell. I would have visited her but she is out for the day. She won't fuss if she knows it is coming and the rebate will pay rent and rates. I can pay bills from the pg.'s as I go along. I have soothed the coal merchant!

---

* Gabbitas Thring was an educational employment agency. Eric was planning to tutor pupils at Thornworthy when his summer relief work at *The Times* came to an end. Richard Livingstone, like Maurice Bowra, was an eminent Oxford don. An old Wykehamist, classicist and president of Corpus Christi College, Oxford, he had been Eric's tutor at Corpus.

Mr Jeffreys had been saying 'No cheque, No coal' to Miss Jeffreys but I put a stop to that! [The boiler at Thornworthy was coal fired and had to burn all summer to heat the water and the cooker].

I am quite determined not to let pressure of money fluster me and now we are dealing with it as best we can I don't see why it should.

London NW8 – 14.6.57

I was much relieved to get your postcard. I had been gloomy and bewildered all yesterday – WOUNDED in fact that the Old Girls should (I now see) dislike and distrust me; as they must if they think I'd take advantage of them ... Quelle betise! Please tell them we are <u>broke</u> [but] we'll pay up ...

I'm also much relieved, having begun my novel – new version. It must be funny and invented. I knew that. But I didn't see how. Now I've found the approach, torn up the pages I read you and written a very funny and original first page ... I mean to finish it in 12 weeks. Above all, I am enjoying writing it – in this new style. It is a STORY ...

My book is a tribute to your heroism ... Best wishes for a happy weekend with Toby, and give him lots of love ...

Thornworthy – 15.6.57

Got home at 2.30 this morning to find all the stoves out and your letter about the rent etc. Stoves soon lit and have slept sound– lessly – I hope – six hours. Toby gone off to the lake ... and we are going to swim this afternoon and tomorrow. The weather is broiling hot ...

There is nothing fundamental to worry about. I told Dick [Dick Waller, their landlady's nephew] what you did not, that <u>a.</u> To let this house at all it has to be done up and have money spent on it and <u>b.</u> That although it has been on all the agents' books for a year there has never been a nibble. I also said that Hughes was a bugbear and Mrs Hughes indispensable to his aunt and mother but not to <u>us</u>, so he will have registered <u>that</u> point ...

A good day at Bryanston [for Toby's school speech day]. *The Lark* <u>transformed</u> by Christopher Fry was very very good.* The Platts-Mills† in good form and we supper picnicked with the Sternsteds by the river first. Were kept awake by police pickets looking for the escaped prisoners‡ all the way home armed with photographs of two nice young men 'in prison overalls'. I had seen them thumbing a lift, in other clothes, on my way up to Bryanston but said nothing ...

Thornworthy – 15.6.57

... Very nice letter from the Bismarck mother, the boy isn't coming but coming next year with a sister, and a very nice letter indeed from Monsieur Hanhart (who telegraphed) who says thanks for trying to put him off, but he and the boy are determined he shall come! So I now have the right number of little dears – seven – one replaces another ... Two are paying eight guineas and all the rest ten. As they are all French or Belgian except Beine Schacht** I expect Roger and Toby will improve their French.

Toby is displaying great charm and beauty, good manners and thoughtfulness – *pour que ca dur*!

... Yesterday was very tiring but very enjoyable. John P-M said, 'We are thinking of moving out of London because of the

---

* A play by Jean Anouilh translated and adapted by Fry in 1955.

† John Platts-Mills QC had been a friend of Mary's and a great influence over her before the war. His son, Joe, was also at Bryanston.

‡ Thornworthy was within audible distance of the siren used by Dartmoor Prison when prisoners escaped. Mary used to leave the house unlocked with a cold meal on the kitchen table and a change of clothes on the washing line.

** Biene was the daughter of Dr Hjalmar Schacht.

cost of living.' 'To Moscow I suppose.' 'To Sussex,' pursing his lips. (Joey is being sent to Moscow with a youth party for 3 weeks of the hols.) ...

London NW8 – 16.6.57: Trinity Sunday

... I have been to mass and slept and slept! Driven mad by the noise I have decided to move to Glyn's slum on Thursday morning (40 Warwick Avenue W9) which I went to see yesterday. It is squalid but quiet. (Alwyn is engaged to an artist who draws on TV Children's Hour.) So that is that. At least I shall be able to sleep and work.

I saw Nancy yesterday, too. She is fed up with her job, is 49, finds life meaningless, and Susan Hibbert told her she had spiritual possibilities. Susan also wisely said that she had replaced God by 'Jack', who has now got his divorce ... but certainly won't marry Nancy. That of course is the core. She needs turning inside out. I told her firmly <u>a.</u> not to think of giving up her job <u>b.</u> to become a Catholic. She is not at all drawn to the sort of church-going she was brought up to. I rang Mangan today, and she will ring him up tomorrow. I think this may be a very good thing indeed (or a failure). She admitted having grown or turned away from us, and 'as soon as she heard we'd become Catholics felt she'd come home to us again'.

Mass was in the most hideous church I've ever seen, which made people look like Belsen warders and wardresses. Very elaborate and hideous. * Nevertheless, as moving in its essentials as ever, and I lit a candle each for you and Billy.*

I am just recovering from having my Dublin Review article returned (in proof) yesterday as unintelligible. The best thing I've ever done! Am I a genius after all? It is a blow and perhaps I am partly to blame ...

---

* Church of Our Lady, St John's Wood.

The Times *people are very nice to me, send me away early,*
say I am 'doing all right'.
I <u>*can't*</u> *wake up. Blazing sun right in this window.*
All my love,
Eric

Thornworthy − 17.6.57

Boiling hot here. We fried like bacon all day yesterday at Tarn
Teign. Toby goes back tomorrow teatime ... [He] and I are brown
as can be − between swims Toby caught a lovely trout in the river
and lots of little ones which were replaced in the water. He is very
well but <u>lost</u> as he has the abroad bug, wants to go to Italy, Austria,
France etc. Good, but I'm glad I have my Bill. Don't forget
Thursday is Corpus Christi [a holy day of obligation when Catholics
were required to go to mass]. I shall be going in the evening to
Okehampton ...

London NW8 − 17.6.57

Dearest Owl,
    ... I am feeling irresponsible and carefree, as it is QUITE
impossible to work here. Traffic roars, sun beats in, and the old
lady of 75 below, of Czech origin, plays the same twiddly piece
from 10 to 1 every morning.

    So I am sure my decision to live in a QUIET slum is right,
and I am looking forward to being alone in a large, dreary room
... I shall dust the room, and make my own breakfast and bed.
Glyn will be there for company. He is, unconsciously, very funny
indeed. He is so glad Alwyn's fiancé is British − and not some
ghastly central European. *

---

* Alwen Hughes, Glyn's daughter, married her 'British' fiancé Rolf Harris in
  March 1958.

Mangan was spare in greetings, but I daresay it's all he can do to get to the telephone ... I have become quite reliable at The Times and was entrusted with the 'lead' story – the weather, all over Europe! As you see, my ambitions are modest. I feel as if I had suddenly become sane. I feel empty.

I had better do some work.

I am reading Jane Austen, who is even more detestable than I imagined. The English ideal; class-conscious, money-conscious, sexless and Refined.

I will say that for the Catholics I saw yesterday, they all looked like murderers.

No drinks, no women ... no cigarettes and damned little company! It's alright if I work, and I like London in summer ...

Thornworthy – 18.6.57

Not Owl please! My love,

I am glad you are not feeling too hot ... Quiet is more important than anything. Jolly unquiet here this morning with a swarm of bloody bees moving into the top attic, Hughes thundering about in a veil and Mrs W. and I replacing baby swallows in their nests while the coalmen bring the anthracite [smokeless coal]. Boaty [Toby], who has always shown grown up tendencies, has gone off to the lake to fish. He goes from Exeter this afternoon. Olive Hepburn* now has cancer of the liver and will die. Nothing to be done. Sennan is the nearest and best beach ... Boskenna very rocky and anyway we can't go there anymore.†

If Father Mangan sounds terse on the telephone it is because he has a phobia about the doorman listening to his conversation. If this letter reads cross, which I see it does, it is that Hughes is

---

* An acquaintance, and resident at Easton Court.

† Betty Paynter, who had been ruined by her second marriage to a dishonest solicitor called Paul Hill, was forced to sell Boskenna in March 1957 to pay off her husband's debts.

driving me mad. 'Are you there, madam?' every minute. 'Have you got a torch?' 'I've fallen through the ceiling.' 'You can't alter bees' minds.' Whatever next? ...

That blasted old Schacht has not yet told me when his child is coming so I have refused fifteen children now for her. Thora says the Hohenzollern is the future Kaiser and that the family 'keep very dark' and 'nobody knows them'. I have heard no more anyway and am full up ...

Everyone grumbling here at the lovely lovely weather ...

If we can shove Nancy over the brink Billy will have one Catholic godparent as I told her ...

London NW8 – 18.6.57

11am – In the traffic

Dearest Pol,

I am less enervated this morning ... Clang go the milk bottles, bang goes the bus, crash go the gears; but I think my novel may be quite funny.

Before me is your letter. You must be delectably brown, so prepare yourself for mortal sin. Which shall not prevent me from taking communion tomorrow. I am quite clear about this. Take it or leave it. Let us enjoy life ...

The novel is about les English as seen by a Frenchman ... It is about how love grows without being logically defined or even consistent. It is about the insanity of Common Sense and the idiocy of trying to defeat it, by reaching out for the Absolute. All this, quite simple in the classical manner of the English comedy. (Much as she annoys, Emma entertains me. Real Woman's Mag stuff. It holds the reader because it tells the story day by day. That is what I am trying to do.) ...

Following a visit to Cornwall with Mary, Eric moved in with Glyn Hughes.

Thornworthy – 19.6.57

... I am being pressed by some bill collector from Peter Jones and have passed the whole baby to Rutherford and told him to give them a brisk telephone talk. They menace proceedings within five days ...

Saw Toby off last night and then visited Carolyn [Cobb] who is lending me blankets on the way home. She looks awful. Norman has rejuvenated – obviously sees his freedom not far off – Miss Hepburn bright yellow and calm and courageous ...

There was a thunderstorm brewing. Got home just in time to shut the doors and windows for the storm which raged for hours. The dogs whined and hid under the counterpane, wouldn't be left alone. The telephone emitted sparks and the house literally shook. It went on for four hours in the darkness of death. So what with the dogs and the telephone which when not sparkling tinkled I didn't sleep much ...

Thornworthy – 25.6.57

... At Torquay for confession and fished a very jolly fat priest out of the presbytery, egged on by a very deaf old woman so that my needs were shouted all over the hideous church. You must have been dreadfully unlucky with that Frenchman. Mine today said, 'Oh well, my child, 5 Hail Marys and keep away from the man.' So I said 'Indeed I will <u>not</u>' and explained the situation. So he said, 'Well, well. Brother and sister I suppose. No children and keep on trying.' 'Indeed we <u>have</u> a child,' I said, 'and a very lovely one too!

A Catholic.' 'Well indeed now, how very interesting it is. You come down off the moor at any time and ring the bell and we'll be here to help you!' And I was bustled out of the church on a wave of well-wishing and blessings. There are no end of surprises ...

Thornworthy – 26.6.57

... The result of my asperity to Hughes was that he rushed at me this morning and expressed great pleasure in working for me. It's poor Dot [his wife] who drives him madder. Got my first cheque for the first three weeks of the timid Belgian boy's visit. Very handy. £31–10-0d.

I have house-maided all day and am now going to have an enormous high tea and so to bed even earlier than usual ...

Had to write lengthily to Carol of course as he has sent no pocket money and not written this term nor to Roger ...

40 Warwick Avenue, London W9 – 28.6.57

My Pol,

Thanks for letter and laundry. I feel very loving. I think I have almost become normal – capable of love ...

It's hot, but my room is shady. Great schemes with Glyn for doing our own laundry and mending. He's going to iron! ...

I am doomed to Lisson Grove, the Catholic Belsen; which is, again, just round the corner here. They are, however, most efficient and have masses of confessions and Masses. I adore your account of the Irish comforter you found at Torquay ...

I get a good breakfast round the corner (Germans or Austrians) between here and the church.

I really think I can do this book in the next 3 months ...

I lunch with Nat Micklem on Wednesday, and (through him) I am invited to a Liberal social at the House of Commons on

9th for tea! I shall go, because I want to meet Grimond, who is now head of the Party (Nat is chairman) and who married Laura Bonham-Carter. No other social life. I haven't even sent out my address cards. No time ... The Times people are very nice ...

———

With this letter Eric enclosed a clipping from the Star, *a London evening newspaper, concerning the case of a young woman who had been detained for three years in Rampton State Mental Institution as a 'mental defective'. An independent doctor commissioned by the* Star *to report on her state of health had decided that she was not mentally defective and that she should never have been detained in Rampton. The National Council for Civil Liberties was taking her case to appeal before a Ministry of Health tribunal. This was the continuation of the 'Jacko case' that Mary had initiated two years earlier when living at Broughton. Jacko, a fifteen-year-old village boy from Broughton, a playmate of Toby's, had been confined to a mental hospital after stealing two pairs of socks from a washing line. With the aid of John Platts-Mills, Mary had started a successful campaign to get Jacko released. According to the newspaper report as many as 20,000 sane people were thought to be confined to mental hospitals under the 1927 Mental Deficiency Act.*

———

Thornworthy – 28.6.57

My Darling,

Will you send me your telephone number in case of need? I haven't got it.

I have nearly got the house ready for *les jeunes* who arrive Monday. <u>Three</u> of them, Germaine's grandson among them ...

Sonya [Paynter] has not turned up or rung up. She would be a great help to me if she came as that ceaseless flow of chatter would make a good start. I don't want her rung up. If she comes it must be under her own volition.

I have read a really funny novel by Margery Sharp called *The Loving Eye* ...

I have booked rooms for little Willie's ménage, if they come, at Easton Court. I expect Carolyn, who loathes Germans, will keep to her bed but Norman, who was drunk, was irresponsibly welcoming. I made specially good terms, for the Germans <u>not</u> for Norman ...

Your socks, sleeping pills and handkerchiefs will come up in relays. I worry about your discomforts ...

Later

Ted Kavanagh isn't dead.* He is coming to stay on December 4th. It is bubbling hot up here ... Write when you can for your letters sustain me.

M.

Thornworthy – 29.6.57

I am glad you are keeping up with Nat Micklem. Thank God you can get breakfast round the corner, it is a load off my mind ...

Sorry to miss Charlie. Ted Kavanagh doesn't seem very fond of him, referring to 'his misguided missiles at us (the BBC) from the United States' ...

Another letter from the Hohenzollern. I can read that it is friendly and that they are next year coming, nothing else ...

Thornworthy – 30.6.57

I went to mass in the village. Get hearty greetings now but don't know their names ... Was slightly surprised this morning when

* Ted Kavanagh was a celebrated radio scriptwriter. He died in September 1958.

the lady in the long black mantilla, who keeps the dotty man quiet, said she was prepared to tell fortunes and had done so at some other Bazaar. I expressed mild surprise and she said 'Yes I know, but it was quite alright because I confessed afterwards' ...

The girl from the pub who has started this ghastly revel ... says that when Father Millerick announced the bazaar last Sunday (when we were in Cornwall) everyone 'rushed for the door as though stung by bees' ...

I am going to bed very early *mit* no alarm – my last for a long time ...

If you hear of a good job for Thora in the autumn she speaks French, English and Deutsch and has le shorthand and typing and English men like her. She wrote a delighted description of a party at Luneberg [*sic*] given by the 8th Hussars who convulsed her by their descriptions of how bad they were at everything. She had just [e]merged from a German horse show where 'the will to win' had nearly killed her ...

Warwick Avenue, W9 – 1.7.57

... Today I got up by mistake at 7am ... [I] did two hours work and went out to see Olivier and Monroe* and had a snack at Lyons' and now I'm back here for more work ... This is my free day and I'm enjoying it ...

My church is too awful. (I confessed at Spanish Place but went again to Mass with Communion at the Lisson Grove Palais des Horreurs.) ... I can take a bus to near St James's, Spanish Place, which is old, beautiful, fashionable and has Mozart. I'll report next Sunday. (It also has Harman Grisewood.†) ...

---

* *The Prince and the Showgirl*, a romantic comedy starring Laurence Olivier and Marilyn Monroe, had just been released.

† Harman Grisewood, Catholic actor, prominent radio broadcaster and novelist.

I've read Jane Austen's Emma *and Max's* [Max Beerbohm]
Seven Men; confirming my view that the English are heartless,
snobbish and prudently-realist: (not say, materialist). I doubt
those throbbing bosoms, alleged by you to accompany the stiff
lip. But the heartless prose makes for good art, in light comedy,
and I know what I am about. The light, English novel ... heartily
infused with French misunderstanding (and intellectualism). That
is __my__ *comedy!*

Everything depends on how it goes. If I can't do the bulk of
it in three months, ought I to explore the Times *and other jobs?*
I propose to see Douglas Woodruff who is wise without being
discouraging, and worldly without being crude ...

The film was the Folies bergères *mixture* à l'anglaise – *King*
George V's Coronation ... laced with bosoms and buttocks.
Real showmanship. I enjoyed it. It is quite, quite awful. And
pansy.

Thornworthy – 2.7.57

... They are all arrived. Michel Cattier very nice, good manners.
Miss Fiertag exquisitely pretty, Jewish I think, also lovely manners.
Germaine's grandson seven feet high and a clown, also lovely
manners ...

━━━

Mary, who had never taken a school exam in her life – though
she did once follow a course on politics at the LSE – now prepared
to transform herself into a language teacher. Her first students
came from Germany, Belgium and France. Both teacher and
pupils found themselves facing a steep learning curve.

━━━

Thornworthy – 3.7.57

... Kleine Miss Schacht is arriving next Tuesday which will even up the sexes as the boys gang up together and leave Gisele Fiertag out. Also I hope for Sonya on Monday ...

I think there is a class difference between les boys and la Fiertag who is jewish, gentle and half German and has an enormous behind ...

It is infra dig to wash up in Belgium but I am altering <u>that.</u> Also they lay the table. The situation until they become less shy, or Sonya and Biene Schacht arrive, is that unless I speak French we might as well be Trappists! ...

True chased a sheep last night and Wonnacott to whom I resorted said calmly 'It doesn't hurt them. Nell did it for years and does still.' ...

I wish we were together but at least some of the bills are getting paid ...

Michel Cattier made a face of enlightened astonishment when after I had said there had been too much bombing of Germany and he had said 'Well they began it' I taught him his first English proverb, 'Two wrongs do not make a right' ...

Thornworthy – 4.7.57

... There is a possible companion for Nick for the autumn arriving by way of Christina – half-Polish half-Swiss, the nephew of her beloved doctor. He has an Armenian millionaire step-father so I have suggested £15. That would make £25 a week till Christmas and you can finish your book ...

Harry [Siepmann] has written to say that he is coping with kleine Schacht. I forgot to tell you yesterday that Horace, as Harry calls him [Schacht], wrote that he was telling Harry to 'deliver her safely' into my hands. Little does he know that it's three hours in the train and Harry is just going to pop her in and leave her!

I have lost my engagement books so all the arrivals and departures will be surprises. One boy who was coming for July and August has 'ratted' *un examen* so is leaving on the 31st. In fact all this lot have ratted and are busily reading Stendhal and Rousseau instead of English. 'Now don't you start Madam,' exclaimed Mrs Wonnacott when I shouted a command in French – as if it were a disease! ...

Authors' Club – 5.7.57

Darling,

I am relieved to hear the first news of les enfants ... *Don't talk politics! You can be startling, but it may sound very differently by letter: without your charm and aplomb to relieve it ...*

It might be delightful if the little Schacht and the little Jewess get together (and relieve each other's timidity!) Anyway, I am sure you do marvels, without any advice from me ...

At LAST, I've found what I wanted. Just across the bridge from The Times *is Clapham Common – which I have always fancied. I went there this morning, having reached breaking point. I have taken a nice attic room in a clean Guest House – the room is quiet, I'll have my table, my own ... bath ... because no one else is on the attic floor. Good breakfast, and room done daily by resident maid. HURRAY. It is 12/6d a night [62.5p]; not bad. The Common is lovely, with a round pond. Beautiful houses abound, and teddy boys and molls. A pauper's lunch is served at a new restaurant, run by a writer (woman) and painter (husband) who have just 'given up'. I've just had lunch there. She is a bore, but was published by Faber; and oddly enough her last book, refused all round, is called* To Hell With Love *and is said to be 'too unpleasant' ...*

At the restaurant I had delicious rice and egg salad, 2/6 [12.5p]. The danger is too much conversation ... She comes from Bideford, is related by marriage to Asquiths, knew Peter Quennell and all the literati ...

I was pretty desolate yesterday, but really my slum is too awful. Poor old Glyn! I am giving a week's notice ...

I brought D. Woodruff yesterday to lunch at this club with Nat Micklem. Most interesting and delightful – mutual suspicions, mutual goodness, much erudition. Nat (a non-Conformist) emerged as intellectually 2nd rate as compared with Woodruff: who had seen the Pope, but not Wyszynski* who was closely watched by the communists but (I think) messages were exchanged ...

Thornworthy – 5.7.57

... Boiling hot here. Germaine's grandson is gigantic, lazy and amiable, rather stupid but very nice. The little girl is half-Jewish (papa). She was hidden in the Ardennes during the war while her father was in a concentration camp and her mother, not Jewish, worked away at hiding and saving Jews. I am gaining her confidence. She is agonizingly shy. Michel Cattier has a vast inferiority complex which takes the form 'that women are only good for cooking and keeping house. There has never been a woman in the world who could do anything intellectual.' He has just failed his English exams but refuses English lessons here.

I had a brain wave today and drove them all to Torquay and abandoned the boys, who were too un-enterprising to take their bathing drawers, and have told them to find their way home <u>separately</u>. Michel has 'I don't speak English' written on a piece of paper and both have the address and telephone number. I wonder what will occur?

Gisele and I, who both have the curse and can't swim, drove agreeably home across the moors chatting – in French – all the way. I shall think up some other tricks as I go ...

---

* Cardinal Stefan Wyszynski, primate of Poland and leader of national opposition to brutal Communist rule, released from 3 years' imprisonment and house arrest in October 1956.

I hope nothing stops Sonya coming as she will bowl them over like ninepins!

Keep my letters. I want to work up a talk [for BBC radio] on foreign guests. The boys look absolutely clean but neither has washed once!

M.

Thornworthy − 6.7.57

How glad I am that you have found other rooms ... On Clapham Common there is a house called Wren House in which lives Betty Stucley that was (now I don't know who) from Bideford. She is nice, fat, was at the London School of Economics with me. Go and see her do. Writes on Boswell ...

The risk of leaving the boys at Torquay worked. Yves arrived home in no time, having got a lift from Father Millerick. Michel being shy and farouche took hours. I have now tamed <u>him</u> ... He has offered to lend me his fishing rod and we have had a long heart to heart in midlake ...

I too get into despair! They don't talk, don't eat, hang about, then suddenly are gay, play tennis, go and work for the exams they have all failed − it's all ghastly adolescence. Longing for Sonya ...

Politics are excellent. Electric shock. Just what they need.

M.

Thornworthy − 7.7.57

Sonya tomorrow I <u>hope</u>. Betty telephoned with her usual adder's tongue yesterday evening and said you had been there and a lot of nauseous things about Sonya. My troop are in hand and I would have no anxieties except that not an English word is spoken and I am rapidly forgetting it myself ...

I am teaching Michel backgammon ... and also how to make beds and Yves lays the table. Giselle dries while I wash up ... Yves follows me about like some colossal puppy when he is hungry. He is about six foot four so I cannot bring myself to ask him whether he is wearing his corset ...

They all listen to the French radio all the time ... Three is a bad number. Never mind by Tuesday it will be six ...

I love you, *du courage!* As we now say at Thornworthy ...
M.

Authors' Club, SW1 – 8.7.57

... The woman who runs the restaurant is obviously Betty Stucley. She told me about Bideford and about Boswell. I am going to move on Wednesday morning ... 'Madam' Wolska [land-lady at Warwick Avenue] *is furious, and I don't like that. So I washed my own laundry this morning ...*

Sonya is due, isn't she? She'll turn up and help a lot ... Betty says Sonya is sex-mad. This will annoy you, but I say it only in case of accidents. Are you to have FIVE tomorrow? You can't!? ...

Thornworthy – 9.7.57

Six now! ... and *kleine* Schacht (who is enormous) is <u>splendid</u>. Thierry also very jolly.

The mystery of why '*le papa de Thierry*' brought [him] '*en personne*' was explained by the fact that he found my letter so funny that he had to come and see for himself. Not very flattering! ... He is a fat little mushroom of a man who is going to send all his friends' children here ...

I am busy from dawn to dusk as it's all so unexpected. If we had not so many bills I would make a good profit ...

Sonya is not sex mad at all. Betty would like her to be what she was herself. Sonya is very natural and madly gay and a great help and simply loathes Betty …

80 South Side, Clapham Common, SW4 – 11.7.57

… Alles in ordnung! … Here I am at a magnificent table, after a trot on the Common. I was called by a maid, had a splendid breakfast (egg and bacon), and my room was done and speckless by the time I wanted to work … This seems like Paradise. The fact that the maid is obviously out of the loony-bin (but nice, she tells me about the bin), that I can hardly fit into the tiny bath in which the geyser drips on me, and that this is an ordinary boarding house – none of this matters …

I had an exceedingly pleasant talk with Iverach Macdonald, the Foreign Editor, who was civil and thought he had met me abroad and was 'delighted to meet me again' and yes, will certainly 'bear in mind' the possibility of trips. We see eye to eye on NEWS not handouts; he even, as Diplomatic Correspondent, refused to attend Press Conferences. There is quite a chance; and it is more likely to be (French) North Africa than anywhere else …

So I am treated as a recognized person, and not – as I had begun to fear – a 'sub' who had sunk into obscurity …

Nice, quiet supper with Nancy. All about sex and religion, I need hardly say. The latest is that as she may want to marry 'Jack' (who, though divorced, shows no signs of marrying her) she had better go slow on Catholicism … She longs to see you, and is really very good though neurotic and pitiable …

Thornworthy – 11.7.57

My Love,

I have taken refuge in your room to write letters …

Biene Schacht is an enormous darling armed with a dictionary and understands a lot already. Sonya is a tremendous help.

Michel spends his life by the lake having silences with Comrade Potter. Thierry is very French and jolly. They are all alright. Impossible to tell now what profit I shall make with them all having parents who chop and change the dates but gradually I am paying bills which is a lot and the tax [rebate] will pay for the rates and rent ...

I have never worked so hard in my life but it's alright. I am making them work too ...

Are you alright? What is the Newsroom like? Good that you are having a repeat in August ...

Being submerged in a bunch of adolescents is very queer indeed! Each one different, each one needing different treatment. It's like having six children all the same age.

I love you,

M.

Thornworthy – 12.7.57

... Mr Langton Lopton comes twice a week to give lessons and is amazed and amused at what he finds. Tried to teach them from Churchill's war memoirs this morning, but caught on sharp when I said <u>No</u>, something Neutral!

They live on chocolate, tea and tomatoes. Very strange. Biene is ably fixed up with a dictionary the size of a pea. She is at <u>least</u> twice my size and has a half-sister of fifty-four ...

I am writing this under the drier in the village hairdresser ... I try to spend a little time alone with each every day – and especially the ones worth cultivating, i.e. the <u>intelligent</u> ones ...

I get up at 7.30 and have the house to myself, *le petit dejeuner* at nine and I get to bed when I can. It's like the War only one isn't terrified. Sonya with all her slovenly faults is <u>splendid</u>. Betty rang up last night to ask whether she was being untidy, sexy etc. I said 'Not at all and my advice to you is to <u>shut up</u> and leave her alone' ...

Biene is Lutheran and will have to go to church with Lady Waller! ...

Glad *The Times* are nice, what a difference it makes.

Your loving M.

Thornworthy – 13.7.57

... My English is becoming practically unintelligible I notice. Teaching five children of the rich to wash up and make their beds is *quelque chose*! ...

The boys do their best. I should like to have seen more of Thierry's papa, obviously a terrific collaborationist in the war. '*Mon appartement, je l'ai emprunté à un grand seigneur Allemand, qui a laissé tout en ordre.*' ...

The Belgian woman hater only likes Sonya and me because he thinks we are both mad. Sonya hit Yves over the head with a chess board which gave pleasure and is teaching him to ride ...

Thornworthy – 14.7.57

... Exhausted I went to bed, only to hear sudden shrieks, cries, thumps and a broken ashtray. Sonya losing her temper with Yves who had hidden her shoes or something equally infantile ...

White with rage I sprang out of bed, put on my pretty pink dressing gown (which I afterwards discovered to be transparent) and made a silent entry, hissing 'I don't care who is to blame, what it is about, clear up the mess and all go to bed'. Wonderful effect! I've never seen sheer terror on so many faces before, Sonya's in particular. 'People do not behave like this in my house,' I added illogically and disappeared. Positively intoxicating as they are all twice my size. *La discipline, hein?* ...

Clapham Common – 15.7.57

My darling and disapproving wife,

I missed you badly this weekend ... I have been worrying as I don't get on with my book and the winter depends on my finishing it ...

There is a Regency church with a negro in stained glass (Wilberforce had some local connections) and I am quite comfortable though lonely. The loony maid, as I foretold to a day, bunked yesterday ...

I shall go mad unless I work, which is the only way to regain my nerve ...

Thornworthy – 16.7.57

Sweet love,

Do not lose your nerve. Leave the first chapter unwritten and go on from there ... The paralysis of not being able to start is most ordinary ...

My adolescents are losing their first gloss ... Thierry, the 'smart' little French boy, has chummed up with Yves and picks up girls in buses. Michel is a gentleman and behaves as such except that <u>a</u>. he never washes and <u>b</u>. wears his gum boots indoors. Sonya is a great help in the house, lays the table etc., but of course as she has never been given any upbringing since the age of nine, does not know how to behave ...

The object of her chase is Michel and this takes the form of a lot of squawking, not unnatural but boring. I have condemned squawking. Michel is fortunately too young and too well-brought up for there to be any danger. After being particularly irritating, talking foul French instead of English, which she is here to do, for two days she took charge of the house [and] left the kitchen in a filthy mess ... At breakfast Michel announced that he and

223

Sonya were riding this morning and Biene this afternoon. Who, I asked, had arranged this? Sonya. And since when does Sonya run this house? Silence. 'Either you all three ride together or not at all.' Sonya sulked. Then Thierry arrived for breakfast. 'Does anyone want any bread?' 'No, but I should like you to say good-morning to your hostess and shake hands.'

Tomorrow Michel is being sent off with Cripps [a local poacher] until 1am and to spend the night with him ... Michel is thrilled! After that Sonya will leave I think. I am dreadfully sorry for her but ... I am very worried that she will turn into another Betty or a Newton and see no means of stopping it. It is perfectly natural that at sixteen she should want men but Betty has let her loose in night clubs, dumped her anywhere, and she hasn't an inkling of how to behave. She can be absolutely wonderful, then she gets excited and becomes a moll ... The result is that I have to sit up until they go to bed ... My *pensionnaires* must be guarded!

It is very amusing, particularly now that they know I have a bad temper when necessary. Very necessary with these six footers! ...

Thornworthy − 17.7.57

... Last night was very peaceful as Michel spent the night fishing with Cripps and only returned this morning after having a lovely time and being taught a lot of poacher's tricks. Sonya, after sulks, came sweetly beaming and apologised and says I am please to tell her as nobody else ever does ...

I <u>think</u> Michel is going to have a bath. I <u>think</u> so. Next to get washed is Thierry and to hell with his shaving. The girl picked up on the bus has disappeared very neatly. '*Pas d'histoires dans mon village, hein?*'

I have written to Malcolm Muggeridge* asking him to return my article thrust into his pocket and out of his mind ...

* Editor of *Punch* at the time.

Clapham Common– 18.7.57

... *Yesterday was my day off. Awful. I couldn't work. I took buses, any bus. I saw* <u>two</u> *movies. A gloom had begun, the night before, when I saw the photograph on the front page of my Standard of the body of a woman who had thrown herself out of the fifth floor of the Strand Palace. Then I read it was John Davenport's wife.* I don't recognise evil when I see it. I am afraid Betty is evil. I don't blame him so much as people like Betty who egged him on and were so foully cruel to and about her. Am I being morbid? Anyway it gives much to think about. Sonya is good at heart, but the influences are worse than silly – evil. I am now sorry I relented as far as I did towards Betty. Yet she was your friend, and* <u>we</u> *are far from perfect! It is a puzzle ... It was a shock ...*

Fed up with yesterday's desperation, I have mailed a dozen address cards – to your real friends only ... I lunch tomorrow in Hampstead chez the 'Mossbachers' (alias Gwenda David: the reader, who wrote).† They are professionals ... and they may have useful advice about e.g. my two plays. NOT about translations where, like Antonia White, rivalry enters. What a life! Mossbacher sounds nice. I may see Tony [Antonia White], at last ...

I am lunching with Nat to meet the MP who runs liberal publications ... I may propose something like The Week‡ *– run from Devonshire?!*

Too many irons in the fire. I've hardly written two thousand words. Your wise, brave words are a real help ...

---

* Davenport was a close friend of Dylan Thomas and a prominent literary journalist and critic. He weighed nineteen stone and was very proud of his physical strength.

† Gwenda David, influential publishers' scout and reader, translator, friend of Iris Murdoch, Muriel Spark, Graham Greene, Elizabeth Jane Howard, Rebecca West, etc. Married Eric Mosbacher, translator, lived in Hampstead where she entertained.

‡ *The Week* was a political newsletter edited and written by Claud Cockburn in the 1930's. (See footnote on p. 108.)

Thornworthy – 18.7.57

... Michel is having a bath. Grand triumph! Thierry writes on p.c.'s, which he gives me to post, that he has some nice *copains* and the food is not bad for England. Yves writes, also on postcards, that 'there is an odd girl called Sonya staying'.

No more.

I packed her off to Betty today. For days she has been working up towards two things, a flirt with Michel who is going to be very attractive – more lipstick, more squawks, more scent, more cigarettes, and he not responding and the other boys bored ...

Then a blistering, disgusting scene made by her on the telephone to Betty. For days she had not written to Betty until I forced her to. Then two mangled lines and later a telegram to ring up urgently. When Betty did ring up yesterday evening, in an agreeable friendly mood, Sonya immediately began to shriek, stamp her foot and be unbearably rude. I removed her from the telephone, told Betty I would put her on the train today and then told Sonya just exactly what I think of her. She tried to make me a scene but it did not work luckily, and after four hours appalling sulks which upset (or if it had not been for Giselle's intuition and Biene's niceness would have upset) my whole apple cart she came and apologised and told me she had never been so frightened in her life 'as by you Mary of all people'.

Poor child. It is all Betty's fault. Sonya wants to be respectable and have a background and marry and have children. Betty would like her to be bohemian. Since no one has taught Sonya Anything since she was nine her manner of setting about being respectable is quite terrifyingly like Betty's. Since she is very stupid, I told her, that she is stupid, that she is behaving like some Teddy boy's moll and that no respectable person will want to have anything to do with her as she is. I love her, so I was able after my initial anger to 'tell her what' lovingly.

Her position is very bad and Betty is a dreadful mother but the child is a fool. I suppose it's her age but she does dangerous things like trying to get Roger to invite her to the Sandhurst ball meaning to meet future guardsmen through him and leave him flat, and accepting invitations from Tom [Paynter, Sonya's cousin] who puts himself out for her then telephoning that she has found somewhere more amusing to go. The chasing of the gentleman is quite naturally done by a child of her age, but she does it unsubtly like the fourteen year old's who hang around American bases.

Anyway I think a little penetrated her thick head and she <u>can</u> be perfectly sweet, gay and everything else but while this 'phrase', as Alice calls it, lasts and I am having all these children here I cannot have her. Later and nearly alone, but not now ...

All my love,
M.

PS Naturally, as I feel like the ham in the sandwich, not a word of Sonya to anybody.

Authors' Club – 19.7.57

... Horrifying lunch with Gwenda David, an old grey trout who wanted once to be a rainbow. She had just been to the Davenport funeral – and was full of anti-Catholic (and other) blasphemies. Then John's daughter by his first wife, a hideous girl of 16, came in for coffee, blaspheming (she is Catholic-trained but in revolt) with stories of how drunk her father was, kissed the girls, and said he will marry again. L'enfer ...

Thornworthy – 19.7.57

... I too was horrified by John D's wife's suicide but proud that she is being given a Requiem mass.* If ever anyone was hounded

---

* A requiem Mass was not usually authorised in cases of suicide. Mary is blaming the suicide of Davenport's wife on the circle of friends revolving round the actor Robert Newton. They included Betty Paynter, and Pauline Gates, who had originally introduced Eric and Mary.

to death by Newtonia, she was. I last saw her in Peter Jones, a despairing terrified woman and thought to myself she would crack soon. Poor John D. will have remorse and I hope it leads to the A.A! It was never necessary for him to do what he did to her, it is never necessary to be <u>led</u> however easy. Damn all those bloody people who killed her. Betty no more than the others, she only 'opened' earlier than the pubs and had a free telephone.

A very nice peaceful day without Sonya ... I wrote a pretty tough note to Betty blaming her for what she sowed. No use being full of self-pity now, as she is, but she is a very unhappy woman.*

Sonya and I parted with all ties (for what they are worth) intact.†
Biene and Giselle have gone to Exeter to buy presents for their families before the bus strike starts. The boys have spent the day playing cards in French ... I am recovering from the shock of Sonya's scenes, which had to be seen to be believed, and <u>heard</u> too, and am taking pills for fibrositis which I have in my right shoulder, arm and neck. A curse.

It will be tremendous joy to see you and I have informed our real friends of your whereabouts. No point in being without me <u>and</u> hiding. You seem to get like that sometimes ... And let it flow, the book, stop bottling it up and riding on buses ...

I wrote a lovely letter to the German papa giving him some pretty hot references and saying that I for my part wish references, that I may possibly have room for his son and that if he comes I wish to be paid in advance and assume that he will behave as my own sons and other visitors do. Quite a lot of fun to be had out of this game.

It's quite wonderful how the Belgians <u>loathe</u> the French – *sales types, ligne Maginot* etc. The Germans seem to be almost popular

---

* After selling Boskenna, Betty Paynter moved to a small flat in Penzance – it was infested with mice, which she used to feed by hand. She separated from Paul Hill and took up with a much younger man who was an antiques dealer. The antiques dealer was subsequently shot dead by Paul Hill. Hill was tried for murder and acquitted by a Bodmin jury. He committed suicide in 1985.

† Sonya Paynter, who was sent home from Thornworthy in disgrace at the age 16, later became very close to Mary who looked on her as an adopted daughter.

by comparison! No destruction in Belgium and *grands seigneurs* in France. A lot of bitterness for '*le bombing par les Américains*' felt by both.

All my children do what I tell them. I love Biene. Michel will be a charmer. No longer wears gumboots in the house and has had a bath. I rather regretted the bath as I took positively hours cleaning it afterwards. Never mind, the other two boys are bathing tonight or else.

They are <u>all</u> except Giselle at least a head taller than me so I feel like those ferocious sergeants in the A.T.S. in cartoons.

Both dogs very well. True sleeps with Michel. I am sorry you won't meet him. He and all of them [have] come on tremendously by being treated as adults ...

We must get Billy back,* at first by degrees and then finally he can go to the Ruegg kindergarten. Do not worry. I am on top of my situation. I communicate every Sunday which helps tremendously and pray a lot. I also have faith in you and Billy and Roger and Toby ...

The boys say my French is coming on splendidly. '*Vous faites de grands progrès, Madame!*'

M.

Clapham Common – 20.7.57

My love,

Having confessed to theft of umbrella, lust, despair and missing mass twice (without saying that I had, for some reason, attended two funerals instead) I got the quickest and lightest sentence: 3 Hail Mary's. Now I can go to Communion tomorrow. Our church (St Mary's) seems quite old, and has a torrent of masses ... And it is just round the corner. I shall try to get to know a priest.

---

* Billy, aged three, had been sent to Penzance to spend the summer with Alice Grenfell, wartime nanny to Roger, Toby and Sonya.

Having got over the contrast with the slum, I need hardly say that I find life in this boarding-house dreary and depressing; the only cure is work and that I've hardly begun ...

No need for Alcoholics, Anonymous or Otherwise. The thing to do is pay all my wages into ... my overdraft account, leaving barely enough to live on (7/6d a day). Drastic, but it works!

This morning I had the story of Sonya. She is certainly best away from your pensionnaires, and Betty seems to have been justified, for once, in what she said! I cannot yet speak about the horrors of la vie bohème as lightly brushed against yesterday: the malice, godlessness, and crudeness (of 'Madame' Mosbacher – she deserves the title. Self-adopted by my late landlady) and the horrors, maybe exaggerated, of John Davenport's behaviour. Maybe God has shown me a slum and a slice of bohemia, to cure me for good ...

I think I lunch with H. and C. (Benita's one good joke)* on Tuesday. The foreign editor has seen my cuttings, and now we await the editor, who is holidaying in Nice. If I get trips, tant mieux; but they pay abominably. Also I'm afraid it is now a second rate paper. Did I tell you Haley[†] was once a telephone-short-hand-writer and married a typist? Vive le snobisme ...

I live in squalor. My failure is complete. These things must be changed ...

Oh dear, how I wish we had achieved security and were together ...

All my love,

Eric

---

* Benita Hume's nickname for Eric's older brothers, Harry and Charles.

[†] Sir William Haley, editor of *The Times*, contributed a column to his own paper under the name 'Oliver Edwards'.

Thornworthy – 20.7.57

As I have an acute attack of fibrositis ... all the children are being made to work. I made the two dirtiest boys bath last night <u>and</u> clean it afterwards ...

Thierry has picked up a grammar school girl and gone to tea with her mum '*pour jouer les disques*'. She speaks perfect BBC English and it is all *très comme il faut* – so far ...

How sad your lunch at Gwenda David's was so gruesome.* Stick to the beaten track of known friends. Thou shalt not judge but I cannot help feeling John Davenport might have protected his wife a little from the detractors and snubbers. One sharp word to Newtonia might have saved her life, not that it can have been an agreeable one. And the insidiousness of Newtonia is its strength. She is not the first to die of it. They flatter, the men pretend to befriend the wives and then watch the suicides. Very jolly.

I like Germaine's grandson who is foolish but well brought up. Biene Schacht who is not only sweet but intelligent, Michel Cattier and Giselle who has all the Jewish gentleness. Her father is Russian Jew her mother German. She and Biene have made friends. I think he probably keeps a shop. Thierry is one of the notable French bores and always knows best.

I shall be very glad when the boys [Roger and Toby] arrive and speak English. It is uphill work forcing them to repeat in English what has been said in French ...

You will only meet of this lot Biene and Giselle and I shall be in the process of breaking in two new French boys and a possible German. '*Fermez la porte s'il vous plait!* ...' Shades of Otto Siepmann ...

The bus strike limits activities and the rain is bloody but they appear happy enough. Cards, chess, darts etc ...

---

* Gwenda David later became a friend of Mary's. Eric's failure to cultivate an influential alliance meant that he missed yet another opportunity to develop his writing talent.

Thornworthy – 21.7.57

... The Germans are now telegraphing madly – Prince George of Hanover for a senior Salem boy the latest, so you may find the house full of Germans instead of the present French/Belgian population when you come ...

There is deep envy felt among them all for the English school system and they are British imperialists to the last child! Too comic for words. My horrid French child who shaves, but does not wash, is lost outside a town and walks twice a day to Chagford – returns as bright as a button and does, to be fair, what I tell him ...

Authors' Club – 21.7.57

... I am feeling a trifle more cheerful, having been rung up and asked to lunch by Rosemary Beddington ... (I refused sherry, and enjoyed a good, icy hock. Nothing after. I am NOT a drunkard, so please don't tell me I am.)

He [Jack Beddington] *drove me here in a gearless Rover; which made me worry very little about their £200 ... Funny stories about being called in as official valuer for objets d'art on which Bill Astor had lent your friend S.* [Simon] *Harcourt-Smith £6000. Value established £800. Embarrassment ...*

Thornworthy – 22.7.57

... Christmas candidate is arriving it appears on September 1st until Christmas, ten guineas a week and I think a bit more for tuition. You are to teach him. He does not sound a bit boring as he has been turned out of every school in Switzerland! He is half Polish, half Swiss and his mother writes delightfully ...

Do not tell H. or C. anything, both are treacherous ...

I shall be in your arms again very soon. Don't tell me like Tom Paynter did that I look tired. He got a very sharp answer!

I took Biene for a ride this afternoon. The moor was wet and beautiful. I rode Sunshine, she a pony which tried to make off with her but she remained aboard. Fitzrandolph [German friend] has written that he has told Schacht to send the other girl here too, so I replied he had better look <u>sharp</u> as Prince George is <u>persecuting</u> me on the telephone. This is an extraordinary whirligig. *Vive le snobbism.* Never again the Universal Aunts and their percentage! I must stop and get supper and push the boys into baths. Thierry smells awful. How do I get a nice winter talk on all this on the BBC?

Lady W. [Waller] got a sharpish retort from me in *plein village* this morning – something about the post. The village were delighted. Poor old thing, it comes of having those enormous English feet.

I love you ...

M.

Thornworthy – 23.7.57

Pebble's 11th Birthday

Last night the above mentioned <u>fiend</u> went off hunting quite alone and was eventually found by Biene who dragged him out of the forest and all the way home by the collar. By this time I had lost my voice shrieking and breath whistling ... Into the bath they went. The girls are delighted. Giselle washes seven pairs of knickers at a time. Biene also. A spectacle worth seeing! ...

When you come home you will find the dear geese everywhere as they have a food shortage, and adolescents everywhere except in your room and our bedroom ...

I have had no time to confess to my nasty thoughts and actions so take communion anyway and too tired for lust ... I

love every bit of you and I never said you were a drunkard! You
are <u>not</u> ...

Clapham Common – 24.7.57

*... My tuition fees are 10/- an hour, or £3.0.0. a week for a
lesson a day ... isn't that right? ...*

*To hell with the geese. I want to help with the adolescents.
Please assign me chores. I want you really to have some let-up,
and I have 4 days. E.g. I can do stoves, breakfasts and all
washing-up with the girls. <u>This is an order</u> ...*

*My work at The Times is very easy: practically non-existent,
and I talk too much in the canteen. Some find me funny, some
have begun to stiffen their lips. Who cares? ...*

*My point about the Catechism was that I know it points to some-
thing psychologically right when it says: don't rely on yourself ...
But (relics of protestantism – incidentally <u>Luther</u> invented Original
Sin, one of my favourite doctrines) I cannot think that anything but
will is effective – and my will fails. I suppose I don't believe enough
in God for him to help me?! I don't think I believe in anything at
all, except the difference between Good and Bad; and that is wholly
mysterious, which I call God. Sometimes I prefer Bad. As for Christ
and so on ... well, it <u>sounds</u> true. But are other religions untrue?*

*As regards failure, I am not so much a failure as forgotten.
Ryan* came up, meaning to be polite: 'I'm supposed to have
known of you ... the name meant nothing to me.' I thought my
name was infamous, which is a sort of fame. Nothing of the sort.
I sit in Clapham, in total obscurity. One feels it in a town. I am
of course depressed; but don't think I am hopeless ...*

*Nick means well. I am taking dinner off him tomorrow, chez
Stucley. I find him quite intolerable: may never see him again.
But one cannot refuse a gesture, at least I can't.*

---

* A colleague at *The Times.*

On Monday evening Charlie [Siepmann] *rang me up at* The Times. *Harry is ill and I was to lunch with him ... and Janey* [Mrs Charles Siepmann].*

I decided to accept nothing. I had them to lunch 'at my club's ladies annexe'† (alias Whitehall Court!) *and gave them cocktails (none for me) and lunch and a bottle of wine. This set me back a fortnight, but I think it was the right thing to do ...*

They have a suburban house and a farm in Vermont ... They were very jealous and I was thoroughly jealous, especially of [their son] *Jeremy's schooling for Harvard and musical brilliance. I MUST get into a position where Billy has a more cultured environment than we can offer him, in our isolation. We can stay at Chagford; but we must achieve a position, and freedom and travel ...*

Anyway, I am not devoured by self-pity, as I concluded, from some remarks, that Harry is. He has another bout of lung-trouble, but he has to live another 5 years till his Insurances mature, for which purpose he has monkey-gland injections.

I am both uncharitable and unChristian. And I am ashamed of my analysis of what I really want. What I really would like is <u>*Money, Success and Popularity*</u> *... Perhaps you are less attached to the world than me? Mangan says you are potentially a 'contemplative' which – for some reason – makes me very angry. I didn't marry a contemplative, but a buccaneer who seems to disappear whenever* The Saint *looms up. I must give you back your confidence, and you will be my Saint-Buccaneer ...*

Jack Beddington just rang up; lunch next Monday, which will be nice. I really like him ...

---

* After falling out with Lord Reith, Charles Siepmann had emigrated to the United States where he had married and enjoyed a successful business career.

† In the 1950s most London gentlemen's clubs did not admit ladies, but some had a dining annexe. Eric hoped to give his brother and sister-in-law the impression that the Authors' Club had a much grander dining room elsewhere.

Thornworthy – 24.7.57

My Darling,

... Appalling long telegram from Herr Muller in German to whom I wrote so rudely. The son is arriving August 1st. I am just back from Exeter where the girls 'wanted to look at the shops'. They were mostly shut but this did not seem to impair their pleasure! They are now playing tennis. Biene attired in very short shorts looking like a Valkyrie. Michel is now on Christian name terms with Potter [local farm worker] and calls him Sidney, and they fish together ...

Comrade Schacht has written to Biene to say he is arriving with Comrade Frau Schacht on August 25th to fetch her home. Either so appalled by Fitzrandolph's description of the charms of Thornworthy or the reverse, no one knows! He will discover his little daughter has learned to iron, wash up and make her bed, even if she has not learnt much English ...

Have you safely weathered your lunch with H. & C? Not long now to August 9th ...

Clapham Common – 25.7.57

... I'm off! It flows ... This is my free day and I've worked till 2pm and done 1500 words and I like my story ...

I've had my first brisk exchange at The Times – about starving the Germans. I cannot pipe down. Must I? No, not necessarily. But I had better lie low. I tease the idiots.

If I can only succeed in my work, Billy's situation and yours will automatically become normal. We are too isolated. I have isolated you. But I shall transform our lives. It is NOT too late, please God.

All this because I've done two and a half hours work. I do enjoy writing though, when once I start! ...

I expect my letter yesterday disgusted you ...

Thornworthy – 25.7.57

Your Tuesday's letter arrived today and saddened me. I <u>do</u> understand. Naturally <u>Will</u> is nothing (unless it turns you into a destroyer) without <u>God</u> ...

I am <u>enjoying</u> what I am doing because I am doing it well. I shall <u>not</u> stay in bed for breakfast as I like to get up but shall be deeply grateful for stoves, geese and above all conversation at meals as I am at the moment carrying all five and it's quite hard to do ...

Of course you believe enough in God for him to help you. I hope Billy won't grow up with the same ideas you had about your elders but be <u>himself</u>. It's as though I wanted to be the Clerk of the Drapers' Company when you tell me you are jealous of Charlie and Jack Houseman.* Pah! Sorry to be so furious ...

Living here at the moment is like expecting the Germans to invade in 1940, only this time the threats come by guttural telephone instead of the wireless and I reply sharply, 'Can he do housework?' It's frightfully funny ...

When you arrive I shall have Biene and Giselle ... two French boys quality yet unknown and one German ditto, being trained ...

We have *petit déjeuner* (no, not like cooked breakfasts), a hearty lunch, tea if they want it and a good supper. Tomatoes and chocolate biscuits are very popular and they spend all their money on sweets and don't have spots! Curious ...

Do not be angry with me, I cannot bear it.

M.

Clapham Common – 26.7.57

... Nick has offered me a bed! It would be far more convenient, and I thought of going there after coming to you as I can

---

* Mary's brother, Hugh Farmar, had been appointed Clerk to the Worshipful Company of Drapers, a wealthy and charitable City livery association, in 1952.

forward my interests and meet people (he lodges with Aidan Crawley, a famous TV News man) during September, to build up connections for freelancing from Devon ... and cultivate Panorama, Brains Trust etc. This is suburbia, but from Hertford Street one can 'drop in' on Margery Vosper, ABC TV etc. What do you think?

I must say I withdraw my nastiness (if not, altogether, my suspicions) about Nicky ... He is a mystery. He pronounces his <u>own</u> street Hurt-ford Street! What is this? ...

I shall be with you in a fortnight, and you <u>will</u> have breakfast in bed.

Amusing too about the Schachts ... I attribute much to your having charmed Fitz! You can tell him to send Biene again when I am there, and she shall learn English ...

I think of sending my Hitler play to Jack Haussmann [Houseman]; but none of them are eager to keep in touch with me, so my pride opposes ...

I need another suitcase; and where do I get the handle of yours mended? ...

I've read three Jane Austens, and quarrelled with a colleague on The Times.

All my love,
E.

Thornworthy – 26.7.57

<u>Friday early</u>

... I must have sounded so ungrateful in my letter yesterday, please forgive me. It is only that this is my show and since you decided to go to London ... it has been very much 'go it alone' ...

I could not possibly give up as then the whole thing would disintegrate and my authority be lost. As it is all's well and although you never believed in it I can and am doing it.

I believe in your talents but not in your envy. You are far too generous, too wide in your outlook. Ordinary people drive one to contemplation perhaps. That is what Mangan saw …

Thornworthy – 26.7.57

Your yesterday's letter and <u>Thank God</u> it flows! My spirits soared …

Smartie Pants [Thierry] has been trying to get off with Huey Hughes' young lady. Result, Huey Hughes on sentry go (looking rather formidable) in Chagford Square and *les pants* stays up here. <u>What</u> has occurred will be told me by the hairdressers who are in stitches of laughter.

Biene fortunately has another interest besides riding – painting. She is a most easy and amiable child, if anything so large can be a child …

If Toni [Antonia White] doesn't answer she is in a huddle trying to finish her book and having taken on three extra translations to allow her to do so.

I hope your gardening knowledge enables you to appreciate my joke about Malcolm [Muggeridge]. I do want the article back all the same and it certainly never came here!

Thornworthy – 27.7.57

… Thank goodness the book is started. It's up to you. I see no prospect of any work chez Nicky and it's extremely noisy also no difference between addresses. The one where you are is becoming chic and the one where he is is The Red Light.* Popping in as opposed to work seems to be the problem. Loneliness at 2 am or pm is general. Whatever the address. Also Nicky is a prize-winner at getting on one's nerves as you know …

---

* Hertford Street by Shepherd Market, a popular area for prostitutes.

I seem to be writing you some very nasty letters! ... This continual moving of addresses is the usual when we are separated ... Be of good courage I beg. Don't imagine my spirits do not also meet the depths because they do daily. Whose would not ...

———

At this stage the correspondence was evidently supplemented by a number of sharp telephone conversations.

———

Thornworthy – 27.7.57

I am sorry my letters are stupid. I had better stick to my chronicle and shut up because although I <u>think</u> I can imagine your difficulties how can I really? Jack may be a good advisor. Marks and Spencer sell excellent suitcases. If you can find a cobbler nearby he would mend the handle of the suitcase ...

A jolly German comrade from the Argentine telephoned this morning to check up that Biene was alright ... The German boy's father has written an ecstatic letter to say my name 'rings loud in Hamburg' at least this is Biene's translation, and that he wants to send his boy by air to Exeter via Paris, will I check up? I did check-up and Exeter airways screamed 'for God's sake don't let him, everyone is getting stranded in Jersey'. One must admit a certain honesty in the English ...

[Yesterday] all the boys were making themselves far too much *comme chez eux*. So to their intense astonishment they found themselves washing up, standing up when I come into the room etc. 'My husband and sons <u>always</u> do', so now they do so too and, 'I don't give a fig for what they do in Paris or Brussels'. Delight from the girls and general amiability all round.

One of the French boys' mama's has written that she hands me her authority and please will I see that Phillippe does this, that and the other … Not to run up debts was one of her commands! And I am to grab all his money at once otherwise he will spend it. She writes extremely funny letters. I wish she were coming not the son! …

My darling, *Vive* the love story, use my horrible mannerisms as much as you like, I must cook supper …

Thornworthy – 28.7.57

… Trooping out of mass this morning like sardines emerging from a tin we ran into Lady Waller with two others emerging from the church. 'Oh! What a <u>dreadful</u> lot of Romans!' I was unable to resist laughing outright and saying 'Yes, isn't it <u>splendid</u>!' She took it in very good part.

The bus strike Thank God is ending so that tomorrow Biene and Giselle can expedite to Torquay which they long to do …

Michel had his second bath since he's been here and the drain was nearly blocked. Meggy, who always produces the home truths, says 'the Belgians are the dirtiest people in Europe'. I think it's just boys myself …

Biene is charmingly frank and childish and says her mother has taken her to see so many sights and churches that she never wants to see another! *Keine Kultur.* She is reading an English book borrowed from Ann Ruegg about <u>horses</u>. Michel reads about <u>fish</u>. The others read Simenon or Steinbeck. They are quite extraordinarily uneducated and ill-informed for 16–17 year olds.

My success with Fitzrandolph was purely snobbish. He was in Ribbentrop's Embassy and deeply impressed by my family and social connections, as he imagined them to be. His wife has married an English millionaire who lives in Switzerland.

Imagine Peter Ustinov acting a Mittel Europo [*sic*] and that's
Fitz ...

I want my Billy back and it would be sheer heaven to have
Alice − even for a week. Father Millerick has lent me the Life of
Abbé Pierre. I hope it is good and not just journalism ...

Thornworthy − 29.7.57

... No wonder the Germans lost the war! Long letter from Prince
George to tell me the boy is coming but not giving me the date.
Am now in communication with his grandmother in Stuttgart.
The parents are in Paraguay, ahem ...

I too took communion, having confessed to God of many things,
lack of charity mostly ...

Clapham Common − 30.7.57

*... Three letters yesterday and two today! ... Which cannot
console me for my stupid remark on the telephone. My vanity,
if you please, was nettled by your assuming that you had sent
me a 'tart note'. None of your letters was tart ...*

*Remember that when I met you I consciously reverted to my
childhood's values: and my parents, as it happens, thought a
very great deal of the world (of which they knew little) and of
success (though not of money) ...*

*I am going out to cheer myself up with a shampoo, and
lunching with Nat and the Liberal MP in charge of publications.
As I say, I am ready to run a News-Letter from Chagford ...*

*The crux is that I've only done a chapter and a half since I
came to London! It's the old story ... It is a matter of Will. (That
is my problem. Can God help?) ...*

[My accountant] *thinks the Tax idiots are unlikely to worry or investigate a 'writer's' position showing a dead loss as this is not uncommon among writers.* * *I've told them to buck up as rates and telephone approach ...*

I can't rise above it, except by finishing book. So I will finish it – but when one can't absolutely tell. I'll have to begin it first of course. ('First chapters' have been my life story ...)

Thornworthy – 30.7.57

... I am fighting furiously to prevent the invasion of the older Comrade Schachts as I am far too busy for them, he, however, with hideous guile is trying to infiltrate his elder daughter and friend for Biene's last week ...

I have replied that if they share a room and help wash up I will. During that particular week two more will make no odds at all but £20 will!

Roger arrives the 11th or 12th. Toby about then too. Perhaps we shall hear some English spoken?

Am reading about Abbé Pierre. Catholic Book Club journalism but what a story!

Biene rode alone this morning and the pony lay down – 'how wet are my trousers!' She is quite imperturbable, a very large good-humoured Gretchen ...

I was amused that Yves's mother wrote to him to take a bath every two days or so, as 'over there they even have one every day!' ...

Another comrade from South America has written to Biene to ask whether she is alright or wants anything, this time in English. Biene has entrusted me with the job of replying! If I

---

* Eric was waiting for repayment of overpaid tax.

don't look out I shall have the whole former S.S. <u>and</u> Reichsbank
here ...

Clapham Common – 31.7.57

... Yesterday was a nice day. I had a hair wash. My man [barber]
*now quietly does the Duke of Edinburgh (I discovered this outside,
<u>never</u> a word inside Penhaligon; and if you ask they don't answer).
But I couldn't get him, so I had the really old man, at least 80
(who does Churchill; some deaf ear if you ask). He, too, lives on
the Common and remembers ... the daily coach and four from
the Plough to the Mansion House. When I said I was delighted
by the negroes in the Crucifixion Scenes of the stained-glass
windows in Wilberforce's church he said: 'Yes, and by what I've
seen of the district lately' (Brixton is full of Jamaicans) 'we'll have
some white men in the windows one of these days' ...*

*I was given lunch by Nat, and made to talk and listen to Holt,
a mediocre but far from witless MP from Bolton. They more or
less offered me job as Vice Chairman of Publicity; Frank Owen
having been sacked some time ago, because he didn't do any
work. Don't worry. I don't think they can pay anything, let alone
my salary. But we had a fascinating talk about policy as well as
publicity, and I expect I shall be asked to meet Jo Grimond, the
allegedly enchanting (but rather colourless) Leader. The party is
in a bad way. No money. No organisation ...*

*The German National Bank has been replaced by a new
Central Bank; and the new Governor is Blessing! (I must find out
if they use Portal's paper, for which I made him the agent ...)*

*Children are playing out in the air ... fishing in the ponds,
someone is spade-ing coal, the cars whizz by and sound like waves
breaking ... I must trot round the ponds, while they make my bed.
My landlady treated me to a tirade at breakfast about ... the
immense superiority of the Germans to the English! She also thinks
'Yorkshire Guest House' a trifle common, and would like to call*

our lodgings 'Cheltenham Lodge'. The young Welsh mother, whose husband is seventeen, showed me two pretty breasts, which I can't possibly turn into anything more sublime than what they are ... so I had better put my spare desires into five pages a day ...

At Thornworthy it is changeover day. Thierry, Yves and Michel leave, but the girls stay on.

Thornworthy – 31.7.57

... My first new boy French (partly black) from Tananarive arrived last night. Being used to giants I firmly stopped the first French boy I saw on the station and led him to the car only to discover he was a white Russian called Vladimir who thought I was a Mrs Fortescue. I disengaged myself and discovered Jacques, who is a very small very dark sixteen.

At eight this morning thankfully pushed Germaine's grandson and Michel into Rice's taxi. '*Au revoir!*' I cried with joy. Michel's spite was dispersed by my casually remarking that as they did not seem to get on very well, the day to be spent in London would be more enjoyably spent apart, before rejoining to catch the plane. Michel was <u>terrified</u>.

Yesterday morning we had the row royal – the children said my command of the French language was something to be heard! While I was fetching Valerie, Michel, knowing full well we have to ask Lady W. each time we borrow the boat, rather than wait twenty minutes, took it. I am glad to say he caught nothing, except from me and I couldn't believe I was saying what I thought with such verve! Later I sent him to thank Lady Waller for the use of the boat. I had of course rung her up and asked for it the moment I found he had gone, so she never knew, but I did not tell him this.

Fin de vacances as you say and he has failed all his exams while Yves and Giselle passed them with ease. [He is now] going to be in the same class as his considerably younger sister. I expected a cool parting but after I had kissed Yves and pushed him into the taxi Michel flung his arms round my neck kissed me and said, '*Au revoir et merci merci pour tout.*' So there were no hard feelings, until I found they had gone off with the lavatory plug as a joke and Yves had left his corsets behind ...

The earnest Salem boy telegraphed optimistically that he was arriving at Victoria at 4 tomorrow. 'We can't have this' I cried to the nice man giving me the telegram. 'Send him the message to catch the 3.30 from Paddington!' 'But madam, he does not arrive till 4. Would it not be better to send him a telegram telling him to catch the 5.30 from Paddington?' 'What would I do without you?' I cried. 'I don't know, madam, but the 5.30 seems to <u>me</u> best and your name is Siepmann isn't it?'

Giselle says that Biene says some English moved away from her and her sister when they heard them talking German ... Schacht seems a bit touchy ...

All my love,

M.

Clapham Common – 1.8.57

... August is here and I have been at my desk. A scorching day. The children are playing some sort of 'ronde' outside, with incantations (as they did outside my window in Spain) ...

The Liberals have sent me literature but (you may be glad to hear) no offer ...

Times continues nice, at what is called my level ... They refused Betty Stucley's excellent article on Clapham and 'Oliver Edwards' is both conceited and shaming (alter ego of the editor's outward personality, which is ultra-reserved, shy. I haven't even met him). I shall put in for trips before I leave ... Peter Fleming has just done one (Russia) so they can afford 'names' (which they don't print) and probably don't need me ...

The late Jane Austen is funny, because spiteful. She wrote 3 in her twenties, and 3 at 40. I prefer the late, spiteful ones ... <u>*Tomorrow week!*</u>

Thornworthy – 2.8.57: 1am

... Gert despatched by Prince George of Hanover into my tender care telegraphs to say that delayed by the Bank Holiday crowds he is arriving at 2.56am at Exeter. The poor boy is on the Penzance train and has been stranded in London ... In an hour without my interpreter I am off to collect because there is no taxi and I cannot go to bed and leave him stranded again sans anything in Exeter which closes shop at eleven ...

Loud shrieks from Brussels that Yves had left his corsets behind ... £10 extra is coming from Brussels because of 'the <u>immense trouble</u>' I have taken and 'Yves <u>looks so well</u>' ...

I am all for you reforming the Liberal Party. You might begin by drowning Violet* in her flow of conversation ...

I have discovered through this caper of mine that what you used to call my talent for men is a form of lunacy which mesmerises the young into doing what they are told and respecting me as well.

Biene, ever practical and extremely clever for fourteen, is delighted that Gert speaks Spanish as she is going to learn from him. Her French is greatly improved where it was pathetically non-existent before, and her English wonderfully so, considering no one speaks anything here but French. She wants to be a doctor but on the other hand she and Conny her sister may take on Schacht's Bank. Steam roller girl, she's a darling.

Philippe Meunier looks like a faun with green eyes and fair hair and rides beautifully. His parents have a house in Paris, a

---

* Violet Bonham Carter, born in 1887, daughter of Liberal prime minister Herbert Asquith, close to Winston Churchill when young, prominent and opinionated public figure, mother-in-law of Liberal Party leader Jo Grimond. Eric had known her since he was a schoolboy.

house in the country and his grandfather at 87 teaches him dres-
sage. I foresee <u>rocks</u> but am amply warned. Also his mother has
cleverly provided him with no money so that he can't go far. So
I hope. Very nice manners ...

I can't wait to see Gert (and get to bed) ...

I am going to be very uppish and snob next year and pick and
choose. After all I have refused twenty! The better bred the better
they wash up and no nonsense about being rich here ...

It <u>was</u> Fitzrandolph who told Biene the English would leave
if they heard German spoken ... Schacht began life by wishing
to be a clergyman but became a banker instead. He must be
greatly misled if he relies on people like Fitz ... Curiously like
Harry ...

All all my love ...

PS I used to ride on Clapham Common (a riding school) and the
man said I had a wonderful seat!

Thornworthy – 3.8.57

... I never found my German boy after all. I am so tired I have
even forgotten his name ... I reached home without him at 4 in
the morning and found two bats in the bedroom. Went to sleep
with the dogs chasing the bats in the dairy ...

At seven the telephone rang and Gert Stoeckle was at Exeter
having become inextricably mixed up with a Bank Holiday World
Jamboree of Boy Scouts of all nations crossing to England where
he has never been before and knows nobody ... Arrived by bus
and the village grapevine about eleven <u>bright green</u> with the
fatigue of fifty hours from Stuttgart! ...

He has really good manners ... *Vive* the Germans! Biene at
fourteen <u>far</u> younger than any of the others shouts commands in
ringing tones. 'Vill you all come and vash up now, it is time!' ...
They all obey her without question ...

Monsieur Philippe Meunier, who is rapidly and to his intense surprise being taught to 'vash up also' will soon be adorning the bar of Chez Francis using whatever funds he can extract from his Mum ...

Gert and Biene have just come to say goodnight and kiss and click heels. The French are smoking and playing Radio Paris. I am in your room and just about to hurry into bed, switching off the telephone as I go ...

All my love,

M.

Authors' Club – 4.8.57

... I have discovered a wonderful bus. I walk two minutes across the Common and find myself on a hill looking down over Battersea Fun Fair. A sixpenny bus ride takes me down the hill to Sloane Square and Knightsbridge ... The Common (if your beautiful seat remembers) is on top of a high hill! This accounts for the breezes.

Breezes or no breezes, I don't like living alone. And I am very worried indeed about Billy. However we have made our plans, and we must try to carry them out ...

But I would like to visit Billy soon ...

Thornworthy – 4.8.57

I have, I think, survived the most ferocious German invasion yet! Good God! We got back from mass and the Mayfair Hotel telephoned to say 'a Mr Siepmann was coming to stay with a Miss Miller'. Instantly after lunch Biene and I dashed to Exeter expecting a timid lost German boy. We did not find him because he was heavily accompanied into enemy territory and camouflaged by an ENORMOUS mama and a still larger German friend to act as interpreter and ... to see the house. Somehow we got them all into the little car and I had German mama and friend to tea, took their money off them, explained it is no use Gustav coming here unless he is prepared to do exactly what I tell him, wash up, make his bed and keep *alles in ordnung*. 'I can't be bothered with all this counting of money' was what hit them hardest.

Gustav looks like a terrified Robert Morley.

[Meanwhile] Biene, Giselle and Gert were collapsed with laughter in the garden room. Gert is my new treasure. Comes of a family who thought Germany too horrible for words and hopped to South America in 1919 ... Like Biene I would gladly keep him for ever.

Meanwhile the three Frogs had escaped my clutches, joined up with more Frogs from Madame Watkinson and rang up from Exeter. 'We are in Exeter ... we can get home by 10 o'clock.' 'You will come home immediately' I said. '*Je m'en fous royalement du cinéma. Prenez le bus.*' '*Bien, madame.*' Later ... I was telephoned again. '*On a manqué le bus.*' '*Je m'en* etc ... You will take a taxi and pay for it. Your parents did not send you to me to talk French and I am not going to sit up and get you supper at ten.'

They came home in a taxi and paid. It cost a lot they said. 'I knew it would' I said. Good humour all round. The top Germans Biene, Gert and Giselle tickled to death. I now have seven till Thursday.

Robert Morley's parents never even bothered to write and say when he was coming here, let alone telegraph. 'Extraordinarily odd and rude,' I explained to the interpreter. They belong to the unsquashed German business class, and were perplexed to death. I was at my most grandiose so they became servile. All Robert Morley needs is a little me and he is going to get it.

Toby has written that he will hitch hyke [sic] from Quarr on the 11th or 12th so we expect that one when we see him. Roger of course is being left to bring all the luggage ...

Much touched by Nat's letter. Unless Edith wishes to step into a madhouse I cannot have her.* That is the week there may be a Schacht invasion.

I am retreating to bed having cruelly put Robert Morley in to sleep with Philippe ...

Philippe is the sort who like Toby wheedles the maids, but being Toby's mother I am not wheedleable ...

Clapham Common – 6.8.57

My love,

Your bulletins have become more amusing than ever ... I beg to point out that 'je m'en fous' is indecent (the 'f' being similar in both languages) ...

I arrive at Exeter Central at 5am on Friday ... Please leave the front door open. Thank God you are relieved of two by Thursday! I am sorry to miss Giselle, as they have become characters in fiction to me ...

I have a plan to interview Schacht for Encounter [I have come] up against the hard fact that at 54, I am more *than unemployable. So vive le plan ... It will be heavenly to have my study ... I stood in the middle of the Common yesterday and was overcome by the smell of people ...*

Clapham Common – 7.8.57

My Pol,

I really do rejoice at these tributes in cash and adjectives to your success ... It's obviously more than a gift; it's genius ...

I could go down to Billy (if necessary) alone by sleeper on September 13th ... I can't afford it of course; but I don't want to 'lose' him.

---

* Eric's sister Edith had proposed a visit to Thornworthy.

Thank you very much for the £1! Which will save me from the annoyance of letting Harry pay for lunch in my own club today ...

I am utterly routed and demoralised by the difficulty of working in London ... I shall tell Harry today that, at least, I am not interested in door-to-door Encyclopaedia salesmanship! On the other hand, I'm not sure I've achieved much by sub-ing at The Times. Respectability, yes. But people so quickly accept that you have accepted to be there – at the bottom of the tree ...

———

Eric took a week's leave from The Times to return to Thornworthy.

———

Thornworthy – 13.8.57

My Love,

Pain at parting, though perhaps you thought not ...

Biene practically in tears of rage and despair on being reminded by her sister to remember her mother's birthday, the 50th ... She emitted what Toby called 'a stream of German' ... so I sent her out round the lake with Toby and this afternoon we bought a horrid piece of pottery ... and cheered her up ...

[Biene said] 'Each year she tells us she is younger and does not let us see her passport ... Now she is fifty I will send her a present but never again, she is too old!' I told her how Vera's son at 27 had asked Vera how old he was to tell his squadron leader [his age], as she [still] said she was 30. This gave great pleasure.

Roger arrived and has rushed out with his new gun ...

Junior Army & Navy Club
Horse Guards Avenue, SW1 – 14.8.57

I had a most agreeable and campari-vin rosé lunch with Jack
[Beddington] and I have just been delivered at the Junior Army
and Navy (of which no one has ever heard) ...

He extended complete [belief] to my statement that drinking
was no longer a problem; and that this was due to Catholicism ...

I begin daily work on The Joys of Marriage *on Friday ...*

Thornworthy – 14.8.57

... The love song which began to worry me last night as 'Steerforth'
Philippe* after a good deal of showing off his prowess and winning
tremendous devotion from Jacques has ceased, and he has had a
considerable tumble. Wonnacott has asked that he should no
longer ride the pony Sally unless accompanied by me or Roger ...
[because] he has strained the pony's back ...

Philippe, dreadfully ashamed, has switched his attention rapidly
to Toby and been taken out on the lake ... Atmosphere of disaster,
saved by Roger and Biene and by a carefully considered joke of
mine. I shout 'I want one "Roast Beef" one "Frog" and one "Sale
Boche" to help me wash up!' This is considered wonderful except
by Gugu (Gusti) who has gone to look it up in his dictionary ...

Jacques sat up far too late alone with Philippe last night so that
I descended, to find them playing cards, and dispatched them to
bed ...

Dear me, what a <u>bore</u>. However it always happens at that age
and I suppose there is nothing I can do to stop it ... I think Jacques
is probably a natural as we thought, and Philippe both. How

---

* Mary has been concerned about the undue attention Philippe has been paying
 to the younger Jacques. She compares Philippe to the brilliant and seductive
 character of Steerforth in *David Copperfield*.

conscious it is I don't know nor how much I can curb it. They all seem to be learning everything but English here ...

M.

Horse Guards Avenue, SW1 – 15.8.57

... I didn't work today as I went to High Mass at Westminster [Feast of the Assumption – holy day of obligation] ... The music was marvellous, and the vestments white. Christ was immense on his huge cross, and the choir tapered away into the green heights behind that gate with its strange yellow pillars and pointed arch through which millions of the dead have gone. When I walked down Victoria Street afterwards the two Abbey towers soared in the sky, but the Abbey needs cleaning.

I suppose the Reformation was necessary – and something was lost for ever; one cannot rebuild what one has destroyed. One can only start again; but, like the English Catholic convert, one recaptures what one can ...

Thornworthy – 15.8.57

... Paul [Ziegler] has told Toby he will help him get into Warburg's. Will you ask Harry or shall I write to him later on? Toby has told Carol and Averil* he is going to decide for himself what he is going to do and <u>not</u> to be interfered with. Apparently Averil torments her son to death to become a chartered accountant and he <u>paints</u> ...

M.

---

* Averil Knowles, second wife of Carol Swinfen. They had married in 1950 and settled in Ireland. Roger and Toby regularly spent part of the school holidays with them.

Clapham Common – 16.8.57

... My gas is on! and outside the winter is cold and dark grey. This makes my attic more attractive. Your delightful letters are beside me. It is worrying about Steerforth. Shall I write and tell him about Lord Montagu* ('en Angleterre, c'est tres grave')?! ...

Now I shall eat my lunch; two bananas and a pint of milk ... and read the New Statesman *– which is what I have done more of than most things, all my life! Lord Londonderry (aged 19, jazz band at Eton; failed exams) attacks the Queen in it. What can they expect if they a. remove the young peers' responsibilities b. set an example of skiffle and racing?* Selon moi, *that Bowes-Lyon* [the Queen Mother] *brought it all in ...*

Clapham Common – 17.8.57

I like the sound of canasta. If Toby organises games your worst troubles are over ... '*What next!' as you once suggested, on presenting one of your beaux to me ... Has Roger's regiment survived? ...*

My confessor was very nice; and I have made a date with him for a talk on Monday, at twelve. He sounded cultured, and is only here on retreat. His name is Father Furey.

I had three bitters at poob with my steak (Saturday night outing, it comes to 14/6) and a talk with the piquante, naughty waitress, and was all set for trouble if the church had not been next door ... What luck! I was horrified at entry, by the sermon and mumbo-jumbo (Assumption) and stayed to be deeply moved and impressed by these crowds of people, on their knees and singing (drearily, in a low-ly anglican manner) and the relic (?) or Host exhibited and worshipped. And I confessed; including, especially, my nastiness

---

* In 1954, Edward Douglas-Scott-Montagu, 3rd Baron Montagu of Beaulieu, was convicted of sexual activity with an adult male on his own property and sentenced to twelve months in prison. The case caused a public scandal, with the Conservative home secretary, Sir David Maxwell Fyfe, ensuring that it received maximum publicity. The eventual consequence was widespread sympathy for the accused and a change in the law.

when I went home (my ungrateful, mendacious outburst ...); and
did penance and came home safe ...

All my love,

Eric

Do not be afraid to sign your name!

Authors' Club – 18.8.57

Mary, my darling –

... I knew from a common-sense point of view that to practice
a religion must help me; yet I couldn't believe it. Now it has begun
to WORK in just the way foreseen; but it seems miraculous.

I mean that <u>in trouble</u> I can turn to it ... Yesterday I had
reached a new depth of desperation, and even went to bed at
noon! I got up at four, and took 'any' bus. I had decided that I
could <u>never</u> recover from my despair and failure. The bus went
to Victoria, and I suddenly remembered Confession; and I had
the fullest and most helpful confession I ever had, at Westminster,
from a priest – who stammered – and who apologised for
speaking so long.

He told me, again, that despair is of the devil, that I must
remember that I am a 'noble' person (Christ has made us all
potentially so). What was new was that he (practically) laughed
merrily at my 'worldly failure' ('<u>That</u> won't matter much in 50
years') – and in that laughter dissolved that obsession with
'money and success' ... which you find so odd in me. I really
think I don't care any more, except to make you happy ...

I do hope you have not been worrying? The <u>principle</u> is solved.
The next 6 months are one more bridge, or rather ridge on our
mountain ... and after that, our troubles may be over. Certainly
(Harry – most materialist – agreed) teaching as a second line,
and by way of using the house, is preferable to anything else
that can be combined with writing ...

I reckon to finish my novel on October 23.

I am wondering whether to write up my notebooks as 'Notes of a Convert' ... I have a lot to say ...

I miss you <u>badly</u> ...

Eric

Thornworthy – 19.8.57

... Roger's regiment is almost the only one left intact.* Toby is so full of interest that the first boring years will not worry him. *La tête* screwed on and grandfather and uncle were bankers.† I think very soon I would like a letter from Harry, also I shall get Kurt Hahn and Paul to pincer movement. I rather think it should be done soon as Averil wants the money and there will be no Oxford.‡

Thora has abandoned her virginity to the gentleman and what is so annoying is that there is a clever cousin of the right age interested. She is prepared to abandon herself to love with tears *pour toujours.* Dear dear! Let's ask St Joseph. No good asking me is it? What folly have I not committed nor what foulness? I must go to bed.

I too feel Catholic. Part of the extraordinary jostle in the village hall, able to confess *sans gene* [*sans gêne* – without embarrassment] to Father Millerick.

I shall sign my letters my love. 'M.' came from a distrust when you shewed my letters to others.

Anyway I am, your dear Pol

---

* Roger, aged 19, had decided to join the Royal Scots, much against Mary's wishes. This regiment was one of the few not to have been affected by severe defence budget cuts.

† Toby's Ziegler family, his grandfather and uncle, were bankers in Prague.

‡ Mary is concerned that Carol's second wife will object to the money he is spending on the education of Roger and Toby.

Clapham Common – 19.8.57

I wrote my 1000 words and went to Father Furey ... He is Irish, fat, tiny fingers yellow with nicotine, burst veins, black eyes that roll in different directions behind strong lenses ...

I asked him what mortal sin was. He began to generalise. I said I wanted to know what I must confess, if I am to take Communion. He said mortal sin was anything serious. Then he began to split hairs. If you got very drunk, it was deliberate. If, drunk, you then fornicate that may not be deliberate: therefore not mortal.

You cannot decide, according to your conscience. But (as far as I can see) you have to decide what the Church says; ie your conscience is used (only) to refer you to the known rules of the Church. It was not wholly satisfactory: but some headway was made.

We went on to redemption. Did Christ die 'for' men – if so how? Answer: he died so that all can achieve salvation, in spite of their sins. But they must want to. Or, if they are ignorant (Eskimos) they may be naturally good, and saved even if they never heard of Christ. Ditto if they are Buddhists. But not if they are Buddhists who have heard of Christ, and rejected him in favour of Buddhism!

He, or the room, smelt sour. But he seemed genuinely delighted at my being a convert: and especially at my enjoyment of the church ... He was better on sex: far from wrong, God-created. If alone, one is bound to be tempted etc ... I did tell him how madly I behaved, or became obsessed at times. He thought all my bad behaviour and thoughts might be a good thing, insofar as they may have saved me from spiritual pride!

I left liking him better ... He was touchingly kind (I told him about the French priest) and touchingly proud of his church and of its being always packed ... which is, indeed, exciting. I have another date on Wednesday ...

I can get Harry to speak to Warburg as soon as you like. BUT can we play the real card, in Warburg's case? I don't suppose English Hons. appeal to him. *

I reckon I cannot sell my novel until November ... Also there is this blasted rebate (but I have a feeling it will be drastically cut). Anyway, do not worry. You have saved the boat single-handed ...

Thornworthy – 20.8.57

Your priest cannot be so stupid if he puts his finger directly on your humility, all the same not '*le top*' as St Teresa would say. Glad though you are seeing him ...

I go to have the car serviced and my hair washed and try to keep an eye on Philippe, though how this is to be achieved with my head in a basin or under the drier is up to St Joseph ...

I don't see how the Income Tax can fail. They are just bloody slow ...

I hope you had tea with Nat. I think proximity to goodness is a great help, in any form. Mrs W's natural goodness helps me ...

Thornworthy – 21.8.57

... Both Roger and Toby want to pop down and see Billy ... I am fed up with Hughes. Nothing but weeds and excuses in the garden and not even a lettuce. I planned so carefully many months ago for vegetables for July, August and September ... Hughes gets worse, not better and ... Dick is going to walk into a bees' nest ...

I wish the Income Tax would fork up as we would be in a far stronger position if the rent were paid ...

---

* The German-Jewish Warburg banking family had emigrated from Hamburg in the 1930s. As the sons of Lord Swinfen, Roger and Toby were entitled to the courtesy title of 'The Honourable'. Eric is suggesting that it might be a good idea to establish that Toby was a Ziegler.

Clapham Common − 22.8.57

I was fed up so I rang up Tony [Antonia White] (tea next week, with me here) and Woodruff, with whom I have just had lunch. He is shrewd and world-wise, in a non-pejorative sense. Because I expect nothing of him (heart) I am never disappointed (head) − and he is both friendly and informative.

Reasons for gloom ... Work: <u>not</u> regular! No letter from you (post, of course): Times experiment really a waste of time, as my idea of being proved steady is useless. To their mind, I am a ghost! Never mind ... I get on with my colleagues (worst paid failures in London) and I have not been rude to my superiors, yet (I won't be) ...

Soon, soon it'll ease off; and we'll be together. I'll try to be less horrible.

Emily* has disappeared into an Abbey; not, it appears, as a nun. But for some time!

Peter Rodd has been in plaster for weeks at Cheam. Accident. I might visit him. Typical ...

Thornworthy − 22.8.57

... I think your explorations in your Graham Greenery [i.e. church on Clapham Common] very interesting but do not forget the Farm Street boys ...

What I want from Harry is what age Warburg's start the boys at. I think if they are to be told the truth it is for me to tell it ... Toby rather wants to go back to Salem to get his German perfect ...

Mrs Grant listened again with pleasure to your broadcast, said it was very good ...

I shall be sad to lose Biene ... Rode yesterday and the whole moor smelt of honey as the heather is out ...

---

* Emily Holmes Coleman, American author of *The Shutter of Snow*, pre-war girlfriend of Eric's, ultra-devout convert to Catholicism, made regular retreats at the Benedictine Abbey of Stanbrook.

We shall get our Billy home. It is far better for him to be away at this age than later ...

Thornworthy – 23.8.57

Accounts

I have in hand £37, and with £40 owed me by Schacht which I will get next week and money promised and yet to come – roughly £100.

From this I must feed the PG's and Roger and Toby and myself until the 20th, and pay wages ...

Toby wishes to return to Quarr.* He says that during his period of atheism he was very unhappy. He takes his missal to church and reads it during the protestant performance which he finds entirely lacks meaning and boring in the extreme. He wishes time and thought before deciding on becoming Catholic. He thinks about religion a lot ...

He is off to stay with best friend at Bath, son of a psychologist who must believe because Toby and the son are so interested in religion. They have 'converted' several other boys [at Bryanston] from atheism back to God. What next? I was profoundly moved at being told.

Money does not matter either. Happiness is what matters, 'like what you and Eric have' ...

Thornworthy – 24.8.57

... This *fin* (*de vacances*) of the summer is trying for us both. I feel like Alice having run very far to remain on the same square, but I have managed the bills and wages and you have managed

---

* Toby wanted to pursue his new friendship with Dom Paul Ziegler, a member of the Benedictine community at Quarr Abbey. Unknown to Toby at the time, Paul Ziegler was his uncle.

... the banks and planned your book. It will be better for me after Wednesday. Naturally they all leave at different hours ...

Tomorrow I can take communion which will help me ... Both Roger and Toby very sweet. Toby suddenly grown mature, like Heinz, only much deeper far less froth. Judgements on people very acute ...

Clapham Common – 26.8.57

Nothing has ever given me so much pleasure as Toby's tribute to God, the unimportance of money, and ... 'happiness like ours' ...

Time and again, I have asked myself if I should give the boys more verbal guidance, and told myself that advice is a boomerang and that example and atmosphere count, and reproached myself that my example was pretty useless. Now, unconsciously, you have reaped this great reward; because 'our happiness', which Toby sees, is your creation and achievement ... After all, he is your son. And so is Roger. They are good boys. Give them my love ...

Your annual 'bash' is wonderful; it really pays for six months! ... You have not run on the same square. In spite of never ending difficulties you have, in fact, solved our problem ...

I am <u>beginning</u> to know what depending on oneself and not on God means ... I feel as if I had developed new sinews, through my wonderful Confession at Westminster. Yesterday I sat in the third row. You see the priests giggle, and the castrated (grown men) sing as choirboys.* This strengthens the faith ...

Darling, I must finish the first 20,000 words of my book ...
Eric

---

* Eric apparently thinks that the counter-tenors in the Westminster Cathedral choir are castrati.

Thornworthy – 26.8.57

... No time for a proper letter. Watch out for Gugu [Mary's name for Gustav, sometimes known as 'Robert Morley', the humourless German boy with the tiresome father and enormous mother] who has your telephone number. <u>Don't see him</u>. His bloody parents are arriving at the Ritz tomorrow and he is joining them there ... I am exhausted and sick to death of him. What a day. I reached the point where I could not be left alone with him ... Biene deeply ashamed for the Germans and Gert cheerful as anything as he is Paraguayan and had his hair cut by the village barber this afternoon who told him 'not <u>nearly</u> enough Germans were killed in the war'. Gert thinks this is frightfully funny and is coming to mass on Sunday ... [he] is one in a million ...

Thornworthy – 27.8.57

Your wonderful letter this morning gave me real joy. No good saying it is I who reap a reward like Toby (Roger is ditto) it is you too. I have always thanked God for your sweetness and cleverness with them ...

What a loss Knox dying ... *

Clapham Common – 28.8.57

I have been at my desk an hour, and read through the 40 foolscap pages of my novel. The big problem is: Can I now get 1000 words a day written, in spite of being mentally diseased? ...

* Monsignor Ronald Knox, Latinist, biblical translator and prominent apologist for Catholicism to which he had converted in 1917; died aged sixty-nine.

Thornworthy – 28.8.57

... So glad you have written to Bowra and Livingstone ...

Hughes really does present a problem. He is deteriorating so fast. Roger is running the electric light and found several faulty cells [in the generator].

If you get a chance of seeing Schacht will you tell him how thoroughly I appreciate Biene? Give the old rogue my love too ...

Authors' Club – 29.8.57

I have just had talks with Schacht ... He sends you his regards, and an inscribed book called Confessions of an Old Wizard. *I had an hour with him, and Frau and Biene, and he is to come over for a two-day's interview ... Can we have him for the weekend October 4–6? ... Don't say yes if it is inconvenient. He will come at any time, and looks forward to meeting you ...*

Thornworthy – 29.8.57

Your letter sounded sad so I rang you up. They said you had gone to Greenwich! ...

The Schacht camerads rang up, all very jolly, to say thank you ... Schacht first, loud exuberance, then Frau S. but she had to talk in English and can't, then Biene, all very sweet. I was pleased as I love Biene and would do anything for her. Gert says her mother is very strict so I must have been quite a change. I was <u>sad</u> to see her go yesterday.

Gert has taken Jacques and Bertrand to swim so Roger and I are alone ...

I enclose Father Mangan's letter. Do see him before you come home. I was afraid my rather racy account of my experiences in the confessional might annoy him but apparently not ...

You did not enclose the pound but keep it, I shall have one for you.

Nice letter from Quarr [Dom Paul Ziegler], says Toby never mentioned banking but is obsessed with helping backward coloured races, but that if he does turn to banking he has an enormous pull with George Warburg, Sigmund's son ...

Don't be silly, you are <u>not</u> mentally diseased ... You are bloody well frustrated that's all and I should think so too! ...

We have been adopted by the new Jane [replacement home help] and I think her husband too. 'One can't easily find people like you to work for.' Am very flattered. Nice to be offered a post as cook at Farm Street but what about my sex? ...

Gert says he was six when the war ended, never knew anything about it and only discovered the horrors of the Hitler regime when sent to school in Germany. He told me, as though I could never have heard it, about gas chambers, anti-semitism and concentration camps, with absolute horror ...

Thornworthy – 30.8.57

... Can you get me Ronald *Knox's Enthusiasm* from the London Library? It's <u>the</u> book on heresy? Tell Woodruff, who ought to know! '*Le petit frère*' arrives this afternoon. Tomorrow the Gymkhana. Heavenly weather. Roger got the Wonnacotts corn in and saved their lives. Great gratitude and bowls of cream ...

Clapham Common – 30.8.57

I have had a polite letter from Haley, who is going to America on Monday; but he has promised to discuss my future when he gets back. This will make it easy to offer him a Schacht article. The Times has some big advantages ... and may fit into my scheme: which includes Television, on which I can appear as the interviewer ...

Schacht is highly irresponsible, at his own expense; rather like a German Bernard Shaw. He may be difficult to place. So I proposed an interview on 'What to do about World Inflation'; and then we drag in his past, and the present Germany, as side-issues. He quite appreciated this tactic ...

Thornworthy – 31.8.57

... I would not have missed '*le petit frère*' for anything (he missed two trains). The answer is l'Indo-Chine, where '*papa a fait la guerre*', and *fait* Jacques too. [He] is twelve, looks like a six-year old geisha girl. Absolutely heavenly.

Baron de la Salle writes, will I keep Bertrand as long as possible ... He is well known in France having blabbed a military secret to his brother-in-law who is a journalist. It was in all the papers the next morning and there was a *proces*! This from Jacques. I now have Gert, Jacques, *le petit frère*, Bertrand, Roger. Toby comes back on Sunday ...

Thornworthy – 31.8.57

My Darling,

Cling to it. The Schacht shot may be a very useful long shot. Now Malcolm is giving up *Punch* do all the Uncle Tom Cobbly's fall off that wagon?* ...

Roger leaves the 16th for Sandhurst ... We are just back from the Gymkhana where a lovely pony had to be shot because it broke

---

* Malcolm Muggeridge resigned the editorship of *Punch* due to proprietorial interference. He said that the last straw was censorship of a cartoon showing an elderly man sitting up in bed beside a naked young lady. There was a tumbler of water on the table within her reach. He was saying: 'Hand me my teeth. I want to bite you.'

its leg. Otherwise it was a success. Roger and Gert ran and Gert went green and collapsed afterwards but he says he always does and Roger says it's usual and he does too! ...

Le petit frère is delicious but bone idle ... He deceived me at first by enunciating various English sentences with a perfect accent. Jacques was deeply mortified. All is well now as it is revealed that <u>a.</u> He has no idea what he is saying and <u>b.</u> Can't understand <u>one</u> word. All we all get is an oriental good-humoured stare – 'Pleeze?' He arrived with a box of conjuring tricks and is as clever as paint and very funny ...

We must plan not to be separated like this. It is horrible for you, you have had quite enough loneliness in your life and beastly for me ditto. I really feel a Catholic now. Not a good one but I have been given the vehicle, the life belt which I needed. *Je tiens au Jesuits et Benedictin's* [sic]. *Je tiens* to you too, Friday week my darling,

    Your Pol

Thornworthy – 2.9.57

I have dispatched Jacques, little brother and all the others to Exeter for the day. Roger and Toby and I have the house and Pebble's howls to ourselves.

Thank you for yesterday's letter ... Roger is faithful and good and, as Toby says, 'There's a lot more there than you can see.'

A sleepless night. Toby came back beautiful and nervous and ranged about my room until 11.30 – so like his father ... A long outpouring over Carol's futility and Averil's – 'I wish to God Eric were my father.' Nothing ever decided or done for him except by us and terrible embarrassing uncertainty as to whether he is to go to university or not.

I must go to London to see Carol, but when? My two-edged sword is overtaking me alright. 'They never read a book!' 'Those idiotic cocktail parties!' ... The sharp cruel judgements of adolescents and the furious sense of not belonging, of being different from other people. A fine turmoil.* I wish he would go fishing which is the only thing that calms him but he is lying on his bed preparing to write letters ...

Naturally I long to tell the truth. I need someone to advise me. You. Father Mangan. God. In a way I am inclined to tell him [Toby] the truth, a terrible risk, and that Carol has been made use of long enough. My sin. What does Carol know? I don't know ... Then how deep, how serious is this? Begun how? Friends who have intellectual fathers? Other values than Carol's? Unworldly?

What is certain is that he now needs you urgently, as you always said he might.

Paul [Ziegler] says never tell and I suppose he is right? I told him [Toby] that we all criticise our parents. That I consider myself very lucky that he even speaks to me ... That Carol with all the negative points is generous and kind. That he must never expect people to be other than they are, that it is waste of breath, that if he considers himself and his few friends 'different' from other people he is a dead duck as I have always been and must accept it. One is! He has been staying with a psychoanalyst called Guirdham at Bath. The boy is his best friend and will come here. Papa anxious to come too apparently to meet me in the flattering sense. I feel astride a bolting horse and can only pray hard ...

All due to a bright idea in a Hungarian restaurant in Soho 18 and a half years ago! ...

Your Polly

---

*Mary is faced with the consequences of her wartime decision to have three children by three different fathers. Toby believes that his father is Carol and is ignorant of the fact that his father was Heinz Ziegler, brother of Dom Paul Ziegler. Meanwhile Carol has not yet committed to paying for Toby to go to university.

Thornworthy – 2.9.57

I told Toby I feel very responsible for my follies* and his position and he said, no, not at all, that he knows a lot of young
whose parents hang together for the sake of appearances and
the results are appalling nervous strain. I feel humiliated, he
is so grown up. I feel it is wrong that he should dismiss my
shortcomings with a loving snap of the fingers as poor Carol
cannot help being what he is or what I have thrust on him and
he has been whether consciously or not as wonderful as he can
manage ...

At Bath Toby was loudly greeted by a restaurant proprietor as a
fellow mittel european and was most amused! Loud German shouts
about Prague and Vienna. What next? The Rabbi I suppose ...

Our next problem child is of Polish (father) Swiss (mother)
parentage and has been tried in every school in Switzerland. He
is an intelligent fourteen and his only hope of English public
school education is to get next Easter a <u>scholarship</u> for
Gordonstoun. I am going to try to get him in to Bryanston and
am playing Hahn. His mother may descend on you in London en
route for Chagford. Her name is Mrs Klossowska and she lives
in sin with an Armenian ... I hope to get hold of the boy and rid
of the mother as soon as possible ...

Mary

Clapham Common – 3.9.57

*Toby is (at last) growing up; and this is adolescence. It rouses all
sorts of memories and responsibilities in you, but these have
nothing to do with his 'problem'. And his problem is an inner
turbulence which might take any form; thank God it's taking the*

---

* In 1958, instead of telling Toby, Mary wrote an account of her life (unpublished), intending to explain herself to her three sons. She called it *The Fruits
of My Follies*, but she kept it to herself.

form of both seriousness and sensibility and wider interest. Carol is an ass, but nothing you can say will alter that. There is not the slightest point in telling Toby anything now, at this stage. But there is an inner (secret) argument for his becoming independent as soon as possible. On the other hand, if he can get to Oxford, that is not to be despised. All you have to do is cope, as usual …

I met Nat at the Authors' yesterday at tea. He has written an article about me in The British Weekly (non-conformist!). He is wild to meet Schacht, and he is doing a Brains trust at Exeter on October 4th, so I am writing to Schacht urging that they should coincide. Especially as … I see Nat as a valuable third party in my 'interview' – he is a friend of Niemoller and was amazed that doors should be shut against Schacht …

Thornworthy – 4.9.57

I am very glad about Nat and Schacht. The combination with you would be very effective especially as you never know what Schacht will say next …

What Toby needs is to be guided into some profession from whence he can tilt at Windmills. He is obsessed by Albert Schweitzer and the Negro problem at the moment …

Would Nat like to stay here? Plenty of room, old gentleman much the same as little boys! Then he and Schacht could get to know each other, you could all have a shouting match together, punctuated by meals …

Clapham Common – 4.9.57

Having had a row yesterday because I couldn't get breakfast until I had waited half-an-hour today the door is slammed in my face … My novel is like stone in the womb, thanks to London landladies …

I believe Landladies in Literature to have played a sinister part – silencing Keats, choking off Chesterton etc. My genius is a tender plant. I would be sad if I did not feel my fingers on your shoulder blades and spine – all my love to you.

Eric

Thornworthy – 5.9.57

You must go on TV with Nat and Schacht. Wonderful. Those pince-nez are the very ticket! The young generation of Germans have never heard of Niemoller.

I feel terrible for you with the landlady. Perhaps she has a liver like Lady Waller? It isn't landladies who have paralysed your novel, it's just London …

Gert and I are collecting anti-German articles in the papers. His idea of fun but it isn't funny. Krupp's yesterday, who now make pots and pans …

Hughes told Roger he was 'in bad odour'. 'Yes,' said Roger, 'you are' … We shall not lose that Albatross! …

Clapham Common – 5.9.57

By Christmas we shall probably have Alice and Billy with us, and my aim is for us to be <u>Alone</u> together by the spring …

I am seeing Jack at 3, about how to play ITV against BBC … BBC may flinch [at Schacht interview] because the Authorities do – Kirkpatrick* refused to see him when he was in Germany; and Harry says City is closed to him. That may frighten BBC, but attract ITV …

---

* Sir Ivone Kirkpatrick, post-war British High Commissioner for Germany, had retired as Permanent Under-Secretary of State for Foreign Affairs – head of the Foreign Office – in February and was now chairman of the Independent Television Authority.

Thornworthy – 6.9.57

Roger is an angel and works hard for me. He gave up his sailing so I can't not have Martin [his friend] to stay. Toby is reading everything at once, Plato, Dostoyevsky and has taken to <u>grunting</u>. When I complained about the grunting he said he 'was agreeing with himself' and grunting agreement ...

I am despatching both Jacques and Gert at dawn on Tuesday ... Gert says both Stauffenberg's sons are complete lollipops ... *

The geese hate everybody but me and when I go and sit beside them they peer into my face and nibble my jersey with their beaks ...

Gert's good humour and balance is I think due to being brought up in a country without war [Paraguay]. He seems to me to belong to another race altogether ... Did you know Schacht started life wanting to be a parson? ...

No news about the landlady. That's the worst of letters. There I was all yesterday, breathlessly waiting for the police to ring up and say you had crowned her with a milk bottle and today no mention ...

Clapham Common – 7.9.57

I fear I have failed badly to be 'a man who looked after you' – which is what you needed ... But Nancy says that though thin you are buoyant; and in good form, compared to some low, worried period when she met you in London a year or two ago ...

I think Schacht is a TV natural, as he is sure to say something unrehearsed – BBC have snootily not answered, so I am going to ITV ...

---

* Colonel Claus von Stauffenberg was the officer who planted the bomb in the conference room at the Wolf's Lair, German military HQ in northern Poland, on 20 July 1944 in an unsuccessful attempt to assassinate Hitler. Von Stauffenberg was executed immediately after the failure of the plot. His sons were aged ten and six at the time.

I do not think Krupp can be called innocent. There is a Protestant convent on Catholic lines, in the Rhineland, where they pray and confess daily about their guilt against the Jews. That seems to me right, and normal; there is something abnormal about ... Schacht's blamelessness. (Grist to the mill of my 'interviews'.)

Thornworthy – 7.9.57

Letters of admonition arriving in droves for Bertrand from his mama <u>and</u> to me. 'Ah! C'est le comble!' 'Encore une autre!' ... [She] is *une emmerdeuse du premier ordre* ...

Toby reading the Bible, Plato, Cicero, Ilya Ehrenburg and two books on religion and busy writing a very boring short story. Hysterical with excitement last night on hearing the Eroica for the first time. Such a nice change from cricket and football pools but as he is suddenly aware of spiritual and intellectual values I have the full shock of the discovery hurled at me. Otherwise he grunts, stalks about and is aloof ...

Thornworthy – 9.9.57

... The wind veers wildly in adolescence. [Toby] came to Mass yesterday with Gert and the Frogs, the banker handing the plate winced visibly at Gert's smiling face. Father Millerick announcing another 'impot' from the bishop made it clear 'these are his lordship's wishes, <u>nothing</u> to do with me, I am fed up with trying to find money for this that and the other thing!' Toby giggled audibly and thinks he is terrific ...

Clapham Common – 10.9.57

BBC want Schacht (and me) for press Conference; but I want a 15-minute programme, 'Dr Schacht' – in which I try to get him to persuade me of his innocence and Germany's ...

Income Tax have now passed the buck to Maida Vale, as they say I 'reside' there ...

It is hot and sticky ... London is a muggy swamp.

Thornworthy – 11.9.57

My Love,

The Klossowska has arrived with Stakhov. He is a tiny very intelligent fifteen. She very rich, I don't know whether I like her or not. The child is furnished with wireless, electric blankets etc obviously used to much luxury. She is I think staying at Easton Court until Saturday so as to see you. She seems to have all her meals here so we are seven again. I wish she would go as it would be much better for the child but of course she must see you. It did not seem to occur to her to leave today and see you tomorrow. I shall be alright as soon as numbers diminish, it is too much in this bloody weather.

All my love, can't wait for Friday,

Your Pol

Clapham Common – 11.9.57

The TV's are (I think) tricky. Geoffrey Cox, the ITV news editor, thought Schacht had been condemned [i.e. to death]. I expect BBC are best, but I'm beginning to doubt if it is the right medium. They will trap him, and ignore me – unless I'm careful ...

I am quite clear now about sex; with us it's love; and I have no intention of giving it up. I had the intention to try, when I became a Catholic – as Tony says, that is genuine and enough (I didn't discuss any further with her than that). I am genuinely sorry that I'm not a wholly spiritual being.

*(I should hate it if you were!) Is this honest? Doesn't it make
sense? ...*

    Hurray for Friday,
    Eric

*PS I find Billy's jokes very funny. (Doctor I had myxomatosis on
Tuesday. – Then why didn't you send for me? – I sent for the
Vet!) Genius.*

Clapham Common – 17.9.57

That was a very fine week-end ...

    *I have fixed for Schacht to appear on TV for about 10 minutes –
if he wants to. If it's* Press Conference *on the Monday (which
would suit) I would be with him ... If* Panorama *(Friday) it would
be without me. I told them I am indifferent, but on second thoughts
I am veering to* Press Conference *– as you never know! ...*

Authors' Club – 20.9.57

Feeling an access [sic] *of Gloom and the Devil I anticipated them
by taking the bus over the hill down to the Oratory (who have full
time confessions). Here I told my confessor exactly what I feel about
sex and our marriage; and I told him clearly that I had no intention
of living as 'brother and sister', although I had recognised that as
the aim when I joined the Church, and still recognised a spiritual
life as preferable ... Well, he said, God would recognise our good
intentions, and knew best; and not to torment ourselves ...*

    *I feel better because I have said clearly to a priest what I told
you was my eventual reaction to it all. What I would not do is
<u>pretend</u> to aim at a sex-less life ... I need you too much. (And,
as I told him, I cannot think it wrong!)*

Almost invariably I go into a church thinking that [it] is perhaps best to give up faith and live courageously and truthfully by admitting that life is a short, sharp struggle full of beauty: but meaningless and finite. I come out thinking <u>There</u> is reality, and see things instead of being blind. Today I even saw the National Gallery for the first time! ...

—————

Eric left The Times subs desk on 25 September, and returned to Thornworthy determined to earn a living as a private tutor while writing his novels away from the distractions of London and the gloom of a solitary life.

In August 1960 Mary and Eric left Thornworthy after five years and moved away from Dartmoor to Basclose Farm, Otterton, near Budleigh Salterton on the Devon–Dorset border. It was a pretty pink house large enough for Eric to continue lodging pupils. He was an outstanding tutor, as a testimonial from the mother of one of his pupils suggests: 'We have just been for a week to Rock and on the way home took the A35 from Exeter and made a detour so that Charles should see Otterton. He really was quite "emotional" and one could see how happy he had been there. He frequently talks of the time he spent with you and of how much he learnt from your husband and how much he loved it all.' Mary and Eric bought Basclose Farm with money given to them by a friend of Mary's, Phyllis Jones, who had come into an inheritance. Phyllis (who, with Antonia White, had acted as godmother when Mary was received into the Church) lived at Callow End, near Stanbrook Abbey in Worcestershire, with the American writer Emily Coleman, also a Catholic. Mary sent Eric to Buckfast Abbey, in Devon, 'on retreat' while she managed the move from Dartmoor to Otterton. Much of the correspondence was conducted in the summer when one or other of them was on retreat with the Benedictine monks of Buckfast or the Benedictine nuns of

Stanbrook, but no letters from Mary from this period have survived.

=====

Buckfast Abbey – 15.8.60 (Assumption)

My darling Pol,

... <u>Very</u> good retreat, so far. The Virgin has played hell with my chapter, but has averted all – or nearly all – destructive moods. The splendours of flame and gold; and the Abbot wore white satin slippers at Pontifical Mass today! We have even had Pontifical Vespers ...

I agree with you about Green [sic].* It shows how dangerous and difficult it is to write about religion – and perversion! He used to write Racine-esque tragedies in the form of novels. Or so I thought. He has (as you said, at the start) genius.

I had permission from the Abbot to have Father Wilfrid bless the house on Thursday but I've cancelled it until we're ready ... (Also, the parish priest had better be squared, said the Abbot.) ...

My missal says November was the date of the dogma; but surely we were there? Or did we invent the story about the Osservatore Romano headline 'Virgin Goes Up'?†

For lack of tennis, the boys take me out for rollicking walks ... and this morning they dragged me up the tower to see bell-ringing and the view. I was terrified by the stairs and heights, but I didn't dare show it.

---

* Graham Greene had just published *A Burnt-Out Case*, described by Evelyn Waugh in a letter to Greene as 'a recantation of faith'.

† Mary and Eric had been in Rome in 1950 when Pope Pius XII, speaking infallibly, had defined the dogma of the Assumption of the Blessed Virgin Mary into Heaven. They had light-heartedly considered making a public demonstration against this proposition.

My thoughts were with you during the arrival. You have managed wonderfully. Fr Charles much amused by your parking me out for the move.

I have found some wonderfully apt books for my subject, and I become madder about Russian history every moment. The history is mad. Full of astounding stories, murders, adulteresses, and the interplay between Russia and Rome a heartbreaking series of malentendus and renewed efforts and mischief made by the (Catholic) Poles ...

I must go to my lavish luncheon ...

Basclose Farm House – 3.9.61

... I've just been to early Mass with the Bretts ... I've had a row with neighbours (children chasing Constable [the cat]) and with a farmer called Carter ... (True 'frightening bullocks'!) ...

Lots of love,
Eric

———

Within two years they had moved again, selling Basclose Farm and heading back towards Dartmoor, to a rented cottage near Ashburton. The house had a distant view of the moor and placed them once more within striking distance of Sunday Mass at Buckfast. It was at Ashburton that, following the visit of an old girlfriend from America, Eric took an overdose of sleeping pills and fell down the stairs. Toby (by then an undergraduate at Oxford) had to carry him up to bed. Mary had told Toby that his father was Heinz Ziegler in December 1960.

———

Priory Cottage, Ashburton – 23.8.62

My darling,

I had a good night, with pills, and feel rested. Vespers (BBC) from our old Carmelite church at Notting Hill contributed to restoring me.

If I can't do my Russian book – which is synthetic (but a bloody good idea, and important) – I do not need (Vespers told me) to despair. I can write comic books, which is (perhaps) my metier. Both, however, involve work, which is not (yet) my habit. I shall have an answer to the conflict by the time we meet. Meanwhile, please suspend judgement.

Did you, thanks to your attraction for young policemen, get shoes? (and whisky?) ... Does Billy get pocket money? ...

Priory Cottage – 27.8.62

Darling (an odd word),

Your writing has become so bad that I can't read it. What is the matter? Betty [a home help] insists on washing blankets. Constable howls for breakfast at 8am.

... Giving Father Gabriel* breakfast on Sunday is a new chore, which I like. He is very uncharitable, rude about his parishioners ('that frightful Captain – yells away') and comes here rather than a squalid cottage whose poverty nauseates him and where he is given 'a really filthy breakfast – alright for Father Stephen'!† These monks are amusing ...

For God's sake write decently; haven't you got a proper pen? I enclose la Mitford [a novel by Nancy Mitford], to spur you on to something better than she can do.

All my love (my lunatic),
Eric

---

* Father Gabriel Arnold, monk of Buckfast, serving the parish of Ashburton.
† Father Stephen was the parish priest, not a monk of Buckfast.

═══

Eric had probably known for some time that he was mentally ill. Mary denied this possibility. In 1963 clinical depression was not commonly diagnosed; sufferers were supposed to 'get a grip' and 'get on with it'. Eric had been displaying symptoms of depression for many years, perhaps since the collapse of his first marriage in 1929. He now began to face this situation, but instead of seeking professional help he turned to his religion. It is clear from Eric's letters that Mary is beginning to feel the strain.

═══

Priory Cottage – 22.4.63

Dearest Pol,

... I have re-written one chapter. It is a hard (and final) test. I still think it can be done. Once started I average 1000–1500 words a day ...

I go my magnificent walk. Anemones and primroses and usually I meet Father Gregory. Fr Wilfrid rang up, but did not come after saying he might. His brother nearly died ('say a prayer please').

On the way back from 8am mass it hailed so hard that it cut my forehead ... Betty is a saint. Now that's what I do call a 'saint'. (I've done no washing up). The dining room walls gleam ...

I shall certainly not make a list of your habits. You must put up with mine. It is I who have grossly failed you, by not ensuring your security. Bad, though possibly not the worst kind of failure. Nerves. That is the worst.

I cannot say that I miss you. The ego-centric, uninterrupted peace is welcome (and I am sure you are glad to be away from my grumbles). But the profitability breaks down as soon as I *fail to keep a rigid regime. Work–walk–work–read (I am training myself to keep a 7 to 10 day). As yesterday. When I retired to bed at 4, and surprised myself – and the animals – by suddenly weeping loudly, and even wilfully though I did not put it on or force it. I just let it go, to see what happened. And I heard myself practically screaming like a lunatic. Kindly reserve two beds in the Insane Asylum, for Phyl [Phyllis Jones] and me. Adjoining. (Explanation: in case you look wider – strain of writing, fury that it just doesn't come right, without effort.)*

I am, of course mentally diseased. The job is to make my neurosis profitable ...

Things are moving fast in Russia (Khrushchev to go) but that suits – not me but – my story ...

We have both been beastly lately. Nothing to forgive – au contraire, don't force yourself to be sweet, like Phyllis: that, I think, is a really false basis. (I had a particularly ardent Mass. Came home. The Devil took over. Anger, idleness ... Muriel Spark says it's the despair of the flesh after all that uplift of spirit. Uplift mixed with scepticism, in my case; perhaps even more hysteria–making) ...

True is ghastly in bed. I've discovered a trick. She has her own hot water bottle, to lure her away ...

What is True supposed to live on? We give her mince (daily); but usually she scorns it. She eats nothing, except chocolate biscuits.

Some respect (mixed with irritation), much Gratitude, and all my love, (whatever that means) –

Eric

Priory Cottage – 24.4.63

... Yesterday Father Gabriel came to lunch (he goes to Oxford today). He is less gauche, due to Oxford – and Priory Cottage's shock treatment. Very nice. He said the best thing for those old

girls at Callow End* would be the hardest – for them: to tell them to mix charitably with the 'bourgeois Catholics'! He was a bit shocked at their arrogant isolation – and ours. He teased me about becoming friends with Catholics now, eg Cdr. Ker!? We both had doubts about the practicability of the advice, as far as Phyllis and Emily are concerned. But, just because it is the toughest advice, it might appeal to Phyl? (I doubt it.)

After a bottle of wine and half a bottle of light port I made him walk through the woods and pretended not to notice his difficulties with the mud. That'll teach him not to appreciate Father Wilfred: whom this time, he praised as saintly, but whose knowledge of human nature he doubted. I told him it was ten times his own.

Just as he left the Vet called in, to inquire after Constable. He had a cup of tea, and a long discussion on education and then left saying he'd 'see pussy another time'. I think he was lusting after you: couldn't see any object in the visit otherwise ...

I hope I'm not as horrid as I think I am. I love you quite a lot ...

Eric

Priory Cottage – 14.8.63

The two days after you left were a sickness (after excesses) but on Sunday I had an invocation of the Spirit and a charming and effective Mass at Ashburton ...

Result: 2250 words on Monday! (after a pill). Next, after a sleepless night, suicide. Despair. Horrors ... I hope for a flow of words tomorrow.

---

* Emily Coleman and Phyllis Jones. Jones was a friend of Antonia White's and typed for her and Coleman. When Coleman moved to a cottage in the grounds of Stanbrook Abbey, Jones had moved in for a time with Mary and Eric at Thornworthy.

I finished Fisherman* *– such rot ought to be censored by the Vatican (Holy Office, Inquisition and all the rest of it). Luckily I have a splendid paper-back on the Eastern Church which holds me as a jig-saw. This is my subject, and as I piece it together it becomes exciting. (I need* some *continuity in my ideas.) ...*

The thought that I have only six weeks (in which I mean to finish my book), and one year until we are flat broke, makes me tremble ... and work! Especially as find I conceive masterpieces nowadays; not just 'funny books' ...

I have just had a splendid new central idea ... as I walked with Madame True across the fields ...

Analyse yourself. Now, analyse yourself! And tell me the results. (And for god's sake don't be meek and self-critical, like Phyllis Jones.) But tell me, who is Mary who is *she? ...*

======

On 15 August, Harry Siepmann wrote to Eric to thank him for sending photographs of Billy. 'As it happens I was thinking (telepathically?) in the night – a prolific period for me nowadays – about the deficiencies of our family relationship, which I deplore as much with reference to a future I shall never see as to a present which is more dissociated than I think it need be.'. After receiving this letter Eric proposed to visit Harry on 6 September, then decided he was not up to it and suggested a postponement to January. Harry Siepmann died on 16 September.

======

* *The Shoes of the Fisherman* by Morris West, a worldwide bestseller about the election of a Slav pope.

Priory Cottage – 19.8.63

Bill sends me a card: 'Happy Hangover!' … The Creator Spiritus is giving me a bad time …

Priory Cottage – 22.8.63

Darling,

This is to greet you chez Phyl. Give her my love. My bad temper has been due to the major crisis, involving my work (or my inability to work). But things are going better, ideas bubbling up just when I have decided that 'I can't do it'. Fr Gabriel spent an afternoon, and helped me. I was still writing three books! – and had to decide which …

Priory Cottage – 24.8.63

This morning's letter rather alarmed me. It looked as though you were drunk, hangover-ed, or had just committed suicide. Are you alright? …

The agreeable thing is that I am able to do a little work after a 3 o'clock tea. The miracle which alone can save us, may have occurred. Certainly the book is taking shape …

I do hope C. Burnett [Ivy Compton Burnett] continues to 'take'. She is, I think, an immortal. I shall be happy in sharing her with you. I am reading the Russian church, interrupted by the superb KUNG* which came from Sheed and Ward …

---

* Hans Kung, a Swiss theologian who had become a leading reforming influence at the Second Vatican Council.

Priory Cottage – 26.8.63 – 6th Anniversary*

... *Post came early, and your letter has arrived. You will certainly be welcomed! ... Please don't bribe me with sex – as, I think, you consciously did before you went ... It is alright, I want you to rest ... However, you are kindly offering me a week getting up at 5.30 and going to church 4 times daily* [i.e. a retreat at Buckfast Abbey]. *'No need to go to' the Imperial Torquay, or anything like that! Harsh, aren't I? (The fact is, I think my <u>vanity</u> is hurt.) ...*

Montini [Pope Paul VI] *is clever. He must know that a statement to anyone but the Eastern hierarchies cannot lead to anything ... I am increasingly pessimist ... Altogether I am sceptical about any get-together, Christian or Christian and Communist. This is my greatest hope (when I believe at all). But it will only come, not by reasoning, but out of blood ...*

Priory Cottage – 30.8.63

Dear Pol,
    All is well ... All my books are written except for the prose ...

═══

In January 1964, Eric, driving to pick Billy up from school, had a serious accident after which Mary's beloved dog, True, had to be put down. Following this accident Eric's handwriting changed. He failed to recover his previous state of health and underwent a long series of hospital tests which were inconclusive.

═══

---

* Anniversary of their reception into the Catholic Church. This had actually taken place in August 1956.

Priory Cottage – 6.4.64

Pol,

    This is a damned exciting play. How can I stick at it till it's done? Glue needed; as when I said 'you'd better stick to me' (December 1944) and you reprimanded me – YOU, ME! – <u>for my English!!</u> ...

Priory Cottage – 9.4.64

Dearest Neurotic,

    <u>*You are not a neurotic! (Repeat, NOT)*</u>*. You are sensitive and loving and anxious, and that's all. Hence the tautness. It was the biggest mistake I ever made, to take pupils for these 4–5 years. From my point of view I've just read what I hadn't realised to be the 'brilliant' notices and letters about my abilities: which I wrote off as 'failure':– it was the 5 vital years lost. As for my using you as housemistress, it was (to use Winston's phrase) 'to harness a thoroughbred to a dung cart'! <u>I am terribly sorry.</u> We must recapture time, and happiness (this can be done, but it needs gifts – which we've got).*

═══

In August 1964, Mary and Eric left their rented accommodation at Ashburton, below the moor, and moved into the last house they lived in together, Cullaford Cottage, a small thatched cottage high up on Dartmoor and not far from Chagford and Thornworthy. It was too small to lodge pupils and Eric's tutoring work had in any case come to an end. In 1965, he was diagnosed with Parkinson's disease, one consequence, in Mary's opinion, of his car crash. No letters survive from this period. As Eric's health deteriorated Mary left him alone less frequently, but in 1966 he felt well enough to travel with his sister Edith to Bristol, to visit Clifton College, where Otto Siepmann, his

German father, had been one of the most celebrated teachers
of his generation, and where he and his brothers and sisters
had been born. He made this journey while Mary was in hospital
for an operation.

═══

2 Sion Hill, Clifton, Bristol 8 – 20.6.66

My dearest Pol,

This is to wish you an easy op. And a complete cure as after-
effect ...

I was delighted with your letter, news and £1!* I feel useless
with all this charity coming in but that can't be helped – in any
immediate future that I can see. Enough. (Did you see Miss Rigg's
marvellous notices? My play 'would have been' perfectly timed.
She is now ripe for lead and play of her own.)†

... [We] called on the Headmaster at Clifton, were made
much of, passed on to the most intelligent housemaster for half-
an-hour's very good chat (chiefly on homosexuality) and invited
to their garden party; it turned out to be 'Commemoration', with
a beautiful cricket match which I enjoyed! Also, as it is term, I
found the High School active and was shown over my house,
including the room in which I was born. It is all traumatic and
magical. As I write I can see Suspension Bridge, and my unconscious gives a twang as if I had suddenly become 8 again ...

I had a most salutary and even entertaining confession. After
I had confessed, sardonic silence. Then an excellent brief discourse
on Redemption, which I never understand. Then: 'If you can
remain in these dispositions for only, say two months ...'

---

* £40 today.

† Diana Rigg, star of the television series The Avengers, had just opened as
Viola in a Royal Shakespeare company production of Twelfth Night.

Me: 'I shan't!'

'Alright, that's irrelevant. Say even two weeks. Say even two days ...' (then with faint but humorous impatience) ... 'if only two minutes'!

A nice man. Cathedral is hideous.

2 The Terrace, Boston Spa, Yorkshire − 27.6.66

... You did not seem anxious to have me back, but I am afraid I must return on Thursday ...

I wish you liked P. [pornography] Lit. I have just read far the most outspoken and improper books ever published − or at least, I thought so − and, at the age of 63 I learned all sorts of things I never knew! Do study a little harder. (They are: My Life and Loves Frank Harris and The Adventurers by Robbens [sic],* read by Toby, 10/6 each, I fear; but I don't like to be innocent, or rather ignorant, at my age.)

Edith is a bit less innocent than I thought, but very sweet and good and not at all boring in her own home. Family sagas, galore. I fear Harry really was the evil genius of our family.

I am cannibalising all I have written − except the play − in last 18 months into open book. Thrilling.

On s'en tirera ... but I am terribly sorry it's a rough patch ... You are a marvel and a help and I love you,

Eric

========

In the summer of 1967 Mary decided to take Billy, then aged thirteen, on a long visit to their friends and family in

---

* My Life and Loves, an imaginative autobiography, was first published in 1922 and promptly banned all over the world. The Adventurers by Harold Robbins was published in 1966. In 1970 it was made into a film − regularly cited as one of the worst films ever made.

Germany. Phyllis Jones moved into Cullaford Cottage to look after Eric.

=====

Cullaford Cottage – 1.7.67

Dearest Pol,

... I have finished Part I (34,000 words) and having it typed helps immeasurably. Like Bill, I can't write decently and a decent size. What <u>is</u> this disease? When I've made money I'll get a tape recorder ...

Cullaford Cottage – 26.7.67

My darling Mary,

We were very glad to get your first letter, and that Billy hound! ... I do hope you flourish in the change of atmosphere. Toby said (he rang up) he had <u>never</u> seen you in better looks or form!

Phyllis is a perfect companion, and cooks delicious lunches ...

Cullaford Cottage – 6.8.67

My darling Pol,

We are flourishing, thanks to a lovely summer ... We see inordinate loads of muck on TV, and I do a little work. Phyl is perfect.

A little work, and a little lust. The current Stern has a photograph of a naked 13-year old negress with a figure like yours, looking down and smiling as if she was being had. And I say to myself, that is how Pol laughed and looked down in the gay times. So hurry home ...

Give Ludwig my love. He married the secretary of the Manchester Guardian (Terence Prittie's), English, I think. They took me to Hammerstein on the Rhine for wine-drinking.* Ask him if he would like a Weekly Letter (radio) from 'an experienced journalist'? Love also to Popsy Donhoff, who takes herself so seriously. (Would <u>she</u> like a Weekly Letter? An outsider's angle, 'Germany's mission as peacemaker' etc?) Don't put yourself out. The time to cash in will be when my political thriller has appeared. (Very good new title – Secret, Tell NO ONE – Maquis International). I still AIM to end in September.

I have all that I want in knowing that you and Bill exist. I love you both, and I am proud of you. 'You are my raison d'etre' ... to be sung to tune of 'You are my heart's delight' ('Du bist mein ganzes Herz', to Billy) ...

I find that I think very highly of you, indeed ...

Your affectionate husband,

Eric

━━━

The correspondence that started in the autumn of 1944 ends in the summer of 1967.

━━━

Maquis International was never completed. In 1969, by which time Eric had become too ill to write, or read, Mary's first two novels – Speaking Terms, for children, and The Sixth Seal, for young adults – were published.

Eric Siepmann died in January 1970. He left his own epitaph in a poem dated 18 December 1964 that lay undiscovered among his papers and is published here in its complete form for the first time.

* Eric is recalling an incident from his days as a Sunday Times correspondent in 1950.

Epitaph of an Idle Artist

Here at my desk I mock my fate,
If help comes now it comes too late.
The valued pictures in my mind
By sheer neglect have made me blind.

My dream deserved a steady look,
I failed to put it in a book,
And now, and now I cannot see,
My dream destroyed reality.

Disliking fact I looked for truth
And patterns new allured my youth,
I would reveal the hidden thing,
But (slothful) I forgot to sing.

So then from truth I turned away
But blinded by the light of day
Found radiant fact too much for me,
I cannot bear reality.

No fact consoles me for my flight,
No truth can give me back my sight,
No dream can make me think I see,
No life is left, so bury me.

===

Mary was devastated by Eric's death and for many years she suffered from extreme depression. On the 30ᵗʰ anniversary of their meeting she wrote in her diary

> *30 years*
> *Hold my hand*
> *Stay close*
> *Don't leave me*
> *Drive carefully*

– a litany that reads like the memory of words exchanged in the moments before she left Eric on a winter's night in 1970 to drive to Cornwall to fetch home their son.

In 1978 she started to write 'Please do NOT resuscitate' inside the front cover of the engagement diary which she kept in her handbag – a habit she maintained until 1981. Eventually she decided to fight back and to imagine her way out of her despair. Jumping the Queue was drawn directly from her experience of those years. It was accepted in 1982 by James Hale and published by Macmillan. The Camomile Lawn followed in 1984 and the next four novels at twelve monthly intervals thereafter.

Mary worked at her writing with great discipline and intensity until 1997 when she completed Part of the Furniture, her tenth and final novel. She made a lot of money from her writing and gave a lot of it away. She enjoyed the unexpected change in her fortunes, and she greatly enjoyed creating the outrageous and outspoken personality of her public appearances and broadcasts. It was the life that she and Eric had once hoped to share, when his life story 'became more than first chapters' and his writing career started to succeed.

Directory of Names

Aragon, Louis: French poet and Communist resister living with his muse, Elsa Triolet, in Paris in 1945

Asquith, Hon. Anthony 'Puffin': film director, school friend of Eric, son of the statesman, H. H. Asquith, 1st Earl of Oxford and Asquith

Astor, Hon. David: owner and editor of the *Observer*

Balfour, Hon. Patrick: later Lord Kinross, writer, became a friend of Eric's while both were stationed in Cairo during the war

Bankes-Jones, Edith: sister of Eric, married to Rev. Roger, a sanctimonious Anglican vicar

Beecham, Alec: National Liberal MP for West Cornwall (including Boskenna), admirer of Mary

Bernsdorf, Bridget: English friend of the Siepmanns who entertained Mary in the family *schloss* in Prussia, married to Hugo, Nazi and wartime member of the SA

Bernsdorf, Thora: cousin of Hugo

Bertaux, Pierre: Republican commissioner for the Toulouse region when Eric was posted there in 1944-5

Blessing, Dr. Karl: director of the Reichsbank under the Nazis, later president of the post-war Deutsche Bundesbank

Bolitho, Billy: wealthy Cornish landowner who first recruited Mary for MI5, Toby's godfather

Bonham Carter, Lady Violet: sister of 'Puffin' Asquith and talkative Liberal party *eminence grise*

Boothby, Robert: Conservative politician, lover of Harold Macmillan's wife Lady Dorothy, friend of Winston Churchill and Eric

Boscence, Joe: a retired dealer in antiques, living outside Penzance, a misanthrope who was fond of Mary

Bowra, Maurice: Oxford academic and wit, friend of both Mary and Eric

Cassou, Jean: French academic and Resistance officer, friend of Eric

Crossman, Richard: millionaire Socialist cabinet minister, once Eric's resentful fag at Winchester

Curtis Brown, Spencer: founder of the literary agency and briefly Mary's agent for her unpublished early work

Dalby, Hyacinthe: Mary's beloved grandmother, wife of Sir William Dalby, a distinguished surgeon

Eady, Toby: literary agent, second son of Mary, grew up in Boskenna during the war

Farmar, Hugh: Mary's elder brother, m. Constantia Rumbold, daughter of Sir Horace, pre-war British ambassador in Berlin

Farmar, Mynors: Mary's father, professional soldier, wounded and decorated veteran of Gallipoli and Passchendaele

Fleming, Ian: managing editor of *Sunday Times*, later novelist

Gates, Pauline: sister of Robert Newton, introduced Mary to Eric, m. Sylvester, chairman of the British Film Institute, school friend of Eric

Gluck: successful painter living with Edith Shackleton

Gow, Nancy: once Eric's secretary at BEA, became a close friend and loyal supporter of both Eric and Mary

Grant, Mrs: merry widow of Penzance, close friend of Mary

Green, Wing-Commander 'Paddy': ace fighter pilot and wartime lover of Mary

Greene, Felix: pacifist cousin of the novelist Graham, once employed by Charles Siepmann at the BBC

Grenfell, Alice: housemaid at Boskenna who took over the nursery and helped to raise all Mary's children

Grimond, Jo: youthful leader of the Liberal Party, his wife, Laura, was the daughter of Violet Bonham Carter (q.v.)

Handley, Michael: security service officer in Hong Kong, later director-general of MI5

Hill, Paul: Penzance solicitor, friend of Col. Paynter and second husband of Betty Paynter

Hughes, Maj. Glyn: owner of the Beverley Court Hotel in Chagford where Mary and Eric sought refuge from Phyllis Siepmann

Ingrams, Leonard St Clair: merchant banker, aviator and friend of Eric; father of Richard Ingrams

John, Edwin: painter son of Augustus, living in Mousehole with a collection of his Aunt Gwen's paintings

Keswick, Sir John: *taipan* of Jardine Matheson in Hong Kong, friend of Chinese prime minister Zhou Enlai, wartime agent for SOE

Kingsmill, Hugh: writer and humourist, friend of Eric

Kirkpatrick, Sir Ivone: British High Commissioner for Germany, 1950-53, head of the Foreign Office, then chairman of the Independent Television Authority

Knox, Mgr. Ronald: Catholic convert, brother of leading Bletchley codebreaker, friend of the Asquith family, translated the Bible

Lee, Raymond: louche French SOE agent and friend of Mary

Maisky, Mikhailovich: wartime Soviet ambassador in London

Mangan, Father Richard SJ: Jesuit priest based at Farm Street who instructed and received Mary and Eric into the Catholic Church

Masaryk, Jan: exiled Czech politician, close friend of Heinz Ziegler

Melikof, Boris: French communist resister and lover of Mary

Micklem, Nat: theologian, academic, politician and friend of Eric

Mitford, Nancy: novelist and pre-war friend of Eric

Morris, Claud: lover of Betty Paynter, later radical printer and publisher

Muggeridge, Malcolm: journalist, briefly editor of *Punch* and friend of Eric

Mynors, Sir Roger: godfather to Mary's son, Roger, twin brother to Sir Humphrey, dep. governor of the Bank of England

Newton, Robert: prominent actor and film star, grew up at Lamorna Cove as a tenant of Col. Paynter

Norman, Montagu: governor of the Bank of England, friend of the Siepmann brothers

Paynter, Betty: daughter of the colonel, heiress of Boskenna, close friend of Mary

Paynter, Col. Camborne: eccentric landowner and generous host

Paynter, Sonya: Betty's only child, grew up with Roger and Toby at Boskenna

Portal, Sir Francis Bt.: chairman of Portals (manufacturers of banknote paper), school contemporary, later employer, of Eric

Quennell, Peter: critic and author, Oxford contemporary and friend of both Eric and Evelyn Waugh

Rodd, Peter: adventurer and conman, Oxford contemporary and long-time friend of Eric

Schacht, Dr. Hjalmar: German economic genius and war criminal, friend of both Eric and Harry Siepmann

Shackleton, Edith: last lover of both Gluck and WB Yeats, wartime visitor to Boskenna

Siepmann, Bill: Mary's third son

Siepmann, Charles: second son of Otto; BBC producer, later American businessman

Siepmann, Harry: first son of Otto; economist, director of the Bank of England

Siepmann, Otto: exile from Bismarck's Germany, master at Clifton College and leading language teacher of his day

Siepmann, Phyllis: née Morris, peppery and vindictive second wife of Eric

Siepmann, Ricardo: cousin of Otto; Hamburg businessman with a finger in every pie

Stopford, Richmond: Bachelor MI6 officer who became a family friend of the Siepmanns

Strauss, Dr. Eric: notable West End psychiatrist who treated both Eric and Phyllis

Sutherland, 'Geordie', 5th Duke of: ladies' man and frequent visitor to Boskenna

Swinfen, Carol, 2nd Baron: Mary's first husband, kindly and generous father to Roger and Toby

Swinfen Eady, Roger: Mary's eldest son, grew up at Boskenna, later 3rd Baron Swinfen

Waller, Lady: pompous neighbour at Thornworthy, sister of Mary's landlady

Waugh, Evelyn: Oxford contemporary and lifelong contemptor (*sic*) of Eric

White, Antonia: author of *Frost in May* and pre-war lover of Eric's, Catholic godmother of both Mary and Eric

Woodruff, Douglas: Catholic polemicist, journalist and author, editor of the *Tablet*

Ziegler, Heinz: Czech economics professor, later rear-gunner in RAF, killed in action in 1943, natural father of Toby

Ziegler, Paul: brother of Heinz, banker, later Benedictine monk

Acknowledgements

My thanks are due to the literary executors of Mary Siepmann and Eric Siepmann for making the publication of this correspondence possible. I am particularly grateful to the late Toby Eady, a steadfast friend and for many years my agent. As a veteran of the wartime nursery at Boskenna, his help in identifying many of the inhabitants, human and otherwise, of the Siepmanns' circle was invaluable. I must also thank Xin Ran Eady for her high-spirits and encouragement, and Kate Ganz, a close friend of Mary's, who gave permission for the use of several of the photographs.

I would also like to thank Veronique Baxter of David Higham Associates. At Random House, I am grateful to Rachel Cugnoni, Beth Coates and Kate Harvey for first recognising the potential of these letters, and to Mikaela Pedlow for seeing the book through the press. My original editor in this project was the late Penelope Hoare. Penny continued to provide invaluable guidance with her habitual enthusiasm and good humour despite suffering a painful illness. She worked on the book with great courage until the week before her sudden death in May 2017.

INDEX